T0185923

Image Texture Analysis

Chih-Cheng Hung • Enmin Song •
Yihua Lan

Image Texture Analysis

Foundations, Models and Algorithms

 Springer

Chih-Cheng Hung
Kennesaw State University
Marietta, GA, USA

Enmin Song
Huazhong University of Science
and Technology
Wuhan, Hubei, China

Yihua Lan
Nanyang Normal University
Nanyang, Henan, China

ISBN 978-3-030-13775-5   ISBN 978-3-030-13773-1   (eBook)
https://doi.org/10.1007/978-3-030-13773-1

Library of Congress Control Number: 2019931824

This Springer imprint is published by the registered company Springer Nature Switzerland AG.
The registered company address is: Gewerbestrasse 11, 6330 Cham, Switzerland

Preface

Hello darkness, my old friend
I've come to talk with you again
because a vision softly creeping
left its seeds while I was sleeping
and the vision that was planted in my brain
still remains
within the sound of silence

—Simon and Garfunkel

Research on image texture analysis has made significant progress in the past few decades. However, image texture classification (and segmentation) is still an elusive goal despite a tremendous effort devoted to work in this area. This is perhaps analogous to what Alan Turing proved, "there are many things that computers cannot do" although he also showed us that there are many things that computers can do [1]. Traditional image texture classification usually consists of texture feature extraction and texture classification. This scheme is flexible as many image and pattern classification, segmentation, and clustering algorithms in literature can be used for texture classification once texture features are available. The separation of features and classification has a limitation that texture features extractors must be well designed to provide a representative set of texture features for the classification algorithm. In the past few years, convolutional neural networks (CNN) have emerged as a popular approach for the advancement of image texture classification. The CNNs are being used in not only image classification but also other applications such as machine vision and language translation. It is quite astounding for the CNN algorithm to extract features automatically without human interactions. Unlike traditional artificial neural networks, CNNs can extract features from the spatial image domain. The concept of receptive field used in CNNs is very similar to the spatial filter in the digital image processing.

Our goal in writing this book is to introduce the basics of image texture analysis to a beginner who is interested in pursuing research in this field. Simultaneously, we wish to present the basic K-views models and algorithms for extracting and classifying image textures, which were developed in our research laboratory and collaborations with other research scientists. We also include the fundamentals of popular textural feature extraction methods and classification algorithms to serve as a solid foundation in this book. The algorithms selected as the basis are carefully decided through our research findings and reformation from the many years of teaching in image texture analysis. Specifically, we divide the book into three parts; Part I consists of Chaps. 1–4 describing the existing models and algorithms. Part II includes Chaps. 5–8 introducing the K-views models and algorithms. Part II is based on the foundation of the papers on the K-views models published in conferences and journals. Part III introduces deep machine learning models for image texture analysis in Chaps. 9 and 10. In order to have complete coverage on image texture analysis in deep machine learning, we present those popular models and algorithms already well developed by many eminent researchers.

If we have learned something from this research area, it is that we are more like the metaphor of "dwarfs standing on the shoulders of giants". We are very grateful to learn so much from the many pioneers who have devoted their time and life to research in this fascinating area. This book is intended for building a foundation and learning the basics of image texture analysis. The recommended audience is senior undergraduate students and first-year of graduate students. Therefore, we have provided examples for the clarification of concepts in the book. We have tried our best to sift through the manuscript. If there are still any errors or typos in this book, it is our responsibility. Please kindly inform us for the correction.

Marietta, USA   Chih-Cheng Hung
Wuhan, China   Enmin Song
Nanyang, China   Yihua Lan

Reference

1. Harel D (2012) Standing on the Shoulders of a Giant: One Persons Experience of Turings Impact (Summary of the Alan M. Turing Lecture), The Weizmann Institute of Science, Rehovot, Israel

Acknowledgements

The skies proclaim the work of his hands;
Day after day they pour forth speech;
Night after night they display knowledge. (Psalm 19: 1, 2)

We are indebted to many students, colleagues, visiting scholars, and collaborators. They have contributed significantly to our research in developing models and algorithms for image texture analysis. The digital age has established a vast "global knowledge library" through the Internet, which brings in many scholars' pioneering works together for us to explore and learn. We have benefited from this global library in writing this book. We are also very grateful to our graduate students who have taught us a great deal about image texture analysis in our research laboratories and classrooms.

C.-C.: My special thanks go to Profs. Jian Zhou, Guangzhi Ma, and Wendy Liu for their research contributions during their visit to the Center of Machine Vision and Security Research (CMVSR) at Kennesaw State University (KSU). My students who have contributed significantly to image processing and analysis research in the CMVSR at KSU (formerly Southern Polytechnic State University): Shisong Yang, Sarah Arasteh, Sarah Sattchi, David Bradford, Jr., Ellis Casper, Jr., Dilek Karabudak, Srivatsa Mallapragada, Eric Tran, Michael Wong, Wajira Priyadarshani, and Mahsa Shokri Varniab. In particular, Shisong Yang has made a great contribution to the K-views model. I also appreciate the Director, Prof. Y. Liu, of Henan Key Laboratory of Oracle Bone Inscription Information Processing in Anyang Normal University for his enthusiastic support for this project. My thanks go to the photographer, Cino Trinh, who provides many beautiful textural images for the book. I give my appreciation to the Center for Teaching Excellence and Learning (CTEL) at KSU for providing me one-semester sabbatical leave to work on this book. It is not possible to list all of the names here. If I miss those who have helped me in this contribution, please forgive my ignorance. The love and support I have received from my late parents and my family are immeasurable. My gratitude goes to Avery, David, and Ming-Huei for their love and encouragement.

E. S.: I give my thanks to my colleagues in the Research Center of Biomedical Imaging and Bioinformatics (CBIB), Huazhong University of Science and Technology (HUST); Professors Renchao Jin, Hong Liu, Lianghai Jin, Xiangyang Xu, and Guangzhi Ma. I have learned a lot from them in the area of medical image processing and analysis through more than 10 years of teaching and research. The brainstorming and discussions with this research group have triggered many valuable ideas. I would also like to give my special thanks to the graduate students in the research center as many works in this book are the results of their research.

Y.-H.: I would like to thank Dr. Xiangyang Xu, Huazhong University of Science and Technology (HUST) and Dr. Qian Wang, School of Information Security, Central South University of Finance and Economics and Law, and Siguang Dai, my senior classmate in HUST, for their helpful discussions in image processing. I appreciate Jiao Long, my junior classmate at HUST who helped to draw a significant portion of figures for the book. I also appreciate the financial support from the National Natural Science Foundation of China (Grant No. 61401242) and Scholars of the Wolong project of Nanyang Normal University for writing the book.

Contents

Part I
Existing Models and Algorithms for Image Texture

Image Texture, Texture Features, and Image Texture Classification and Segmentation

The journey of a thousand miles begins with a single step.

—Lao Tzu

In this chapter, we will discuss the basic concept of image texture, texture features, and image texture classification and segmentation. These concepts will be the foundation to understand image texture models and algorithms used for image texture analysis. Once texture features are available, many classification and segmentation algorithms from traditional pattern recognition can be utilized for labeling textural classes. Image texture analysis strongly depends on the spatial relationships among gray levels of pixels. Therefore, methods for texture feature extraction are developed by looking at this spatial relationship. For example, the gray-level co-occurrence matrix (GLCM) and local binary patterns (LBP) were derived based on this spatial concept. Traditional techniques for image texture analysis, including classification and segmentation, fall into one of the four categories: statistical, structural, model-based, and transform-based methods. The rapid advancement of deep machine learning in artificial intelligence and convolutional neural networks (CNN) has been widely used in image texture analysis. It would be essential for us to further explore image texture analysis with deep CNN.

1.1 Introduction

Image texture analysis is an important branch in digital image processing and computer vision. Image texture refers to the characterization of the surface of a given object or phenomenon present in the image. Texture occurs in many different types of images such as natural and remote sensing and medical images. In order for machine interpretation and understanding, image texture analysis is used to investigate the contents of image textures, characterize each texture, and categorize different types of textures. In general, image texture analysis consists of four types of problems: (1) texture segmentation, (2) texture classification, (3) texture

© Springer Nature Switzerland AG 2019
C.-C. Hung et al., *Image Texture Analysis*,
https://doi.org/10.1007/978-3-030-13773-1_1

synthesis, and (4) shape from texture [33, 34, 37, 41]. Broadly speaking, texture segmentation is similar to image segmentation in which a priori information is unknown. Image segmentation is defined as the meaningful partitioning of an image into homogeneous regions. Due to the repetition of pixel elements in each texture, some algorithms used in image segmentation may not be suitable for texture segmentation. Texture classification assumes that a priori knowledge about image texture is known, for example, the number of different textural classes in an image. Texture synthesis refers to the generation of textures using mathematical models by providing some parameters for texture models. Shape from texture is the construction of three-dimensional shapes of texture surfaces.

Techniques for texture analysis can be classified into four categories: (1) statistical, (2) structural, (3) model-based, and (4) transform-based methods (also called signal processing methods) [40]. In other words, the objective of texture analysis is to characterize and discriminate image textures using the methods of statistics, structural, models, and transforms. This book focuses on the fundamentals of feature extraction, classification, and segmentation of image texture. Hence, we will explore models and algorithms for these fundamentals. Some related algorithms, clustering algorithms in particular, will be discussed in detail. An image texture classification platform is divided into two components as shown in Fig. 1.1a: texture feature extraction and texture classification and segmentation. This model is exactly the same as those used in the traditional pattern recognition system. It provides flexibility for each component to use algorithms available in pattern recognition literature. Texture feature extraction is a process of extracting the intrinsic features from the original dimensional space [13, 25]. Simultaneously, feature extraction technique also reduces the original high-dimensional image space

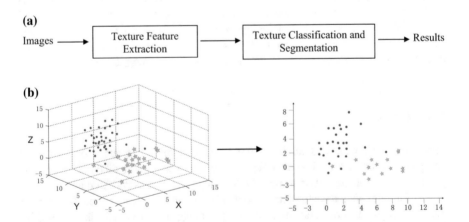

Fig. 1.1 **a** An image texture classification platform that consists of texture feature extraction and texture classification and segmentation is very similar to a traditional pattern recognition system and **b** texture feature extraction not only extracts intrinsic features but also reduces the three-dimensional image space to a two-dimensional subspace

to a lower dimensional subspace as shown in Fig. 1.1b. Texture classification and segmentation is a partition of an image such that each texture can be separated from other different types of textures for efficient machine interpretation and understanding.

As stated in their books by Haralick and Shapiro [14, 15], gray-level and texture are not independent concepts. Both bear an inextricable relationship similar to a particle and a wave. Hence, their conclusion is that "to characterize texture we must characterize the gray-level primitive properties as well as the spatial relationships between them." Based on this concept, we developed a texture feature called "characteristic view", which is directly extracted from an image patch corresponding to each texture class. Depending on the number of classes, the K-views template method (called K-views model, K is an integer to specify how many templates will be used) is then established to classify texture pixels from those classes based on the characteristic views. Here, the template is identical to the spatial smoothing filter used in digital image processing such as a 3 × 3 template. Therefore, the characteristic view is to characterize the image texture features. Figure 1.2 shows one example of K-views templates. The characteristic view concept is based on the assumption that an image taken from nature will frequently reveal the repetitions of some certain patterns of features. The characteristic views are translation invariant. Different "views" can be derived to form feature vectors from different spatial locations. Several image texture classification algorithms have been developed based on the concept of the characteristic view [1, 2, 19, 20, 23, 24, 30, 31, 38, 43, 44]. We will discuss the strength and weakness of the K-views model and its advanced models in a comparison with other different models and algorithms in this book.

In the following sections, we will explain the concept of image texture in Sect. 1.2, texture features in Sect. 1.3, and image texture classification and segmentation in Sect. 1.4.

Fig. 1.2 **a** A numerical image and **b** an example of K-views templates where K is an integer to specify how many templates will be used

(a)

0	0	100	100	100
0	0	100	100	100
0	0	100	100	100
0	0	100	100	100
0	0	100	100	100

(b)

0	0	100
0	0	100
0	0	100

1.2   Image Texture

Image texture has been an active area of research in pattern recognition and image analysis. Although a formal definition of image texture is not available in the literature, image texture is a natural characteristic in many images that we perceive in our environment. In general, a texture can be informally defined as a set of texture elements (called texels) which occurs in some regular or repeated pattern such as the image in Fig. 1.3a. Some pattern in textures may be random as shown in Fig. 1.3b. Texton is a commonly used term that is the fundamental microstructure in image texture [22]. Many different image textures have been collected in several databases [4, 18]. These image textures include bio-medical image textures such as magnetic resonance imaging (MRI) brain images, natural images such as Brodatz Gallery [5], and material image textures such as the OUTex database [35]. Some of the image textures are shown in Fig. 1.4. There are also many other databases for image textures such as KTH-TIPS [7, 16], describable texture datasets (DTD) [8], CUReT [9], UIUC [26], Drexel texture database [36], and UMD [42].

Many approaches for characterizing and classifying image texture have been proposed by researchers [14, 15, 34, 40, 41]. As stated above, these approaches are classified into categories of (1) statistical method, (2) structural method, (3) model-based method, and (4) transform-based method [40]. Some of these methods are more or less adopted from statistical pattern recognition [11]. In other words, if the statistical method is used for image texture characterization, an image texture is represented as feature vectors, which can be used for algorithms from statistical pattern recognition.

The GLCM is one of the pioneering methods for the statistical feature extraction [14, 15]. It describes a texture with spatial relationships by using second-order statistics in a user-defined neighborhood. Features are then extracted from the co-occurrence matrices and used for image texture classification. In the statistical method, a texture is described by a collection of statistics from selected features.

(a)   **(b)**

Fig. 1.3 Examples of image textures: **a** brick arranged in regular pattern and **b** tree leaves grew in random pattern

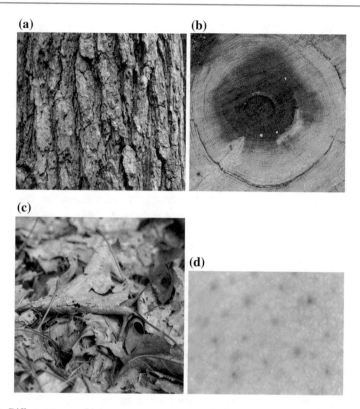

Fig. 1.4 Different types of image textures: **a** tree trunk, **b** wood ring, **c** piled tree leaves, and **d** skin of human face

These features may include first-order statistics, second-order statistics, and higher-order statistics. Then, a histogram is used for representing the distribution of statistics of the features. Hence, GLCM and histograms are commonly used in the statistical method [14, 15, 40]. The basic statistical method can be expressed by Eq. 1.1 as shown below:

$$L = d(F(p)) \tag{1.1}$$

where p is a pixel (a variable) in the image, symbol F(p) is the features of variable p and its neighboring pixels in a user-specified window, and $d(F(p))$ is the decision function which maps the features to a class label (L). Hence, d(.) in Eq. 1.1 is an image texture classification algorithm which gives variable p a class label (L). This is a general model of image texture analysis for the platform shown in Fig. 1.1a.

On the contrary, for the structural method, grammar is used for association with spatial relationships which characterize the placement rules of a set of primitives (equivalent to texels or textons) [29]. This will create symbol strings for each texture. Texture categorization and recognition are then performed on the parsing of symbol strings which describe the spatial relationship. The model-based approach is to characterize texture based on the probability distributions in random fields such as Markov random fields (MRF) [34, 41]. The model-based methods for texture analysis include autoregressive model, Gibbs random fields, Wold model, and others [34, 41]. As the coefficients of the model-based methods are used to characterize the texture, it becomes critical to choose an appropriate model for the texture and correctly estimate the coefficients [44].

The transform-based method is to decompose an image texture into a set of basis images (also called feature images) by using a bank of filters such as Gabor filters [12, 21]. The transform-based method is a multichannel filtering approach based on the studies from psychophysiology [6, 10]. The wavelet transform is another frequently used method in this category. Among the four categories consisting of statistical, structural, model-based, and transform-based methods, each of them has its own advantages and drawbacks. The hybrid combination of different types of texture features extracted using a hybrid of different methods has also been successfully applied for image texture classification.

1.3 Texture Features

Texture features describe the characteristic of image textures. Image texture can be characterized by a set of features based on the operators specifically defined for extracting textural properties. Another term, texture representation is frequently used for the extraction of texture features that describe texture information [32]. Some popular textural operators such as the GLCM [14, 15], the LBP [33, 38, 39], and texture spectrum (TS) [17] fall in the category of textural operators. As texture is considered as a set of texture elements (Texels) arranged in a particular fashion, these elements are also called *texture units* [17]. In turn, these texture units are characterized by a specific feature description which is the result of using the textural operators.

Statistical texture features are the most commonly used texture measures. Figure 1.5a shows a simple numerical image which consists of four different textures with 2×2 pixels in each texture. The first-order statistic of mean and variance for each texture is calculated and shown in Fig. 1.5b. The second-order statistics refers to the joint probability distribution of pixels in a spatial relationship such as the gray-level co-occurrence matrices (GLCM) [14, 15]. Features are then used for texture recognition and classification. Similar to any non-textural feature extraction methods, defining features from the image textures will be the most common task for image classification [14, 15, 29, 34, 40, 41, 44]. However, as most textural operators work on a spatial neighborhood of a pixel (we may refer it as the patch or kernel) in an image texture, it is critical to define the patches for computing distinguished features which will be suitable to describe the local patterns. In other words, for texture classification, texture features are not a property of a single pixel, it is a characteristic in the spatial neighborhood surrounding a single pixel. Liu et al.

(a)

1	1	4	4
1	1	4	4
8	8	6	6
8	8	6	6

(b)

Texture Class	Feature #1 (mean)	Feature #2 (variance)
Texture 1	1	0
Texture 2	4	0
Texture 3	8	0
Texture 4	6	0

Fig. 1.5 a A simple numerical image which consists of four different textures assuming each texture occupies a 2 × 2 block and **b** each texture is represented by the mean and variance as features

give a great comprehensive survey on image texture representation for texture classification [32]. Texture representation in their survey focuses on the bag-of-words (BoW) and convolutional neural networks (CNN) which have been extensively studied with impressive performance [32].

1.4 Image Texture Classification and Segmentation

Image texture classification is the process of assigning each pixel of an image to one of many predefined classes (also called clusters). We usually call them spectral classes as the features are derived from spectral signatures of pixels. In general, each pixel is treated as an individual unit composed of values in one (gray-scale image) or several spectral bands such as color, multispectral, and hyperspectral images. In other words, it ranges from one-dimensional to high-dimensional space. A pixel with multiple images can be treated as a vector which is formed by linking the corresponding pixels from all multiple images. In remote sensing, each image is called a band. Hence, the feature vector of a pixel is formulated by taking the corresponding pixels in multiple bands. By comparing the feature vector of each pixel with the representative features of classes, each pixel will be assigned a class label based on the similarity measure. Pixels belonging to the same class should contain similar information. Such a class is usually called the spectral class. Some of these spectral classes may be combined to form an informational class in an image due to the variety of spectral signatures for an object or region. We may use different colors to denote different spectral classes in a classified image. Figure 1.6 shows an original remote sensing image, the corresponding classified image (sometimes called a classified map), and ground truth map. The ground truth map can then be used for the classification accuracy assessment which will determine the quality of a classification algorithm.

(a)   **(b)**   **(c)**

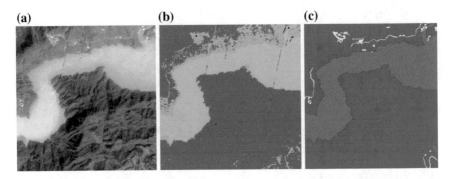

Fig. 1.6 **a** An original remotely sensed image, **b** the corresponding classified image, and **c** the corresponding ground truth map. Please note that the ground truth map may not be available in many applications

Compared with image texture classification, image texture segmentation divides an image into several nonoverlapping and meaningful regions. Similar to a general image segmentation, image texture segmentation has been very challenging due to varying statistical characteristics present in an image such as sensitivity to noise, reflectance property of object surfaces, lighting environments, and so on [3, 14, 15, 34, 41, 44]. Since the goal of image texture segmentation is to interpret the contents of an image, it is necessary to label each pixel after the segmentation. With the labeled pixels, both texture classification and segmentation are used to interpret an image. An image classification or segmentation algorithm for texture is either a pixel-based or a region-based approach. In a pixel-based classification, spectral and textural information (called features) is commonly used to classify each pixel in an image. In a region-based approach, an image has to be segmented into homogeneous regions, and a set of meaningful features can be defined for each region. Once features are well defined, image regions (blocks/patches) can be categorized using pattern recognition techniques. One of the main drawbacks of the per-pixel classifier is that each pixel is treated independently without the consideration for its neighboring information.

Image texture segmentation methods are generally based on two basic characteristics of image textures: discontinuity and similarity. In the discontinuity-based approach, it uses discontinuities of texture features in an image to obtain the boundaries of textures. An example of this approach is the edge detection method. In contrast, the similarity-based approach looks for the homogeneity of texture features associated with the pixels in an image. In this approach, an image is partitioned into regions in which all pixels in a region are similar according to the homogeneity measure of features. The characteristics of spectral, spatial, and textural information are used as three fundamental feature elements [14, 15]. Even though color is an important feature in image segmentation, there are situations where color measurements may not provide enough information, as color is sensitive to local variations. However, by combining color and texture features, an image texture segmentation can be improved and a better segmentation result can be obtained. Many image segmentation methods have been proposed and well developed in the past few decades [15, 29, 40].

Due to the recent development in the deep machine learning, the man-made feature extraction module (as shown in Fig. 1.1a) is being replaced by deep neural networks such as the CNN shown in Fig. 1.7 [27, 28]. A basic CNN consists of a convolutional layer which extracts features to form feature maps and a subsampling layer which produces shift and distortion invariant feature maps. These two layers can be duplicated to form a deeper neural networks. A fully connected layer, which is identical to the traditional artificial neural networks, is then used for image texture classification following the convolutional and sampling layers in many CNNs. There are some hyperparameters associated with the architecture of CNN needed to be specified for defining and training a CNN. As deep machine learning is in rapid advancement, image texture analysis using deep machine learning will also be included in this book.

Image texture classification methods are also categorized into supervised and unsupervised modes. Unsupervised classification algorithms aggregate pixels into natural groupings in an image [3]. Many unsupervised classification methods, such as K-means clustering algorithm, have been widely used. Supervised classification procedures require considerable analyst interaction. The analyst must guide the classification by identifying areas on the image that belong to each class and calculate statistics from the samples in those areas. A supervised classification algorithm requires the analyst's expertise. The classification result of supervised classification usually is better than that of unsupervised methods.

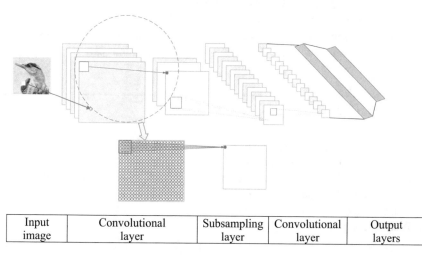

Input image	Convolutional layer	Subsampling layer	Convolutional layer	Output layers

Fig. 1.7 A typical deep machine learning platform for image texture classification consists of an input layer, convolutional layers for generating texture feature maps, subsampling layers, and the output layer. Both convolutional and sampling layers are duplicated to make a deeper convolutional neural network

1.5   Summary

We frequently encounter image texture in many applications of pattern recognition and computer vision. Hence, several models and algorithms for image texture analysis have been developed in literature. Early research in image texture analysis was mainly focused on statistical methods and structural methods from pattern recognition discipline. Later, the model-based and transform-based methods are also introduced to characterize the texture. In the model-based methods, a texture image is described by a probability model. The coefficients of these models are then used to characterize each texture. The key issues are how to choose the correct model that is suitable for the selected texture and how to estimate their coefficients. The transform-based methods use different transformation functions to decompose an image texture into a set of basic feature images. An image texture will then be projected onto these basis images to derive the coefficients for characterizing textures.

The accuracy of image texture classification (and segmentation) depends on two factors: the first is the features that represent the texture and the second is the algorithm using these features to classify the texture. Both texture features and classification algorithm have a significant impact on the classification accuracy. It is only possible to distinguish two texture classes by an algorithm if the two textures are not similar. Sometimes, even the texture features are well defined, but one may obtain different results using different algorithms. For example, if the K-means algorithm is used, due to its heavy dependency on the initialization of the cluster centers, the clustering result may not be the same. Due to the rapid advancement of deep machine learning in artificial intelligence, deep CNNs are making a break-through in image classification and segmentation. It would be essential for us to further explore image texture analysis with deep CNNs.

In the following chapters, we will discuss different methods for measuring and extracting texture features and classifying image textures in detail.

1.6   Exercises

1. Informally define an image texture using your own language.
2. What are image texture features?
3. In terms of image texture feature extraction, contrast and compare the traditional feature extraction method and the CNN approach.
4. What is image texture classification?
5. What is image texture segmentation?

References

1. Arasteh S, Hung C-C (2006) Color and texture image segmentation using uniform local binary pattern. Mach Vis Graph 15(3/4):265–274
2. Arasteh S, Hung C-C, Kuo B-C (2006) Image texture segmentation using local binary pattern and color information. In: The proceedings of the international computer symposium (ICS 2006), Taipei, Taiwan, 4–6 Dec 2006
3. Beck J, Sutter A, Ivry R (1987) Spatial frequency channels and perceptual grouping in texture segregation. Comput Vis Graph Image Process 37:299–325
4. Bianconi F, Fernández A (2014) An appendix to texture databases – a comprehensive survey. Pattern Recognit Lett 45:33–38
5. Brodatz P (1966) Textures: a photographic album for artists and designers. Dover Publications, New York
6. Campbell FW, Robson JG (1968) Application of Fourier analysis to the visibility of gratings. J Physiol 197:551–566
7. Caputo B, Hayman E, Mallikarjuna P (2005) Class-specific material categorization. In: ICCV
8. Cimpoi M, Maji S, Kokkinos I, Mohamed S, Vedaldi A (2014) Describing textures in the wild. In: Proceedings of the IEEE conference on computer vision and pattern recognition (CVPR)
9. Dana KJ, van Ginneken B, Nayar SK, Koenderink JJ (1999) Reflectance and texture of real world surfaces. ACM Trans Graph 18(1):1–34
10. Devalois RL, Albrecht DG, Thorell LG (1982) Spatial -frequency selectivity of cells in macaque visual cortex. Vis Res 22:545–559
11. Fukunaga K (1990) Introduction to statistical pattern recognition, 2nd edn. Morgan Kaufmann
12. Garber D (1981) Computational models for texture analysis and texture synthesis, University of Southern California, USCIPI Report 1000, Ph.D. thesis
13. Guyon I, Gunn S, Nikravesh M, Zadeh L (2006) Feature extraction: foundations and applications. Springer
14. Haralick RM (1979) Statistical and structural approaches to texture. In: Proceedings of IEEE, vol 67, issue 5. pp 786–804
15. Haralick RM, Sharpio L (1992) Computer and Robot vision, vol I, II. Addison-Wesley
16. Hayman E, Caputo B, Fritz M, Eklundh J-O (2004) On the significance of real-world conditions for material classification. In: ECCV
17. He D-C, Wang L (1990) Texture unit, texture spectrum, and texture analysis. IEEE Trans Geosci Remote Sens 28(4):509–512
18. Hossain S, Serikawa S (2013) Texture databases – a comprehensive survey. Pattern Recognit Lett 34(15):2007–2022
19. Hung C-C, Pham M, Arasteh S, Kuo B-C, Coleman T (2006) Image texture classification using texture spectrum and local binary pattern. In: The 2006 IEEE international geoscience and remote sensing symposium (IGARSS), Denver, Colorado, USA, 31 July–4 Aug 2006
20. Hung C-C, Yang S, Laymon C (2002) Use of characteristic views in image classification. In: Proceedings of 16th international conference on pattern recognition, pp 949–952
21. Ji Y, Chang K-H, Hung C-C (2004) Efficient edge detection and object segmentation using gabor filters. In: ACMSE, Huntsville, Alabama, USA, 2–3 April 2004
22. Julesz B, Bergen JR (1983) Textons, the fundamental elements in preattentive vision and perception of textures. Bell Syst Tech 62:1619–1645
23. Lan Y, Liu H, Song E, Hung C-C (2010) An improved K-view algorithm for image texture classification using new characteristic views selection methods. In: Proceedings of the 25th association of computing machinery (ACM) symposium on applied computing (SAC 2010) – computational intelligence and image analysis (CIIA) track, Sierre, Swizerland, 21–26 March 2010, pp 960–964
24. Lan Y, Liu H, Song E, Hung C-C (2011) A comparative study and analysis on K-view based algorithms for image texture classification. In: Proceedings of the 26th association of computing machinery (ACM) symposium on applied computing (SAC 2011) – computational intelligence, signal and image analysis (CISIA) track, Taichung, Taiwan, 21–24 March 2011

25. Landgrebe D (2003) Signal theory methods in multispectral remote sensing. Wiley-Interscience
26. Lazebnik S, Schmid C, Ponce J (2005) A sparse texture representation using local affine regions. IEEE Trans PAMI 28(8):2169–2178
27. LeCun Y, Bengio Y, Hinton G (2015) Deep learning. Nature 521:436–444. https://doi.org/10.1038/nature14539
28. LeCun Y, Bottou L, Bengio Y, Haffner P (1998) Gradient-based learning applied to document recognition. In: Proceedings of the IEEE, pp 1–44
29. Levine MD (1985) Vision in man and machine. McGraw-Hill
30. Liu H, Dai S, Song E, Yang C, Hung C-C (2009) A new K-view algorithm for texture image classification using rotation-invariant feature. In: Proceedings of the 24th association of computing machinery (ACM) symposium on applied computing (SAC 2009) – computational intelligence and image analysis (CIIA) track, Honolulu, Hawaii, 8–12 March 2009, pp 914−921
31. Liu H, Lan Y, Wang Q, Jin R, Song E, Hung C-C (2012) A fast weighted K-view-voting algorithm for image texture classification. Opt Eng 51(02), 1 Feb 2012. https://doi.org/10.1117/1.oe.51.2.027004
32. Liu L, Chen J, Fieguth P, Zhao G, Chellappa R, Pietikainen M (2018) BoW meets CNN: two decades of texture representation. Int J Comput Vis 1–26. https://doi.org/10.1007/s11263-018-1125-z
33. Maeanpaa T (2003) The local binary pattern approach to texture analysis – extensions and applications, Oulu Yliopisto, Oulu
34. Materka A, Strzelecki M (1998) Texture analysis methods – a review, Technical University of Lodz, Institute of Electronics, COST B11 report, Brussels
35. Ojala T, Pietikainen M, Maenpaa T (2002) Multiresolution gray-scale and rotation invariant texture classification with local binary patterns. IEEE Trans Pattern Anal Mach Intell 24(7):941–987
36. Oxholm G, Bariya P, Nishino K (2012) The scale of geometric texture. In: European conference on computer vision. Springer, Berlin/Heidelberg, pp 58–71
37. Pietikainen MK (2000) Texture analysis in machine vision (ed). Series in machine perception and artificial intelligence, vol 40. World Scientific
38. Song EM, Jin R, Lu Y, Xu X, Hung C-C (2006) Boundary refined texture segmentation on liver biopsy images for quantitative assessment of fibrosis severity. In: Proceedings of the SPIE, San Diego, CA, USA, 11–15 Feb 2006
39. Song EM, Jin R, Hung C-C, Lu Y, Xu X (2007) Boundary refined texture segmentation based on K-views and datagram method. In: Proceedings of the 2007 IEEE international symposium on computational intelligence in image and signal processing (CIISP 2007), Honolulu, HI, USA, 1–6 April 2007, pp 19–23
40. Sonka M, Hlavac V, Boyle R (1999) Image processing, analysis, and machine vision, 2nd edn. PWS Publishing
41. Tuceryan M, Jain AK (1998) Texture analysis. In: Chen CH, Pau LF, Wang PSP (eds) The handbook of pattern recognition and computer vision, 2nd edn. World Scientific Publishing Company, pp 207–248
42. Xu Y, Ji H, Fermuller C (2009) Viewpoint invariant texture description using fractal analysis. IJCV 83(1):85–100
43. Yang S, Hung C-C (2003) Image texture classification using datagrams and characteristic views. In: Proceedings of the 18th ACM symposium on applied computing (SAC), Melbourne, FL, 9–12 March 2003, pp 22–26
44. Zhang J, Tan T (2002) Brief review of invariant texture analysis methods. Pattern Recognit 35:735–747

Texture Features and Image Texture Models

2

A smooth sea never made a skillful sailor.

—American proverb

Image texture is an important phenomenon in many applications of pattern recognition and computer vision. Hence, several models for deriving texture properties have been proposed and developed. Although there is no formal definition of image texture in the literature, image texture is usually considered the spatial arrangement of grayscale pixels in a neighborhood on the image. In this chapter, some widely used image texture methods for measuring and extracting texture features will be introduced. These textural features can then be used for image texture classification and segmentation. Specifically, the following methods will be described: (1) the gray-level co-occurrence matrices (GLCM) which is one of the earliest methods for image texture extraction, (2) Gabor filters, (3) wavelet transform (WT) model and its extension, (4) autocorrelation function, (5) Markov random fields (MRF), (6) fractal features, (7) variogram, (8) local binary pattern (LBP), and (9) texture spectrum (TS). LBP has been frequently used for image texture measure. MRF is a statistical model which has been well studied in image texture analysis and other applications. There is one common property associated with these methods and models which use the spatial relationship for texture measurement and classification.

2.1 Introduction

Texture is used to describe a region in which textural elements are characterized in a spatial relationship. An image may consist of one or more textures. If multiple textures exist in an image, the boundary between two textures can be detected and discriminated using texture measure. Texture measure can provide important information for image segmentation, feature extraction, and image classification. Texture measure is very useful in the interpretation of images taken from satellite remote sensing, medical magnetic resonance imaging, materials science, and aerial

© Springer Nature Switzerland AG 2019
C.-C. Hung et al., *Image Texture Analysis*,
https://doi.org/10.1007/978-3-030-13773-1_2

terrain photographs. For example, the study of urban and rural land development in satellite images can benefit from using the image texture analysis.

There exist many texture measures for characterizing a texture. The characterization is called texture feature. Regional properties such as coarseness, homogeneity, density, fineness, smoothness, linearity, directionality, granularity, and frequency have been frequently used as texture features. Many approaches which consist of autocorrelation functions, grayscale co-occurrence matrices, and LBP are used to describe and extract texture features in an image. All of these approaches fall in the four categories: statistical methods, structural methods, model-based methods, and transform-based methods [23–25, 63]. In most cases, texture features are represented numerically by feature vectors, which are composed of feature components derived from a neighborhood of the corresponding texture class.

Each of these approaches has its own advantages and drawbacks. For example, statistical approach is suitable for micro-texture (i.e., random texture) while structural approach is good for macro-texture or well-defined texture patterns such as periodic texture [53, 54]. Many methods for describing texture features depend on the parameters used such as the neighborhood size for a texture region, the quantization of gray levels, and the orientation to measure the relationship among pixels such as the distance and angle [25].

Once the texture features are extracted from a texture, the next phase is to perform the image texture classification (or segmentation). Image texture classification methods fall in one of the two major categories; the first category is based on features with a high degree of spatial localization. In this category, most edge detection methods can use texture features for spatial localization. The major problem with this type of approach is that it is difficult to distinguish the texture boundaries and the micro-edge found in the same texture. The second category is based on discrimination functions with texture features. The classification accuracy in this approach depends on the discriminative power of texture features. The most important step for the second approach is to extract texture features, which can discriminate different types of textures in the image [16, 18, 34, 36, 55, 61, 64].

Haralick et al. have defined a primitive as a set of connected pixels characterized by a list of attributes [23–25]. The primitive is a texture element which can be called "texel" or "texton". A texture pattern can be described by a primitive or a set of primitives. The smallest primitive is a pixel itself. The properties of a primitive are distributed in the neighborhood. This concept has been used in many approaches, and among which are texture unit spectrum [26, 27] and local binary pattern [42, 50]. In the texture unit spectrum approach, a textural element is a texture unit while in the local binary pattern, the texture element, the neighborhood, is called the texture primitive. Both the texture unit spectrum and the local binary pattern approaches are considering only the spatial relationship not the color features.

Color images are seen everywhere nowadays. Color features are potentially useful for texture classification. Hence, many texture classifiers have combined both color and texture features to improve the discriminative capability [1]. Color features were used with texture features to improve the performance on color texture classification [2]. The LBP features and histogram-based method were combined for texture classification on color images [1]. Each texture class has a specific pattern that can distinguish the class from others. To determine whether a pixel belongs to a texture class, the neighborhood of a pixel (a small image patch) is taken and the image patch is examined to measure its similarity to one of the textures and color spectra classes.

Fractal features (frequently called fractal dimensions) are useful in characterizing certain types of objects. Mandelbrot described that "clouds are not spheres, mountains are not cones, coastlines are not circles, and bark is not smooth, nor does lightning travel in a straight line" [45]. Apparently, fractal features are suitable for measuring those objects and regions that have irregular geometry. Frequency features are also very useful in describing certain types of textures. A combination of different types of features will improve image texture classification and segmentation if we properly select some of them for applications.

2.2 Gray-Level Co-Occurrence Matrix (GLCM)

The gray-level co-occurrence matrix (GLCM) is one of the earliest methods using spatial relationships for describing image texture features [23–25]. The GLCM is a statistical method which calculates properties of the spatial relationships among pixels. The spatial relationships between a pair of two pixels in a neighborhood are recorded in the co-occurrence matrices which are then used to calculate textural features [23–25]. The spatial relationships are measured using distances and angles between two pixels in a textured region. This relationship is the joint probability density of two pixels for the transition (or relation) of gray levels in both locations. The GLCM matrices are not used directly. However, certain texture features can be derived from the GLCM such as correlation, homogeneity, and others can be obtained [23–25].

The GLCM is a two-dimensional matrix in which each element p_{ij} represents the frequency of occurrences of a pair of pixels (where i and j are the gray levels) in a spatial relation separated by distance δ and angle α. Let G be an image texture with the size of $M \times N$. An element p_{ij} can be calculated by counting the number of relationships with the following equation:

$$p_{ij} = \{G(m,n) = i, G(m+\delta, n+\delta) = j\} \text{ for each } \alpha, \qquad (2.1)$$

where $m = 0, 1, \ldots, M - 1$, $n = 0, 1, \ldots, N - 1$, and $\alpha = 0°, \ldots, 360°$.

Suppose Q is the number of pairs of pixels i and j separated by δ and α. The probability of p_{ij} is the number of frequency in p_{ij} divided by Q. A hypothetical image and its GLCMs are shown in Example 2.1.

Example 2.1 An example of GLCMs with angles at 0°, 45°, 90°, and 135° and the distance is one unit. Please note that we use the symmetric GLCMs for the frequency count. (a) a hypothetical textured region with a size of 4 × 4 and a value assigned to each pixel, (b) an example of frequency counting in GLCM recording the spatial relationships for pairs of pixels, and (c), (d), (e), and (f) are results of GLCMs with α = 0, 45, 90, and 135 degrees, respectively.

0	1	1	0
1	0	0	1
2	2	1	1
2	2	0	0

(a) A numerical image

		Gray-Level		
		0	1	2
Gray-	0	#(0,0)	#(0,1)	#(0,2)
Level	1	#(1,0)	#(1,1)	#(1,2)
	2	#(2,0)	#(2,1)	#(2,2)

(b) Frequency count for each pair of pixels for spatial relationships

4	4	1
4	4	1
1	1	4

(c) $\alpha = 0°$

2	2	2
2	4	1
2	1	2

(d) $\alpha = 45°$

0	7	1
7	2	1
1	1	4

(e) $\alpha = 90°$

1	4	1
4	2	1
1	1	2

(f) $\alpha = 135°$

Haralick et al. proposed several textural features based on the GLCM method [23–25]. Some texture features including cluster tendency (Clu), contrast (Con), correlation (Cor), dissimilarity (D), entropy (E), homogeneity (H), inverse difference moment (I), maximum probability (M), and uniformity of energy (U) can be computed from the GLCMs as shown in Eqs. 2.2–2.10. Here p_{ij}, similarly defined as in Eq. 2.1, represents the probability of occurrence of pairing pixels as defined above, μ is the overall mean, σ is standard deviation, i and j are the row and column indexes of gray levels in the co-occurrence matrices, and $||$ is the cardinality.

$$Clu = Cluster\,Tendency = \sum_{i,j}(i+j-2\mu)^2 p_{ij} \qquad (2.2)$$

$$Con = Contrast = \sum_{i,j}|i-j|^2 p_{ij} \qquad (2.3)$$

$$Cor = Correlation = \frac{\sum_{i=0}^{M-1}\sum_{j=0}^{N-1} ij\,p_{ij} - \mu_1\mu_2}{\sigma_1^2\sigma_2^2}\;where \qquad (2.4)$$

$$\mu_1 = \sum_{i=0}^{M-1} i \sum_{j=0}^{N-1} p_{ij}$$

$$\mu_2 = \sum_{i=0}^{M-1} j \sum_{j=0}^{N-1} p_{ij}$$

$$\sigma_1^2 = \sum_{i=0}^{M-1}(i-\mu_1)^2 \sum_{j=0}^{N-1} p_{ij}$$

$$\sigma_2^2 = \sum_{i=0}^{M-1}(j-\mu_2)^2 \sum_{j=0}^{N-1} p_{ij}$$

$$D = Dissimilarity = \sum_{i,j}\frac{p_{ij}}{1+|i-j|} \qquad (2.5)$$

$$E = Entropy = -\sum_{i,j} p_{ij}\log p_{ij} \qquad (2.6)$$

$$H = Homogeneity = \sum_{i,j}\frac{p_{ij}}{1+|i-j|} \qquad (2.7)$$

$$I = Inverse\,Difference\,Moment = \sum_{\substack{i,j \\ i \neq j}}\frac{p_{ij}}{|i-j|^k} \qquad (2.8)$$

$$M = Maximum\,Probability = \max_{i,j} p_{ij} \qquad (2.9)$$

$$U = Uniformity\,of\,Energy = \sum_{i,j} p_{ij}^2 \qquad (2.10)$$

Haralick and Bosley [24] performed classification experiments on multi-images using features calculated from the GLCM. These features include uniformity of energy, entropy, maximum probability, contrast, inverse difference moment,

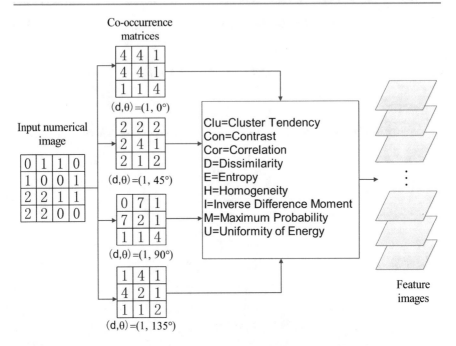

Fig. 2.1 A diagram shows the flow of extracting textural features using the co-occurrence matrices to form a set of feature images for image texture classification

correlation, probability of a run of length, homogeneity, and cluster tendency [23–25]. Feature statistics calculated in Eqs. 2.2−2.10 will then be mapped into the corresponding feature vectors as in Eq. 2.11 and the classification can be performed using any clustering techniques such as the K-means algorithm.

$$\textit{feature vector} = (Clu, Con, Cor, D, E, H, I, M, U)^T, \text{ where T is the transpose} \tag{2.11}$$

Please note that there is no specific order in the list of features for a feature vector. Figure 2.1 shows a diagram for extracting textural features to form a set of feature images. The GLCM is widely used for land cover classification because of its effectiveness. The main drawbacks of GLCM are its sensitivity to background noise, difficulties in determining proper spatial parameters and extensive computation [23–25]. Example 2.2 demonstrates the calculation results based on the GLCM in Example 2.1.

Example 2.2 Each element in the GLCM is converted to the probability and then features are calculated based on Eqs. 2.2−2.10.

0.17	0.17	0.04
0.17	0.17	0.04
0.04	0.04	0.17

(a) $\alpha = 0°$

0.11	0.11	0.11
0.11	0.22	0.06
0.11	0.06	0.11

(b) $\alpha = 45°$

0.0	0.29	0.04
0.29	0.08	0.04
0.04	0.04	0.17

(c) $\alpha = 90°$

0.06	0.24	0.06
0.24	0.12	0.06
0.06	0.06	0.12

(d) $\alpha = 135°$

Hence, the feature vector is *feature vector* = $(Clu, Con, Cor, D, E, H, I, M, U)^T$. For four different directions, four feature vectors will be calculated as in the following:

$\alpha = 0°$

Feature vector = $(4.04, 0.74, -15.84, 0.75, 2.92, 0.75, 0.44, 0.17, 0.15)^T$

$\alpha = 45°$

Feature vector = $(4.02, 1.22, -19.54, 0.68, 2.82, 0.68, 0.40, 0.22, 0.13)^T$

$\alpha = 90°$

Feature vector = $(3.91, 0.98, -19.85, 0.61, 2.51, 0.61, 0.68, 0.29, 0.21)^T$

$\alpha = 135°$

Feature vector = $(3.68, 1.08, -18.77, 0.64, 2.94, 0.64, 0.63, 0.24, 0.16)^T$

Then, an average of above four feature vectors will be used to represent a feature representing a pixel (or neighborhood) for the classification. Alternatively, we may combine all of the four feature vectors with the corresponding weights, which can be calculated with the ratio of norm for each feature vector over the sum of norms of four feature vectors.

2.3 Gabor Filters

Gabor filter is a time–frequency analysis method, which was introduced in 1946 by Dennis Gabor [20]. Gabor filters are the product of Gaussian with sine or cosine functions at different frequencies and different orientations. Gabor filtering provides

a method of textural feature extraction, which is widely used for textural classification and analysis [3, 19, 31, 33, 35, 46, 58, 62, 68, 70]. As a matter of fact, Gabor
filters can be viewed as detectors of edges and lines (stripes) with both directions
and scales. The statistics of these microstructure features in a given textured region
can be used to represent textural features.

Gabor filters, also called Gabor wavelet transforms, were developed based on the
multichannel filtering theory for visual information processing which emerged from
human visual system. This visual system theory was proposed by Campbell and
Robson [6]. Their psychophysical experiments suggested that the mammalian
vision system decomposes the image received by the retina into a number of filtered
images and each of which contains intensity variations over a narrow range of
frequency (size) and orientation. Hence, the spatial domain features and frequency
domain features should simultaneously be used for characterizing textural features.
Gabor filters have been shown to be the best description of the signal space domain
and the frequency domain in the case of two-dimensional uncertainty [20].

There are several different approaches for performing the Gabor transform. Some
methods are computationally intensive. We introduce the multichannel filtering
technique, which uses specified filters to select the information at particular space/
frequency points. Gabor filters implemented as multichannel and wavelet-like filters
mimic the characteristics of the human visual system (HVS) [10, 17, 60]. Although
the wavelet transform is an excellent technique used in image processing, Nestares
et al. point out that Gabor expansion is the only biologically plausible filter with
orientation selectivity that can be exactly expressed as a sum of only two separable
filters [49]. This unique property has made Gabor filter an important transformation
in image processing and computer vision.

There are several forms of 2-D Gabor filter, and a version similar to Daugman's
model that is used in spatial summation properties (of the receptive fields) of simple
cells in the visual cortex is defined in Eqs. 2.12 and 2.13 [12, 13].

$$G(x, y) = \frac{\alpha\beta}{\pi} \exp\left(-\alpha^2 x_g^2 + \beta^2 y_g^2\right) \exp(j2\pi f_0(x_g, y_g)) \tag{2.12}$$

$$\text{with } x_g = x\cos\theta + y\sin\theta \text{ and } y_g = -x\sin\theta + y\cos\theta \tag{2.13}$$

where the arguments, x and y, specify the position of an image, f_0 is the central
frequency of a sinusoidal plane wave, θ is the counterclockwise rotation of the
Gaussian plane wave, and α and β are the sharpness values of the major and minor
axes of the elliptic Gaussian.

When an image is processed using a Gabor filter, the output is the convolution of
the image I(x, y) and the Gabor function $G_k(x, y)$,

$$i.e. \, R_k(x, y) = G_k(x, y) * I(x, y) \tag{2.14}$$

where * denotes the two-dimensional convolution. This process can be used at
different frequencies and different orientations, and the result is a multichannel filter
bank. Figure 2.2 illustrates a multichannel filtering system.

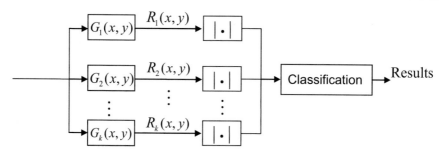

Fig. 2.2 A Gabor multichannel filtering system. The operator |.| is the magnitude operator, and $G_k(x, y)$ is the Gabor function in the kth channel, which denotes a specific frequency and orientation [33]

In Fig. 2.2, symbol |.| is the magnitude operator, and $G_k(x, y)$ is the Gabor function in the kth channel, which denotes a specific frequency and orientation. With the multichannel filtering system, an image will be processed by all the channels simultaneously. The result is a stack of filtered feature images which are defined at various frequencies and orientations corresponding to all the channels in the system. Hence, the characteristic (textural) features at each particular frequency and individual orientation can be obtained.

Although Clausi and Jernigan [10] concluded that the results of every 30° (degrees) will provide a robust and universal feature set, it is very common to use four values of 0°, 45°, 90°, and 135° to save computation time. According to the literature [3, 10, 17, 19, 20, 31, 33, 35, 46, 49, 58, 60, 62, 67, 68, 70], the central frequency is selected according to the image dimension. Low frequency corresponds to smooth variations and constitutes the base of an image while high frequency presents the edge information which gives the detailed information in the image. Using different frequencies and orientations, the Gabor multichannel filters will present an image in different multiple feature images.

2.4 Wavelet Transform (WT) Model and Its Extension

Fourier transformation (FT) is a useful technique which can reveal the frequency information in the Fourier domain [9, 22]. The FT is to decompose an image into a summation of sine and cosine functions with different phases and frequencies. These sine and cosine functions constitute a set of basis functions for the FT. Due to its global property of processes, it is difficult for FT to capture the local transient signals. The short-time Fourier transforms (STFT) are therefore proposed to obtain the frequency and phase content of local transient signals [1]. The window size used in the STFT is fixed. This limitation has some drawbacks [1]: a wide window is good for frequency localization, but poor for time localization. On the other hand, a narrow window is poor for frequency localization, but good for time localization. It

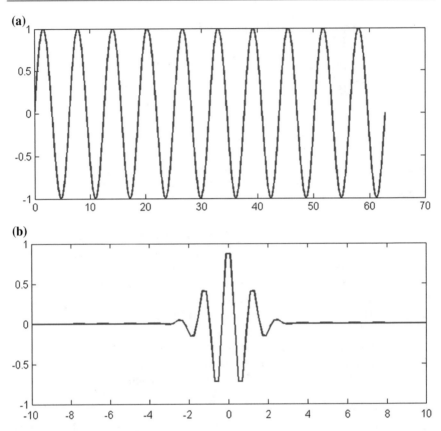

Fig. 2.3 Two different wave functions; **a** infinite duration (i.e., sinusoid) used in the Fourier transforms and **b** limited duration (i.e., wavelet) [11]

would be more appropriate to have a varying length of window which can capture both low-frequency and high-frequency signals. Therefore, wavelet transform (WT) is then proposed to overcome those problems [9, 22]. WT has properties of varying frequencies, limited duration, and zero average value. This is quite different from the FT which uses the sinusoidal functions with infinite duration and constant frequency. The contrast between WT and FT is shown in Fig. 2.3. WT has been widely used in many applications such as imaging medical diagnosis, coding theory, and image compression. Unlike the Fourier transform (FT), there is a difference between the FT and the WT [9, 22, 43]: Fourier basis functions are localized in frequency, but not in time/position. A small change in the frequency in the FT will produce changes everywhere in the time domain. However, the WT is localized in both frequencies (also called scale) via dilations and in time via translations. In addition, many functions can be represented by the WT in a more compact way compared with sine and cosine functions used in the FT.

Similar to any basis functions (will be discussed in Chap. 4), which are used to decompose a complex function. The wavelet transform is a symmetric transformation such as Haar basis functions that is a set of wavelet functions. The transformation usually consists of several Haar wavelet basis functions for extracting certain properties. In the wavelet transform, a basic function, called the *mother wavelet*, is used for performing the *scaling* and *translation* used to generate several wavelet basis functions. These generated wavelet basis functions are called the *child wavelets* [11, 57, 64]. These wavelet basis functions will span the spatial frequency domain of an image.

There are three types of wavelet transforms: continuous, discrete, and wavelet series expansion [9, 22]. Any type of wavelet transforms has the scaling and translation properties. Hence, a Haar function is specified by a dual indexing scheme [9]. A wavelet function fluctuates above and below a horizontal axis with the properties of varying frequency, limited duration, and zero average value. Many different wavelet functions satisfy those three properties. As shown in Fig. 2.4, these are some examples of the wavelet functions; Haar, Morlet and Daubechies wavelets [9, 11, 22].

Among many popular discrete wavelets developed in the literature, we introduce the Haar wavelets [9, 22]. The Haar wavelet transform is one of the earliest orthonormal wavelet transform. Similar to sine and cosines functions in the FT, the Haar wavelets, $f(t)$, can be defined as a set of basis functions $\psi_k(t)$ as shown below:

$$f(t) = \sum_k a_k \psi_k(t) \tag{2.15}$$

where k is the number of basis functions and a_k is a coefficient for the kth basis function. The basis functions can be constructed by applying the translations and scalings (stretching/compressing) on the mother wavelet $\psi(t)$, which is represented in Eq. 2.16 with translation parameter (τ) and scaling parameter (s). For example, if we take a mother wavelet as shown in Fig. 2.5a, we will be able to construct many basis wavelet functions as shown in Fig. 2.5b by applying translation and scaling. It would be convenient if a constraint was used for selecting the values of translation parameter, τ, and scaling parameter, s, with the constraint $s = 2^{-j}$ and $\tau = k2^{-j}$, where k and j are integers. An example with different integers of k and j is shown in Fig. 2.5c.

$$\psi(s, \tau, t) = \frac{1}{\sqrt{s}} \psi\left(\frac{t - \tau}{s}\right) \tag{2.16}$$

We assume that a family of N Haar basis functions, $h_k(t)$ for $k = 0, \ldots, N-1$ with $N = 2^n$, is defined in the interval of $0 \leq t \leq 1$. The shape of each function $h_k(t)$ with index k is defined by Eq. 2.17.

$$k = 2^p + (q - 1) \tag{2.17}$$

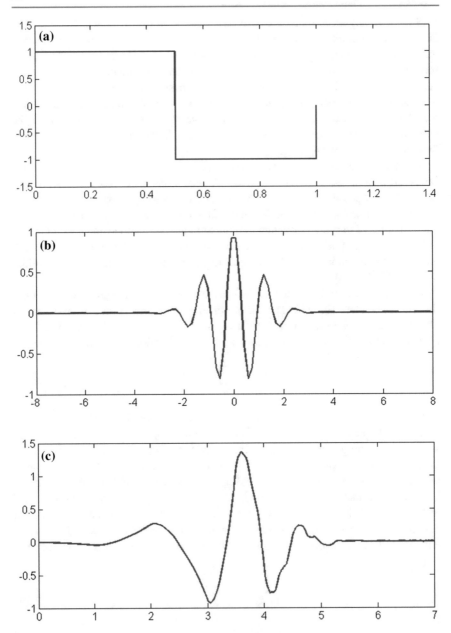

Fig. 2.4 Examples of wavelet functions: **a** Haar wavelet, **b** Morlet wavelet, and **c** Daubechies wavelet [11]

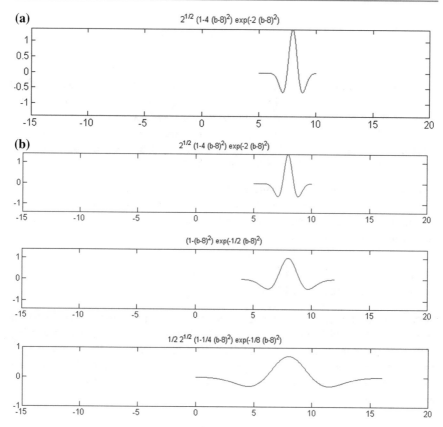

Fig. 2.5 **a** A mother wavelet $\psi(t)$ and **b** the wavelet basis functions obtained by applying the translations and scalings to $\psi(t)$ with values of $s = 2^{-j}$ and $\tau = k2^{-j}$. All wavelets are generated using the equation listed on the top of each wavelet where parameter b in each equation is the value of x-coordinate in each coordinate system

For an index k, parameters p and q are uniquely determined so that 2^P is the largest power of two with the constraint $2^P < = k$. Hence, q − 1 is the remainder of k subtracting 2^P (i.e., k–2^P).

Now, the Haar functions can be defined recursively as:

If k = 0, the Haar function is defined as a constant (Eq. 2.18), then

$$h_0(t) = \frac{1}{\sqrt{N}} \tag{2.18}$$

If k > 0, the Haar function is defined as in Eq. 2.19 [9, 22], which is given below:

$$h_k(t) = \frac{1}{\sqrt{N}} \begin{cases} 2^{p/2} & (q-1)/2^p \le t < (q-0.5)/2^p \\ -2^{p/2} & (q-0.5)/2^p \le t < q/2^p \\ 0 & otherwise \end{cases} \tag{2.19}$$

From the definition, it can be seen that p determines the amplitude and width of the nonzero part of the function (i.e., the scaling parameter), while q decides the position of the nonzero part of the function (i.e., translating parameter).

To use the Haar transform, Example 2.3 shows the Haar wavelet transforms with a set of eight wavelet basis function (i.e., k = 8) by specifying the dual indexing scheme of p and q and their relationship with k.

Example 2.3 The following example illustrates the steps listed above. If we take an example of the Haar wavelet transforms with k = 8, (t is between 0 and 1), index k and its corresponding p and q values are calculated based on Eq. 2.17 and are shown in the following table:

k	0	1	2	3	4	5	6	7
p	0	0	1	1	2	2	2	2
q	0	1	1	2	1	2	3	4

Similar to the rotation, scaling, and translation operations used in image geometry and computer graphics, the Haar transformation can be implemented in a kernel transformation matrix [9, 22]. The Haar transform, similar to the Fourier transform, can be represented in the matrix format. For example, if we assume that there are N Haar functions sampled at the interval of t which is defined in Eq. 2.20, and given below:

$$t = \frac{m}{N}, m = 0, 1, \ldots, N-1 \tag{2.20}$$

to form an N x N matrix for discrete Haar transform.

If $N = 2$, we have

$$\mathbf{H}_2 = \frac{1}{\sqrt{2}} \begin{bmatrix} 1 & 1 \\ 1 & -1 \end{bmatrix} \tag{2.21}$$

A simple Haar transformation using a Haar transformation matrix is shown in Example 2.4. In addition, a normalization on the Haar transformation will make the constructed images more smooth.

Example 2.4 Assume a feature vector with four components $f_v = [1, 2, 3, 1]^T$.
The 4×4 Haar transformation matrix is

$$H_4 = \frac{1}{2} \begin{bmatrix} 1 & 1 & 1 & 1 \\ 1 & 1 & -1 & -1 \\ \sqrt{2} & -\sqrt{2} & 0 & 0 \\ 0 & 0 & \sqrt{2} & -\sqrt{2} \end{bmatrix} \tag{2.22}$$

The Haar transformation coefficients are obtained by multiplying H_4 by f_v:

$$H_{Coefficients} = \frac{1}{2} \begin{bmatrix} 1 & 1 & 1 & 1 \\ 1 & 1 & -1 & -1 \\ \sqrt{2} & -\sqrt{2} & 0 & 0 \\ 0 & 0 & \sqrt{2} & -\sqrt{2} \end{bmatrix} x \begin{bmatrix} 1 \\ 2 \\ 3 \\ 1 \end{bmatrix} = \begin{bmatrix} 7/2 \\ -1/2 \\ -1/\sqrt{2} \\ \sqrt{2} \end{bmatrix} \tag{2.23}$$

The inverse transform will express the feature vector as the linear combination of the basis functions:

$$H_{Inverse} = \frac{1}{2} \begin{bmatrix} 1 & 1 & \sqrt{2} & 0 \\ 1 & 1 & -\sqrt{2} & 0 \\ 1 & -1 & 0 & \sqrt{2} \\ 1 & -1 & 0 & -\sqrt{2} \end{bmatrix} x \begin{bmatrix} 7/2 \\ -1/2 \\ -1/\sqrt{2} \\ \sqrt{2} \end{bmatrix} = \begin{bmatrix} 1 \\ 2 \\ 3 \\ 1 \end{bmatrix} \tag{2.24}$$

Note that the functions $h_k(t)$ of Haar transform (defined in Eq. 2.19) can represent not only the details in signals of different scales (corresponding to different frequencies) but also their locations in time. A set of Haar wavelet basis functions is shown in Fig. 2.6 [9].

The Haar transform matrix is real and orthogonal:

$$\mathbf{H} = \mathbf{H}^*, \qquad \mathbf{H}^{-1} = \mathbf{H}^T, \qquad \text{i.e.,} \qquad \mathbf{H}^T\mathbf{H} = \mathbf{I} \tag{2.25}$$

where $\mathbf{I}$ is an identity matrix. For example, when $N = 4$, we get

$$\mathbf{H}_4^{-1}\mathbf{H}_4 = \mathbf{H}_4^T\mathbf{H}_4 = \frac{1}{4} \begin{bmatrix} 1 & 1 & \sqrt{2} & 0 \\ 1 & 1 & -\sqrt{2} & 0 \\ 1 & -1 & 0 & \sqrt{2} \\ 1 & -1 & 0 & -\sqrt{2} \end{bmatrix} \begin{bmatrix} 1 & 1 & 1 & 1 \\ 1 & 1 & -1 & -1 \\ \sqrt{2} & -\sqrt{2} & 0 & 0 \\ 0 & 0 & \sqrt{2} & -\sqrt{2} \end{bmatrix}$$

$$= \begin{bmatrix} 1 & 0 & 0 & 0 \\ 0 & 1 & 0 & 0 \\ 0 & 0 & 1 & 0 \\ 0 & 0 & 0 & 1 \end{bmatrix} \tag{2.26}$$

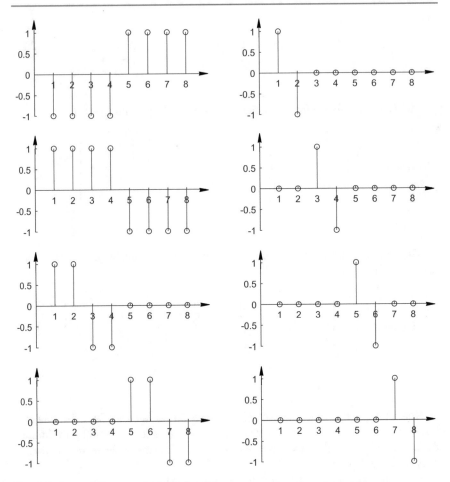

Fig. 2.6 A set of Haar wavelet basis functions

The Haar transform was frequently used for signal and image compression, and noise removal before the more advanced wavelet transforms such as Daubechies and other wavelets were developed. The Haar transform conserves the energy of signals and possesses the compaction of energy [65].

A general discrete wavelet transform (DWT) can be implemented by two basic operations using the averaging and differencing operators on a feature vector [32, 47]. The averaging operator is similar to the low-pass filter such as the averaging filter while the differencing operator is similar to the high-pass filter such as the Laplacian filter commonly used in digital image processing. To calculate the transform of an array of n samples, the following DWT algorithm is used.

A General Discrete Wavelet Transform (DWT) Algorithm:

Step 1: Divide the array into $n/2$ pairs called (L, R) for each pair in an input.

Step 2: Calculate $(L + R)/2$ for each pair, these values, called *approximation coefficients*, will be the first half of the output array.

Step 3: Calculate $(L - R)/2$ for each pair, these values, called *detail coefficients*, will be the second half.

Step 4: Repeat the process on the first half of the array (the array length should be a power of two) until no pair is left for the calculation.

Example 2.5 illustrates the steps listed above:

Example 2.5 Assume that we have a feature vector with eight components $f_v = [1, 2, 3, 1, 4, 6, 7, 5]^T$. We show the step-by-step calculation using the DWT transform algorithm.

The one-level DWT transform of $f_v = [1, 2, 3, 1, 4, 6, 7, 5]^T$:

$$DWT_1(f_v) = [Approximation\ Coefficients | Detail\ Coefficients]$$
$$= \left[\frac{1+2}{2}, \frac{3+1}{2}, \frac{4+6}{2}, \frac{7+5}{2} \middle| \frac{1-2}{2}, \frac{3-1}{2}, \frac{4-6}{2}, \frac{7-5}{2} \right]$$
$$= \left[\frac{3}{2}, \frac{4}{2}, \frac{10}{2}, \frac{12}{2} \middle| \frac{-1}{2}, \frac{2}{2}, \frac{-2}{2}, \frac{2}{2} \right]$$

The two-level DWT transform of $f_v = \left[\frac{3}{2}, \frac{4}{2}, \frac{10}{2}, \frac{12}{2} \right]^T$:

$$DWT_2(f_v) = [Approximation\ Coefficients | Detail\ Coefficients]$$
$$= \left[\frac{\frac{3}{2}+\frac{4}{2}}{2}, \frac{\frac{10}{2}+\frac{12}{2}}{2} \middle| \frac{\frac{3}{2}-\frac{4}{2}}{2}, \frac{\frac{10}{2}-\frac{12}{2}}{2} \right]$$
$$= \left[\frac{7}{4}, \frac{22}{4} \middle| \frac{-1}{4}, \frac{-2}{4} \right]$$

The three-level DWT transform of $f_v = \left[\frac{7}{4}, \frac{22}{4} \right]^T$:

$$DWT_3(f_v) = [Approximation\ Coefficients | Detail\ Coefficients]$$
$$= \left[\frac{\frac{7}{4}+\frac{22}{4}}{2} \middle| \frac{\frac{7}{4}-\frac{22}{4}}{2} \right]$$
$$= \left[\frac{29}{8} \middle| \frac{-15}{8} \right]$$

Table 2.1 is a summary of computations above.

Table 2.1 A summary of average and difference computation

1	2	3	1	4	6	7	5
3/2	4/2	10/2	12/2	−1/2	2/2	−2/2	2/2
7/4	22/4	−1/4	−2/4	−1/2	2/2	−2/2	2/2
29/8	−15/8	−1/4	−2/4	−1/2	2/2	−2/2	2/2

2.5   Autocorrelation Function

Autocorrelation function is a two-dimensional function which can detect repetitive patterns of texels [22, 25]. It works by comparing the dot product (energy) of a non-shifted image with a shifted image as shown in Eq. 2.27. The coarseness and fineness of a texture can be determined by the speed the function drops off. For a coarse texture, the function drops off slowly while for a fine texture, the function drops off rapidly. This indicates that the size of coarse texels is larger than that of fine texels. The function can drop off differently for different sizes of the image. For regular textures, the function will have peaks and valleys with peaks repeating far away from the origin. For random textures, peaks occur at the origin. The breadth of peaks determines the size of texels.

The autocorrelation function $\rho(dr,dc)$ of an $(N+1)$ x $(N+1)$ image, I, for displacement d = (dr, dc) is defined by Eq. 2.27.

$$\rho(dr, dc) = \frac{\sum_{r=0}^{N} \sum_{c=0}^{N} I[r,c] I[r+dr, c+dc]}{\sum_{r=0}^{N} \sum_{c=0}^{N} I^2[r,c]}$$
$$= \frac{I[r,c] o I_d[r,c]}{I[r,c] o I[r,c]} \tag{2.27}$$

where r is the number of rows, c is the number of columns, and symbol o represents a correlation operator.

2.6   Markov Random Field (MRF) Model

Image classification algorithms that incorporate contextual (i.e., spatial) information are called spatial image classifiers. There are two approaches for utilizing spatial information for image classification. The first method is to extract (spatial) features from the neighborhood and use any pattern classification algorithm to assign a pixel to a predefined class. The second method is to segment an image into small homogeneous regions and then extract features from each region for assigning the entire region into a predefined class [22, 25]. The spatial classifier attempts to capture the spatial relationships encoded in the remote sensing images for improving the classification accuracy.

Markov Random Field (MRF) model is a stochastic process that can describe the spatial relationships of pixels in a local neighborhood of an image [14]. The model utilizes both spectral and spatial information for the characterization and computation of features for each pixel and its neighboring pixels. The temporal information can also be used in the model if it is available. In such a case, a three-dimensional (3-D) MRF model is utilized. The MRF characterizes the statistical relationships between a pixel and its neighbors in a user-defined window. It is assumed that the intensity of each pixel is dependent on the intensities of only neighboring pixels [14]. This is called Markovian property which is similar to that used in the Markov chain.

The development of the MRF can be traced back to the Bayes theory [22, 25]. A popular classification algorithm based on the Bayes theory is called the naïve Bayes classifier. The algorithm is based on two criteria, the prior probabilities and conditional probability density functions (PDF) (also called likelihood function) as shown in Eqs. 2.28 and 2.29.

$$P(Y|X_1,\ldots,X_n) = \frac{P(X_1,\ldots,X_n|Y)P(Y)}{P(X_1,\ldots,X_n)} \tag{2.28}$$

$$Class_Y = \underset{Y}{\operatorname{argmax}} P(Y|X_1,\ldots,X_n) \ where \ Y = 1,\ldots,C \tag{2.29}$$

We assume that there is C number of classes. Notation $P(Y|X_1, \ldots, X_n)$ represents the probability of classifying a pixel to a class label Y based on the observed features $X_1, \ldots, X_n$. Notations $P(X_1, \ldots, X_n \mid Y)$, $P(Y)$, and $P(X_1, \ldots, X_n)$ denote the likelihood function, prior probability, and normalization constant, respectively.

The naive Bayes classifier employs a decision rule to select the hypothesis that is most probable; this is known as the *maximum a posteriori* (MAP) decision rule. In the applications of remote sensing images, the Gaussian distribution is usually assumed for image classification. Hence, the maximum likelihood criterion is used in the naïve Bayes classifier. In such a case, we will call the maximum likelihood (ML) classifier. With the Gaussian distribution for modeling the class conditional PDF, we can calculate the mean and variance for each class of the classification.

Although the prior probability is used in the ML classifier, this is an estimate without considering any contextual information from the neighboring pixels. If a prior model can be used in the ML classifier, it should improve the classification result. The MRF which uses the contextual information for modeling the prior conditional probability density functions (PDF) has been well developed [14, 16, 34, 63]. The MRF uses this contextual information as a priori for improving the classification accuracy. However, it is difficult to establish a MAP estimate in the MRF model using the conditional probability density functions (PDF). The Hammersley−Clifford theorem provides an efficient method for solving this problem [14]. The theorem states that a random field is an MRF if and only if it follows a Gibbs distribution [14]. This theorem provides us a means to define an MRF model through clique potentials. Cliques are used to capture the dependence of pixels in a neighborhood.

We assume that the MRF model used is noncasual (i.e., stationary) in which the intensity, $y(s)$, at site s is a function of the neighbors of s in all directions [38, 69]. The conditional probability density function (PDF) defining the MRF models is given in Eq. 2.30.

$$p(y(s)|\text{all } y(s+r), r \in N) \tag{2.30}$$

where N is a neighborhood system and r is one of the neighboring pixels in the defined neighborhood. The neighborhood structure specifying dependencies among pixels in a region are given in Fig. 2.7 in which different orders are defined with respect to the central pixel x [14, 16, 28, 55, 69]. In many of the texture classification, the higher order of the neighborhood in the MRF model is used since it contains most of the statistical characteristics of the original textures [14, 16, 22, 25, 55, 69].

If we assume that $P(\omega \mid f)$ measures the probability of a labeling (i.e., classification), given the observed feature f, our goal is to find an optimal labeling $\omega^\wedge$ which *maximizes* $P(\omega \mid f)$. This is called the *maximum* a posteriori (MAP) estimate as shown in Eq. 2.31.

$$\omega^{\wedge MAP} = \text{argmax } P(\omega|f), \omega \in \Omega \tag{2.31}$$

where Ω is a set of class labels and f is a feature vector. To find f that maximizes $P(\omega|f)$, it would be sufficient to minimize the system energy function U(w) in Eq. 2.32:

$$U(w) = \sum_{c \in C} V_c(w) \tag{2.32}$$

where V_c (w) is the clique potentials of class label c. A clique is defined as a subset of pixels if every pair of pixels in this subset is neighbor in a set of pixels. A set of

5	4	3	4	5
4	2	1	2	4
3	1	x	1	3
4	2	1	2	4
5	4	3	4	5

Fig. 2.7 Neighborhood systems represent different orders with respect to the center pixel (x): **a** the first order (all pixels labeled as 1), **b** the second order (all pixels labeled as 1 and 2), **c** the third order (all pixels labeled as 1, 2, and 3), **d** the fourth order (all pixels labeled as 1, 2, 3, and 4), and **e** the fifth order (all pixels labeled as 1, 2, 3, 4, and 5)

pixels is a patch or neighborhood as defined in Fig. 2.7. A clique containing n pixels is called nth order clique [14].

We can rewrite $P(\omega \mid f)$ in terms of the energy function as in Eq. 2.33:

$$p(w|f) = \frac{1}{Z}e^{\frac{-U(w)}{T}} \tag{2.33}$$

where e is an exponential function, T is temperature, and Z is a normalization constant defined in Eq. 2.34.

$$Z = \sum_{c \in C} e^{\frac{-U(w)}{T}} \tag{2.34}$$

where notations used are defined above.

Since the Gibbs random field model is the characterization of the system energy, our goal is to determine the lowest energy of the system that gives the optimal solution. Our problem becomes choosing the most probable labeling (ω) to minimize the energy. However, this is an NP-hard problem [14]. There exist several optimization methods such as simulated annealing and Gibbs sampler, which are frequently used in the MRF modeling for applications [14].

2.7 Fractal Dimensions

Fractal geometry is a branch of mathematics for the study of complex patterns in irregular geometry objects. Fractals refer to irregular geometry objects that may illustrate a degree of self-similarity at different scales [37, 44, 45, 51, 63]. When the spatial distribution of local image textures exhibits irregular shapes for the texture, fractals can be used for characterizing image textures. Fractal dimension that is different from the dimension defined in the Euclidean space is commonly used for measuring the fractal geometry [44, 45, 51, 63]. The Euclidean dimension is defined as a number of coordinates. For example, a line, which has one coordinate, is one dimensional, a plane, which has two coordinates, is two dimensional, and a space, which has three coordinates, is three dimensional. A fractal is a set in which the Hausdorff–Besicovitch dimension strictly exceeds the topological dimension according to the definition given by Mandelbrot [44, 45]. This generalized dimension, called the Hausdorff dimension (often called *fractional dimension*), invented by German mathematician Felix Hausdorff, is a clear concept in explaining the fractal dimension. If we take an object located in Euclidean dimension D and reduce its size by $1/r$ in each spatial direction linearly, its measure (i.e., number of objects) is increased to $N = r^D$ magnitudes of the original. This is shown in Fig. 2.8.

Considering the relationship $N = r^D$, if we take the log function of both sides and rearrange the formula, the relationship is rewritten as in Eq. 2.35.

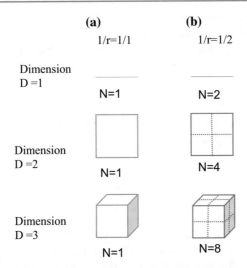

Fig. 2.8 The number of dimensions in Euclidean space (D) is increased from one to three; the measure (number) of lines, squares, and cubes are increased. **a** in this column, since r = 1, N is 1 for all dimensions and **b** r is 2, N is 2, 4, and 8, respectively. (https://www.vanderbilt.edu/AnS/psychology/cogsci/chaos/workshop/Fractals.html)

$$D = \log(N) / \log(r) \tag{2.35}$$

Now, the value of D may become a fraction as used in the fractal dimension. A set with a non-integer dimension is a fractal. However, the formula in Eq. 2.35 may result in an integer dimension which is still considered as a fractal. This generalized dimension is very useful for describing natural objects and chaotic trajectories which are fractals.

There exist several methods for estimating the fractal dimension of complex patterns [63]. Mallat proposed a theory using the wavelet transform for calculating the fractal dimension [43]. Pentland proposed a 3-D fractal model which characterizes the 3-D surfaces and their images for measuring the fractal dimension [52]. Another approach is the box-counting method based on the self-similarity concept developed by Mandelbrot [63].

Fractal features are mainly used in texture description and image recognition for characterizing different textures of the objects [63]. Lacunarity is one of the fractal features used for characterizing image textures [38, 40, 48, 56, 59]. Ling et al. have shown that the fractal dimension is a poor descriptor of surface complexity while the lacunarity analysis can successfully quantify the spatial texture of an SEM image [39]. Lacunarity is a scale-dependent measure of heterogeneity of texture in an image. The index of lacunarity is large when the texture is coarse [39, 59]. Texture feature can be constructed by concatenating the lacunarity-related parameters, which are estimated from the multi-scale local binary patterns of an image [59]. By using the lacunarity analysis and its ability to distinguish spatial patterns, the method is able to characterize the spatial distribution of local image structures for multiple scales.

Fractal dimension may not give different values for characterizing different image textures. However, lacunarity may provide unique characteristics for each different texture although they may have the same fractal dimension [48]. If an object is homogeneous because all gap sizes are the same, its lacunarity will be low while a high lacunarity value indicates that an object is heterogeneous [48]. Myint and Lam use different sizes of moving windows such as 13×13, 21×21, and 29×29 for calculating the lacunarity as the features from urban spectral images and observing the effects of the size of moving windows in characterizing urban texture features [48]. They discovered that the lacunarity approach can improve the accuracy of urban classification significantly using spectral images.

There exist different methods to calculate the lacunarity. The method of blanket is used to calculate the lacunarity in [37, 40, 51]. Images can be viewed as a mountain surface whose height from the normal ground is proportional to the image gray levels. Then, we can create a blanket with the thickness of 2ε covering on the surface of both images. The estimated surface area is the volume of the blanket divided by 2ε. For different values of ε, the blanket area can be iteratively estimated. Gilmore et al. implement the lacunarity as a measure of the distribution of color intensity (i.e., RGB) for an image [21]. The first moment and second moment of the gray-level distribution for each band are calculated first. Lacunarity is defined as the ratio of the second and first moments of mass distribution. Their algorithm is listed below.

The Lacunarity Algorithm

Step 1: Calculate the first moment which is the same as the mean of the gray level of all pixels, s_i, inside the box, and N is the number of pixels for an input image.

$$M_1 = \frac{1}{N} \sum_{i=1}^{i=N} s_i \qquad (2.36)$$

Step 2: Calculate the second moment which is the same as the variance of the gray level of all pixels, s_i, inside the box, and N is the number of pixels.

$$M_2 = \frac{1}{N-1} \sum_{i=1}^{i=N} (s_i - M_1)^2 \qquad (2.37)$$

Step 3:   Calculate the lacunarity, $L(s^2)$, for a box size, s^2, using Eq. 2.38.

$$L(s^2) = \frac{M_2 + M_1^2}{M_1^2} \qquad (2.38)$$

Please note that the algorithm will calculate the lacunarity for the red, green, and blue components of the image separately.

As reported in the literature, the maximal box size used is one-half of the length of the smallest axis of the image. Three maximal box size diameters of one-eighth, one-half, and one-quarter of the length of the smallest axis of the image were used for the lacunarity calculations for each image in [21]. They also used the random sampling to choose the center of each box. The algorithm will generate a feature vector of lacunarities for each component of RGB color image. Depending on the maximal box size, these feature vectors contain different number of elements. Images are thus assigned nine lacunarity values according to the mean of their red, green, and blue vector values for each of three maximal box sizes in their experiments [21].

2.8   Variogram

Geostatistics is the study of phenomena that vary in space and time in geology and remote sensing images [5, 15, 30]. It is used to measure the spatial correlation and its properties. There are some basic components of geostatistics which are frequently used for the spatial characterization, variogram analysis, and Kriging and stochastic simulation [5]. The variogram (also called semivariogram), which is a second-order statistics, is to extract the texture features from the image. Unlike the GLCM, the variogram is to capture the covariance of pixel values as a function of distance between pixels [7, 8, 41]. It measures the difference between pixel values relative to a given distance separating them in a specific orientation [7, 8, 41]. A pair of pixels representing the measurement of the same variable is used for measuring the spatial similarities at a distance between the pair. This distance is usually referred to as "lag", as used in the time series analysis [5]. A variogram shows a peak of the variance, which is called sill. The lag interval to the sill is known as the range. That range indicates the limit of spatial dependence and the distance over which values are similar.

Similar to the GLCM, the variogram has been used in the classification and analysis of image textures [7, 8, 41]. However, they are quite different from the classification point of view [8]. In the GLCM method, different features are extracted from the co-occurrence matrices to form a feature vector for the classification. In the variogram approach, a set of lags is used to calculate the variogram for each pixel located in a neighborhood. Similarly, the variogram is calculated for each textural class using the training sites within a neighborhood in an image. Based on the minimum distance principle, a pixel will be classified based on the minimum distance obtained between the variogram of each pixel and that of the textural classes. The variogram model is described in detail below [7].

Let $G(x, y)$ denote a grayscale image. The variogram for describing this image is formulated as in Eq. 2.39.

$$2\gamma(h) = \frac{1}{2} \int_x \int_y [G(x, y) - G(x', y')]^2 dy dx \qquad (2.39)$$

where h is the Euclidean distance (i.e., lag distance) between a pixel at a location (x, y) and another pixel value G at location (x', y'). For a digital image, this integral is approximated as Eq. 2.40.

$$\gamma(h) = \frac{1}{2N} \sum_{i=1}^{N} [G(x, y) - G(x', y')]^2 \qquad (2.40)$$

where N is the total number of pairs of pixels and $G(x, y)$ and $G(x', y')$ are represented as a pair of pixels that are separated by a distance h.

The variogram $\gamma(h)$ can be computed with a particular spatial direction. Four directions including East−West (E−W), North−South (N−S), Northeast−Southwest (NE−SW), and Northwest−Southeast (NW−SE) are usually used for the spatial directions. These are defined in Eqs. 2.41−2.44:

E−W:

$$\gamma(h) = \frac{1}{2N} \sum_{i=1}^{N} [G(x, y) - G(x + h, y)]^2 \qquad (2.41)$$

N−S:

$$\gamma(h) = \frac{1}{2N} \sum_{i=1}^{N} [G(x, y) - G(x, y + h)]^2 \qquad (2.42)$$

NE−SW:

$$\gamma(h) = \frac{1}{2N} \sum_{i=1}^{N} [G(x + h, y) - G(x, y + h)]^2 \qquad (2.43)$$

NW−SE:

$$\gamma(h) = \frac{1}{2N} \sum_{i=1}^{N} [G(x, y) - G(x + h, y + h)]^2 \qquad (2.44)$$

The variogram is often calculated using the absolute value (Eq. 2.45), rather than the square of pixel difference [7].

$$\gamma(h) = \frac{1}{2N} \sum_{i=1}^{N} |G(x, y) - G(x', y')| \tag{2.45}$$

The training sites of size $M \times M$ pixels are extracted and computed for each class. A variogram is also computed for a region with a size of $M \times M$ around each pixel to be classified. The minimum distance (Eq. 2.46) is used to determine the similarity of variograms.

$$Distance = \sum_{i=1}^{k} |\gamma_t(c) - \gamma_p(c)| \tag{2.46}$$

where K is the number of increments of h allowable given the constraint of the window size M, the subscripts t and p are the variograms of training site and a neighborhood, respectively, c is a particular class. A pixel is then classified into a class when the distance is minimum. The variogram is one of the examples to extract features using a spatial autocorrelation function. Compared with GLCM, it is very useful in the microwave image classification [7].

2.9   Texture Spectrum (TS) and Local Binary Pattern (LBP)

He and Wang stated that a texture image can be decomposed into a set of essential small units called texture units (TU) [26, 27, 66]. A texture unit is represented by a 3×3 window. The central pixel X_0 in the window is the pixel being processed, and the given neighborhood of X_0 is denoted as $X = \{X_1, X_2, X_3 \ldots X_8\}$ as shown in

Fig. 2.9 a A 3×3 window for a texture unit, **b** the corresponding texture unit, **c** a numerical example of texture unit, and **d** its corresponding texture unit

(a)

X_4	X_3	X_2
X_5	X_0	X_1
X_6	X_7	X_8

(b)

E_4	E_3	E_2
E_5		E_1
E_6	E_7	E_8

(c)

1	3	2
9	6	4
6	9	8

(d)

0	0	0
2		0
1	2	2

Fig. 2.9a. The corresponding texture unit set is $TU = \{E_1, E_2, E_3, E_4, E_5, E_6, E_7, E_8\}$ by using Eq. 2.47 such that:

$$E_i = \begin{cases} 0 & \text{if } X_i < X_0 \\ 1 & \text{if } X_i = X_0 \\ 2 & \text{if } X_i < X_0 \end{cases} \quad \text{for } i = 1, 2, \ldots, 8. \qquad (2.47)$$

A number is associated with a texture unit which is calculated with the corresponding weights (i.e., 3^{i-1}) using Eq. 2.48.

$$N_{TU} = \sum_{i=1}^{8} E_i * 3^{i-1} \qquad (2.48)$$

Therefore, N_{TU} has $3^8 = 6561$ standard textural units which are considered the smallest unit covering all possible patterns in all eight directions from the central pixel.

Texture spectrum (TS) is a distribution of the frequency of texture unit numbers. While the texture unit is used to characterize the local texture in the neighborhood of a corresponding pixel, the TS is used to characterize each unique type of textures in the image. Once the texture features are extracted using the TS, a histogram can be used to represent the distribution of textural units. Most classification algorithms can be used to discriminate the texture patterns. The simplest classification algorithm which uses the minimum distance can be found in [26, 27, 65].

Ojala et al. introduced the local binary pattern (LBP) operator to measure the texture pattern [42, 50]. In this method, each neighboring pixel inside the 3×3 neighborhood is compared with the center pixel using Eq. 2.49 to obtain either 0 and 1 for each neighboring pixel. Each binary value is then multiplied by the corresponding weight as shown in Fig. 2.10. An LBP number for a texture unit is obtained by adding all the multiplications. The LBP can produce up to $2^8 = 256$ texture patterns.

$$E_i = \begin{cases} 0, & \text{if } x_i < x_0 \\ 1, & \text{if } x_i \geq x_0 \end{cases} \quad \text{for } i = 1, 2, 3, 4, 5, 6, 7, \text{ and } 8 \qquad (2.49)$$

where x_0 is the center pixel of 3×3 window.

Although a 3×3 kernel neighborhood is used as an example to illustrate how the LBP works, its kernel size can be extended to a different size such as 5×5. To facilitate the invariance of rotation of an image, an invariance rotation operator $LBP_{P,R}$ which characterizes the spatial structure of the local image texture, is defined based on a circularly symmetric neighboring set of P members on a circle of radius R (Fig. 2.11a). Parameters P and R control the quantization of the angular space and spatial resolution, respectively. Figure 2.11b shows some samples of nonuniform patterns and Fig. 2.11c illustrates some samples of uniform patterns which contain very few spatial transitions from 0 to 1.

(a)

1	3	2
9	6	4
6	9	8

(b)

0	0	0
1		0
1	1	1

(c)

2^0	2^1	2^2
2^7		2^3
2^6	2^5	2^4

$$\text{LBP number} = 0 \times 2^0 + 0 \times 2^1 + 0 \times 2^2 + 0 \times 2^3 + 1 \times 2^4 + 1 \times 2^5 + 1 \times 2^6 + 1 \times 2^7$$
$$= 240.$$

Fig. 2.10 **a** A numerical texture unit, **b** its corresponding local binary pattern (LBP), and **c** the weight for each neighboring pixel and the LBP number

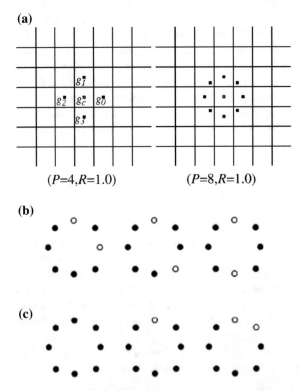

(a)

$(P=4,R=1.0)$ $(P=8,R=1.0)$

(b)

(c)

Fig. 2.11 **a** A circularly symmetric neighboring set (P is angular resolution and R spatial resolution) and **b** samples of nonuniform patterns, and **c** samples of uniform patterns [50]

The $LBP_{P,R}$ number is defined in Eq. 2.50 [42, 50]:

$$LBP_{P,R} = \sum_{p=0}^{P-1} s(g_p - g_c) 2^p \qquad (2.50)$$

where s(x) is defined as

$$s(x) = \begin{cases} 0, & if \ x < 0 \\ 1, & if \ x \geq 0 \end{cases} \quad where \ x = g_p - g_C$$

The $LBP_{P,R}$ operator produces 2^P different patterns. When a texture unit is rotated, each pixel g_p will move along the perimeter of the circle. In order to remove the effect of rotation and assign a unique identifier (number) to each pattern, a rotation invariant local binary pattern is defined in Eq. 2.51 [42, 50]:

$$LBP_{P,R}^{ri} = \min\{ROR(LBP_{P,R}, i) \quad | \quad i = 0, 1, \ldots, P-1\} \qquad (2.51)$$

where ROR(x, i) is a circular bit-wise right-shift on P-bit number x at i times. It is observed that certain local binary patterns are fundamental properties of textures which provide the majority of texture patterns. Sometimes it is over 90% for all 3×3 patterns present in the observed textures. These fundamental patterns are called "uniform" patterns. Other patterns are called nonuniform as shown in Fig. 2.11b. The "uniform" patterns have uniform circular structure that contains very few spatial transitions from 0 to 1. Some samples of uniform patterns are shown in Fig. 2.11c. Using uniform patterns, we are able to distinguish microstructures such as bright spots, flat areas, and dark spots [42, 50]. By this definition, using Eq. 2.52, the pattern obtained is called uniform with U value of at most 2. Therefore, texture operator $LBP_{P,R}^{riu2}$ (Eq. 2.53) detects uniform local binary patterns at circular neighborhoods of any quantization of the angular space and at any spatial resolution [42, 50].

$$U(LBP_{P,R} = |s(g_{P-1} - g_c) - s(g_0 - g_c)|$$
$$+ \sum_{p=1}^{P-1} |s(g_p - g_c) - s(g_{p-1} - g_c)| \qquad (2.52)$$

$$LBP_{P,R}^{riu2} = \begin{cases} \sum_{p=0}^{P-1} s(g_p - g_c) & if \ U(LBP_{P,R}) \leq 2 \\ P+1 & otherwise \end{cases} \qquad (2.53)$$

According to Eq. 2.53, there are exactly $P + 1$ uniform binary patterns in a circularly symmetric set of P pixels in a window and Eq. 2.53 assigns a unique label to each of them. Similar to the texture spectrum (TS), a histogram of uniform binary patterns and minimum distance can be used to measure similarity and dissimilarity of textures for the image texture classification.

2.10   Local Binary Pattern (LBP) and Color Features

The texture spectrum (TS) and the local binary pattern (LBP) methods take only the spatial relationship into account among the neighboring pixels in the defined window. Spectral color is one feature that can be used for discriminating textures within the texture regions. Spectral color is the occurrence of the gray level of pixels in each band. Spectral color provides multi-histograms formed with respect to different bands of multispectral images [2]. The multi-histograms provide quantitative occurrence of the gray levels for each band. Hence, if both the LBP and spectral color are used simultaneously, it may improve the classification accuracy by capturing the features of spectral colors. In order to classify a texture into different texture classes, a correlation-matching method can be used. To find the similarity based on the LBP and spectral color from a small image patch to a kernel (neighborhood), an average absolute difference D(i) is used and defined as in Eq. 2.54 (here we assume that an 8-bit color image is used for the calculation).

$$D(i) = \frac{1}{2}\left(b * \left(\sum_{T=0}^{255}|W_T(j) - S_T(i,j)| + \sum_{C=0}^{255}|W_C(j) - S_C(i,j)|\right)\right) \quad (2.54)$$

where $W_T(j)$ is the occurrence value of the LBP and $W_C(j)$ is the occurrence value of the color spectra in a window superimposed on an image being classified. Notations $S_T(i, j)$ and $S_C(i, j)$ are the occurrence values of the LBP and color spectra j, respectively, in the sample i, and b is the number of bands. The algorithm that combines the LBP texture and color spectra is described as follows:

Step 1: Select a sample patch with the size of M x M for each texture class randomly in the area of the texture class from the original image. In other words, a set of N sample patches will be selected for N texture classes.
Step 2: Calculate and extract an LBP texture spectrum and color spectra from each of sample patches.
Step 3: Scan the image with an M x M window and calculate the LBP texture spectrum and color spectra for each window.
Step 4: Calculate the absolute difference of the LBP texture spectrum and color spectra (Eq. 2.54) between the image window and each sample patch.
Step 5: Assigned the central pixel of the window to textural class i such that the distance D(i) is the minimum among N classes.
Step 6: Repeat Steps 3 to 5 for each pixel in the original image being classified.

To include all texture patterns, a larger window has to be chosen. This indicates that more computation time is necessary. The advantages of this algorithm are easy implementation and able to capture micro, macro, and color features.

2.11   Experimental Results on GLCM, TS, and LBP

In this section, some experiments for different textures were tested with different texture feature extractions. The classification algorithms were tested on a set of both micro- and macro-textures from Brodatz images [4] to examine the effectiveness of features extracted using different models.

There are a variety of GLCM techniques used for implementation in the current literature. For our experiments, simple GLCMs are developed for classification and to compare with the others. The features used in these experiments were dissimilarity (D), entropy (E), and correlation (C). The GLCMs were used with parameters; distance = 1, angle = 0, gray level = 8, and window size of 30×30. For the TS measure, the texture unit of size 3×3 and the window size of 30×30 were used as He and Wang suggested for the optimal classification [26, 27, 66]. Similar to the TS, the LBP uses the texture primitive size of 3×3 and the window size of 30×30.

By observing the experimental results shown in Fig. 2.12, the measures of TS and LBP produce satisfactory results, and many different textures can be discriminated successfully. The TS and LBP methods perform well if the textures are periodic (Fig. 2.12g, j). On the other hand, the GLCMs are good for random textures. The GLCMs, TS, and LBP perform well if the patterns are different such as those including both periodic and random texture patterns (Fig. 2.12f, i, l). However, it is challenging to find the right parameters for the GLCM. The classification results based on the GLCM depend on the selections of orientation parameters such as distance, angle, and the number of gray levels. There is not much difference in accuracy between the TS and LBP.

2.12   Summary

Many image textural classification algorithms apply contextual (spatial) information for distinguishing and characterizing textures. These types of spatial classification techniques can be categorized into four groups; (1) the statistical approach such as co-occurrence probabilities, (2) the structural approach which the texture is viewed as containing many primitive elements such as a texel, texton, or texture unit, (3) the model-based approach such as Gaussian Markov random fields and Gibbs random fields in which a texture image is modeled as a probability model or linear combination of a set of basic function, and the coefficients of these models are the texture features, and (4) the transform approach. Gray-level co-occurrence matrices (probabilities), texture spectrum (TS), and local binary pattern (LBP) extract contextual information for classification which are given in this chapter.

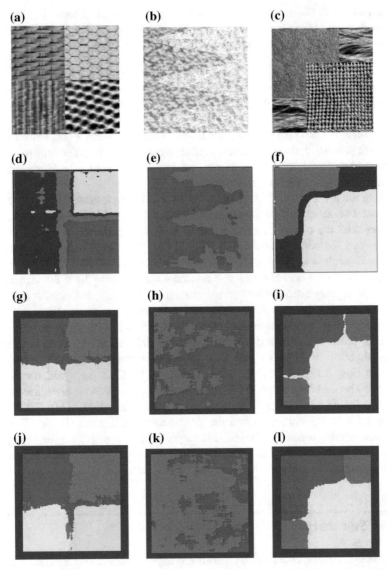

Fig. 2.12 Classified results of texture images; **a**, **b**, and **c** are original images; **d**, **e**, and **f** are results of the GLCMs (with distance = 1, angle = 0, gray level = 8, and the window size of 30 × 30); **g**, **h**, and **i** are texture spectrum (TS) results (with the window size of 30 × 30). **j**, **k**, and **l** are local binary pattern (LBP) results (with the window size of 30 × 30) [29]

Although the spatial classification algorithm is more accurate than the per-pixel-based classification, it is more complex to characterize the properties of the texture in a multispectral image. In general, image texture is defined as a function of the spatial variation in pixel intensities although there is no formal definition of texture given in the literature. Extracting features can reduce the dimension of data to a computationally reasonable amount for better image texture interpretation. Texture image classification has been successfully applied to many practical applications such as automated materials inspection, medical imagery, document processing, and satellite images.

2.13 Exercises

For a hypothetical image shown below:

0	1	2	3
1	2	3	0
2	3	0	1
3	0	1	2

1. Calculate the features using the GLCM method.
2. Compute the features of fractal dimensions.
3. Calculate the features using texture spectrum (TS).
4. Calculate the features using the LBP method.
5. Calculate the features using the variogram.
6. Classify the image using the minimum distance classification algorithm using the features extracted in exercises #1−#5 and compare their classification accuracy.

References

1. Allen JB (1977) Short time spectral analysis, synthesis, and modification by discrete fourier transform. IEEE Trans Acoust, Speech Signal Process ASSP-25 (3):235–238
2. Arasteh S, Hung C-C (2006) Color and texture image segmentation using uniform local binary pattern. Mach Vis Graphics 15(3/4):265–274, 2006
3. Bigun J, Hans du Buf JM (1994) N-folded symmetries by complex moments in gabor space and their application to unsupervised texture segmentation. IEEE Trans Pattern Anal Mach Intell 16(1)
4. Brodatz P (1966) Textures: a photographic album for artists and designers. Dover Publications, New York
5. Bohling G (2005) Introduction to geostatistics and variogram analysis, 17 Oct 2005. http://people.ku.edu/~gbohling/cpe940
6. Campbell FW, Robson JG (1968) Application of fourier analysis to the visibility of gratings. J Physiol 197:551–566
7. Carr JR (1999) Classification of digital image texture using variograms. In: Atkinson PM, Tate NJ (eds) Advances in remote sensing and gis analysis. Wiley, New York, pp 135–146

8. Carr JR, Pellon de Miranda F (1998) The semivariogram in comparison to the co-occurrence matrix for classification of image texture. IEEE Trans Geosci Remote Sens 36(6):1945–1952
9. Castleman KR (1996) Digital image processing. Prentice Hall, Upper Saddle River
10. Clausi DA, Jernigan ME (2000) Designing Gabor filters for optimal texture separability. Pattern Recognit 33:1835–1849
11. Daubechies, I., *Ten Lectures on Wavelets*, SIAM 1992
12. Daugman JG (1980) Two-dimensional Spectral Analysis of Cortical Receptive Field Profiles. Vis Res 20:847–856
13. Daugman JG (1985) Uncertainty relations for resolution in space, spatial frequency, and orientation optimized by two dimensional visual cordial filters. J Opt Soc Am 2(7):1160–1169
14. Demirkaya O, Asyalif MH, Sahoo PK Image procesing with MATLAB applications in medicine and biology. CRC Press, Boca Raton
15. Deutsch CV (2002) Geostatistical reservoir modeling. Oxford University Press, Oxford
16. Dubes RC, Jain AK (1989) Random field models in image analysis. J Appl Stat 16:131–164
17. Dunn D, Higgins WE (1995) Optimal gabor filters for texture segmentation. IEEE Trans Image Process 4(7)
18. Frankot RT, Chellapa R (1987) Lognormal random-field models and their applications to radar image synthesis. IEEE Trans Geosci Remote Sens GE-25(2)
19. Frichtinger HG, Stroher T (1998) Gabor analysis and algorithms, theory and applications. Birkhauser, Basel
20. Gabor D (1946) Theory of communications. J Inst Elec Eng 93:429–457
21. Gilmore S, Hofmann-Wellenhof R, Muir J, Soyer HP (2009) Lacunarity analysis: a promising method for the automated assessment of melanocytic naevi and melanoma. PLoS ONE 4(10): e7449
22. Gonzalez RC, Woods RE (2002) Digital image processing, 2nd edn. Prentice Hall, Upper Saddle River
23. Haralick RM (1979) Statistical and structural approaches to texture. In: Proceedings of IEEE, vol 67, Issue 5, pp 786–804
24. Haralick RM, Bosley R (1973) Texture features for image classification. In: Third ERTS symposium, NASA SP-351, pp 1219–1228
25. Haralick RM, Shapiro LG (1992) Computer and robot vision, vol 1. Addison Wesley, Boston
26. He D-C, Wang L (1989) Texture unit, texture spectrum, and texture analysis. In: Proceedings of IGARSS' 89/12th Canadian symposium remote sensing, vol 5, pp 2769–2772
27. He D-C, Wang L (1990) Texture unit, texture spectrum, and texture analysis. IEEE Trans Geosci Remote Sens 28(4)
28. Hung C-C, Karabudak D, Pham M, Coleman T (2004) Experiments on image texture classification with K-Views classifier, Markov random fields and co-occurrence probabilities. In: IEEE international conference on geoscience and remote sensing symposium (IGARSS), Anchorage, Alaska, USA, 20–24 Sep 2004
29. Hung CC, Pham M, Arasteh S, Kuo B-C, Coleman T (2006) Image texture classification using texture spectrum and local binary pattern. In: The 2006 IEEE international geoscience & remote sensing symposium (IGARSS), Denver, Colorado, USA, 31 July to 4 Aug 2006
30. Isaaks EH, Srivastava RM (1989) An introduction to applied geostatistics. Oxford University Press, Oxford
31. Jain AK, Farroklmia F (1990) Unsupervised texture segmentation using gabor filters. In: IEEE interactional conference on systems, man and cybernetics conference proceedings, pp 14–19,
32. Jensen A, La Cour-Harbo A (2001) Ripples in mathematics: the discrete wavelet transform. Springer, Berlin
33. Ji Y, Chang K-H, Hung C-C (2004) Efficient edge detection and object segmentation using gabor filters. In: Proceedings of the 42nd annual ACM Southeast conference, Huntsville, Alabama, USA, 2–3 Apr 2004
34. Jung Y, Swain PH (1996) Bayesian contextual classification based on modified M-estimates and Markov random fields. IEEE Trans Geosci Remote Sens 34:67–75

35. Kamarainen J, Kyrki V, Kalviainen I (2002) Fundamental frequency gabor filters for object recognition. In: Proceedings of 16th international conference on patten recognition, vol I, pp 628–631
36. Kashyap RL, Chellappa R (1983) Estimation and choice of neighbors in spatial-interaction models of images. IEEE Trans Inf Theory 29:60–72
37. Keller JM, Chen S (1989) Texture description and segmentation through fractal geometry. Comput Vis Graphics Image Process 45:150–166
38. Krishnamachari S, Chellappa R (1997) Multiresolution Gauss-Markov random field models for texture segmentation. IEEE Trans Image Process 6(2)
39. Ling E, Servio P, Kietzig AM (2016) Fractal and lacunarity analyses: quantitative characterization of hierarchical surface topographies. Microsc Microanal 22(1):168–177
40. Liu W, Wu L, Hung C-C (2012) Texture segmentation based on AdaBoost classifier using fractal feature – lacunarity. J Inf Comput Sci 9(1):1–11
41. MacDonald JA, Miranda FP, Carr JR (1990) Textural image classification using variograms. In: Proceedings of SPIE 1301, digital image processing and visual communications technologies in the earth and atmospheric sciences, (1 Nov 1990). http://dx.doi.org/10.1117/12.21411
42. Maenpaa T (2003) The local binary pattern approach to texture analysis – extensions and applications. Oulun Yliopisto, Oulu
43. Mallat S (1989) A theory for multiresolution signal decomposition: the wavelet representation. IEEE Trans Pattern Anal Mach Intell vol II(7)
44. Mandelbrot B (1967) How long is the coast of britain? Statistical self-similarity and fractional dimension. Science 156(3775):636–638
45. Mandelbrot B (1982) The fractal geometry of nature. W. H. Freeman and Company, New York
46. Mittal ND, Mital P, Chan KL (1999) Features for texture segmentation using gabor filters. In: Image processing and its applications,vol 465. Conference Publication
47. Mulcahy C (1996) Plotting and scheming with wavelets. Math Mag 69(5):323–343
48. Myint SW, Lam N (2005) A study of lacunarity-based texture analysis approaches to improve urban image classification. Comput Environ Urban Syst 29(5):501–523
49. Nestares O, Navarro R, Portilla J, Tabemero A (1998) Efficient spatial-domain implementation of a multiscale image representation based on gabor functions. J Electron Imaging 7:166–173
50. Ojala T, Pietikainen M, Maenpaa T (2002) Multiresolution gray-scale and rotation invariant texture classification with local binary patterns. IEEE Trans Pattern Recognit Mach Intell 24(7)
51. Peleg S, Naor J, Harteley R, Avnir D (1984) Multiple resolution texture analysis and classification. IEEE Trans Pattern Anal Mach Intell PAMI-6:518–523
52. Pentland AP (1984) Fractal-Based Description of Natural Scenes. IEEE Trans Pattern Anal Mach Intell 6(6):661–674
53. Petrou M, Sevilla PG (2006) Image processing: dealing with texture. Wiley, New York
54. Pietikainen MK (2000) Texture analysis in machine vision. Series in machine perception and artificial intelligence, vol 40. World Scientific, Singapore
55. Pham MM, Xiang C, Hung C, Kuo B-C (2005) A comparative study on the k-views classifier and markov random fields for image texture classification. Proceedings of the 43rd ACM-SE Conference, Kennesaw, Georgia, USA, 18–20 Mar 2005, pp 1–96–1-97. https://doi.org/10.1145/1167350.1167386
56. Plotnick RE, Gardner RH, Hargrove WW, Prestegaard K, Perlmutter M (1993) Lacunarity analysis: a general technique for the analysis of spatial patterns. Phys Rev E 53(5)
57. Pollen DA, Ronner SF (1983) Visual Cortical Neurons as Localized Spatial Frequency Filters. IEEE Trans. SMC 13(5):907–916
58. Qian S, Chen D (1993) Discrete gabor transform. IEEE Trans Signal Process 41(7)

59. Quan Y, Xu Y, Sun Y, Luo Y (2014) Lacunarity analysis on image patterns for texture classification. Comput Vis Pattern Recognit
60. Shao J, Forstner W (1994) Gabor wavelets for texture edge extraction. In: Commission III Symposium
61. Solberg AHS, Jain AK, Taxt T (1994) Multisource classification of remotely sensed data: fusion of LANDSAT TM and SAR images. IEEE Trans Geosci Remote Sens 32(4)
62. Tao L, Kwan HK (2001) Real-valued discrete gabor transform for image representation. IEEE Int Symp Circuits Syst 2:589–592
63. Tso B, Mather P (2009) Classification methods of remotely sensed data, 2nd edn. CRC Press, Boca Raton
64. Vidakovic B, Mueller P (1994) Wavelets for kids: a tutorial introduction. Duke University, Institute of Statistics and Decision Sciences
65. Walker J (2008) A primer on wavelets and their scientific applications, 2nd edn. Chapman and Hall/CRC, Boca Raton
66. Wang L, He D-C (1990) A new statistical approach for texture analysis. Photogramm Eng Remote Sens 56(1):61–66
67. Weldon TP, Higgins WE (1996) Integrated approach to texture segmentation using multiple gabor filters. In: Proceedings, international conference on image processing, vol 3, pp 955–958
68. Wen J, You Z, Li H (1994) Segmentation the metallograph images using gabor filter. In: International symposium on speech, image processing and neural networks Hong Kong, pp 13–16
69. Woods JW (1972) Two-dimensional discrete Markovian fields. IEEE Trans Inf Theory IT-18:232–240
70. Yao J, Krolak P, Steele C (1995) The generalized gabor transform. IEEE Trans Image Process 4(7):978–988

Algorithms for Image Texture Classification

3

The tao that can be told is not the eternal Tao. The name that can be named is not the eternal Name.

—Lao Tzu

Image texture classification utilizes either unsupervised or supervised algorithms as a classifier based on textural features extracted from images. Many of these algorithms are from early research in the statistical pattern recognition. It has been proved that if the priori probabilities information are available about datasets, Bayes decision theory gives the optimal error rates in classification. However, this priori information may not be available in many applications. Hence, many classification algorithms using other measures such as similarity on the dataset are developed for categorization. There are also many variations of these algorithms which have been developed and used in image texture classification. This chapter will explain the basic concept of the following algorithms: (1) K-means, (2) K-Nearest-Neighbor (K-NN), (3) fuzzy C-means (FCM), (4) fuzzy K-Nearest-Neighbor (Fuzzy K-NN), (5) fuzzy weighted C-means (FWCM), (6) new weighted fuzzy C-means (NW-FCM), (7) possibility clustering algorithm (PCA), (8) generalized possibility clustering algorithm (GPCA), (9) credibility clustering algorithm (CCA), and (10) support vector machine (SVM). Some algorithms utilizing optimization techniques are also introduced. This includes the ant-based K-means algorithm, the K-means algorithm using genetic algorithms, the K-means algorithm using simulated annealing and the quantum-modeled clustering algorithm (quantum K-means). In addition, a pollen-based bee algorithm for clustering is included. These methods can be used in image textures for classification. Algorithms from neural computation [2, 15, 34] for image texture classification will be discussed in Chap. 9.

© Springer Nature Switzerland AG 2019
C.-C. Hung et al., *Image Texture Analysis*,
https://doi.org/10.1007/978-3-030-13773-1_3

3.1   The K-means Clustering Algorithm (K-means)

The K-means clustering algorithm (K-means) is an unsupervised clustering algorithm which partitions a set of pixels (or samples) into a number of clusters [45]. The K-means algorithm is based on the minimization of a performance index ($J_{K-means}$) which is defined as the sum of the squared distances from all pixels in a cluster domain to the cluster center as shown in Eq. 3.1 [50].

$$J_{K-means}(U,A) = \sum_{i=1}^{K} \sum_{\substack{j=1 \\ \&x_j \in a_i(I)}}^{n} (\mu_{ij})\|x_j - a_i(I)\|^2 \tag{3.1}$$

where U represents the collection of μ_{ij} which is a membership function value of each pixel, x_j, belonging to each cluster center, $a_i(I)$ where I is the number of iterations. The value of μ_{ij} is either 0 or 1 in the K-means. If a pixel belongs to a cluster, its membership is 1. Otherwise, it is 0. Hence, the μ_{ij} is often omitted in the formulation of the objective function in the K-means. The symbol A, which is a matrix, denotes the collection of $a_i(I)$. The total number of clusters specified is K and the total number of pixels is n. An example with K = 2 and n = 4 is shown in Example 3.1 which demonstrates the first iteration of the K-means algorithm. Whichever Euclidean distance is the smallest between a pixel and a cluster, the pixel will be classified into the corresponding cluster.

Example 3.1 A dataset of four pixels which will be classified to one of two clusters based on the distance similarity using the K-means algorithm. (a) a set of four pixels in two-dimension, and (b) the Euclidean distances calculated and the assignment of each pixel to one of two clusters, C_1 and C_2. We assume that the first two pixels, x_1 and x_2, are arbitrarily selected as the initial cluster centers of C_1 and C_2, respectively, and represented as $C_1(1)$ and $C_2(1)$ for one iteration.

$$\left\{ x_1 = \begin{bmatrix} 1 \\ 0 \end{bmatrix}, x_2 = \begin{bmatrix} 1 \\ 2 \end{bmatrix}, x_3 = \begin{bmatrix} 3 \\ 2 \end{bmatrix}, x_4 = \begin{bmatrix} 3 \\ 3 \end{bmatrix} \right\}$$

(a)

	x_1	x_2	x_3	x_4
$dist(x_i, C_1(1))$	0	2	2.828	3.605
$dist(x_i, C_2(1))$	2	0	2	2.236
Class assigned	C_1	C_2	C_2	C_2

(b)

The algorithm starts with a user-specified number of clusters, K, and their initial random cluster centers. Each pixel is then assigned to a cluster based on the minimum Euclidean distance to the cluster centers. New cluster centers will then be updated by calculating the average of pixels assigned to each cluster at each iteration. The procedure will be repeated until each cluster center has no significant change compared with the previous cluster center, or meet with the maximum number of iterations. K-means needs to have the initial parameters including the number of clusters and initial cluster centers, the convergence criterion, and the maximum number of iterations. The number of clusters defined by the analyst is fixed. The convergence criterion is usually given a small epsilon value. The maximum number of iterations can be used when this convergence criterion is not met. The algorithm is summarized in the following steps:

The K-means Algorithm:

Step 1: Determine the number of clusters, K, their initial cluster centers, the convergence criterion, δ, a counter for iterations, I and the maximum number of iterations (Max-It). We use S to denote a set of training samples and C a set of clusters, K, below.

$$S = \{x_i \in R^d | i = 1, 2, \ldots, n\}$$

$$C = \{c_j(I) \in R^d | j = 1, 2, \ldots, K\}$$

Repeat the following steps for each pixel in the image.

Step 2: Each pixel is assigned to a cluster based on the minimum distance to the cluster centers.

$$x_i \in c_q(I) \, if \, \|x_i - c_q(I)\| \leq \|x_i - c_j(I)\| \, for \, j \neq q \qquad (3.2)$$

Notations are similarly defined as in Step 1.

Step 3: Each of cluster centers is updated by calculating the average of pixel values assigned to each cluster.

$$c_j(I+1) = \frac{1}{|c_j(I)|} \sum_{x_i \in c_j(I)} x_i \, for \, j = 1, 2, \ldots, K \qquad (3.3)$$

where $|c_j(I)|$ is the number of samples assigned to cluster j.

Step 4: If the difference between each of current cluster centers and previous cluster centers is less than or equal to δ or the number of iterations meets Max-It, the procedure stops. Otherwise, the procedure continues.

$$\text{i.e. } |c_j(I+1) - c_j(I)| \leq \delta \, for \, j = 1, 2, \ldots, K \qquad (3.4)$$

Step 5: (Clustering) Classify each of all the pixels to one of clusters based on the minimum distance between the pixel and the clusters.

The K-means algorithm tends to find the local minima rather than the global minima. Therefore, it is heavily influenced by the choice of initial cluster centers and the distribution of data. The clustering results are more acceptable when the initial cluster centers are well separated since the main clusters in the image (or a given dataset) are usually distinguished in such a way. This distribution is shown in

Fig. 3.1 **a** Clusters are well
separated and **b** clusters are
overlapped with two types of
patterns

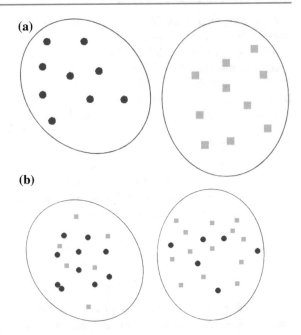

Fig. 3.1a. A scenario in Fig. 3.1b demonstrates that it is more challenging to obtain
an ideal clustering result. An improvement of the K-means algorithm can be done
with some optimization techniques to be less dependent on a given dataset and
initialization of cluster centers [47].

3.2 The K-Nearest-Neighbor Classifier (K-NN)

The K-Nearest-Neighbor (K-NN) algorithm uses similarity measures to determine the
majority of nearest neighbors for classification [11, 14, 26, 51]. A similarity measure can
depend on the distance; the shorter the distance, the higher the similarity is. A new pixel
is assigned to the most common class among a set of sample pixels (the number of
samples is defined by K) that are most similar to it. In other words, K-NN uses the
majority vote among a set of K representative pixels for all classes. Unlike K-means,
K-NN does not need any training. The following algorithm outlines the K-NN procedure.

   To determine the class of a new pixel P:

Step 1: Define an initial value of K given a set of sample pixels (N), where N is
             greater than K.
Step 2: Calculate the distance (i.e., feature similarity) between pixel P and each of
             a set of sample pixels (N).
Step 3: Select K-nearest sample pixels to P in the dataset.
Step 4: Assign P to the most common class among its K-nearest neighbors.

   The K-NN algorithm is a nonparametric function which does not depend on any
assumption for the functional distribution of the dataset. Theoretically, the K-NN will
become the Bayes classifier if the density estimates converge to the true densities with

Fig. 3.2 An example of
3-NN rule in
three-dimensional space

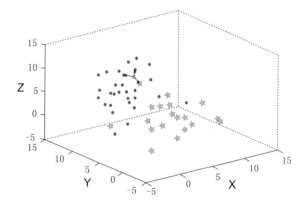

an infinite number of pixels used [11]. In practice, the number of pixels is limited in many applications, particularly, in a high-dimensional space. To have a good performance of the K-NN, all representative pixels belonging to a class should be as close as possible. Although the K-NN classifier is a suboptimal algorithm, its computational simplicity and classification performance allows this classifier to be widely used. If the number of sample pixels is large, its computation and space complexity will be high. It has a good performance on many problems with small sample size [14, 51]. An example of the K-NN algorithm is shown in Fig. 3.2 which demonstrates a 3-NN rule with two classes and three features for each pixel represented with X-, Y-, and Z-coordinates. An incoming pixel with the color black will be classified as the red class using the 3-NN rule as the majority of the class is the red pixel although one green shaded pixel appeared in the neighborhood of red pixels.

3.3   The Fuzzy C-means Clustering Algorithm (FCM)

Fuzzy clustering is a popular method which depends on the foundation of fuzzy set theory for data grouping in pattern recognition. Fuzzy set theory provides some advantages over traditional crispy set theory in many applications. Hence, a clustering algorithm that uses the fuzzy theory is able to solve the problems that a non-fuzzy clustering method cannot do. In the traditional clustering algorithm such as the K-means method, each pixel is assigned to only one cluster. Mathematically, if we define a membership function as shown in Eq. 3.5 to represent this assignment, the membership function will assign a value of one to the pixel assigned to a cluster and zero for the remaining clusters.

$$f_{c_j}(x_i) = \begin{cases} 1 & \text{if } x_i \in c_j \\ 0, & \text{otherwise} \end{cases} \tag{3.5}$$

where x_i is a sample pixel and c_j is a cluster.

In real-world applications, a dataset might be incomplete or corrupted with noise such that each member in the set is uncertain if it carries correct or imprecise information. In such an environment, the belongingness of a pixel to a cluster cannot be completely determined. In other words, this kind of assignment becomes the nondeterministic problem. Hence, the fuzzy set theory provides a solution for the application domain where the nondeterministic problems exist. For example, if clusters are well separated, a hard classification of pixels may give a correct result by using the non-fuzzy method. But, if the clusters are overlapped as appeared in many datasets, a nondeterministic solution may be more appropriate. The fuzzy clustering technique assigns a degree of membership for each pixel to each cluster in a dataset. A degree of membership is in the range of between 0.0 and 1.0, including 0.0 and 1.0. It is called the fuzzy membership function. In the literature, the hard clustering method (without using the fuzzy technique) versus the soft clustering method (using the fuzzy technique) are frequently used. These types of soft clustering methods use fuzzy set theory which was introduced by Zadeh in 1965 [60, 61].

In order to explain the fundamental principle of fuzzy clustering methods, let us first review the concept of fuzzy set and notations used in the fuzzy clustering algorithms [3, 60, 61, 64]. Table 3.1 lists all the notations which will be used to explain fuzzy clustering. Definition 1 given below defines a typical fuzzy subset and its fuzzy membership function. Some typical fuzzy membership functions are given in Fig. 3.3.

Definition 1 A fuzzy subset A of a universal set U is defined by its membership function μ which assigns to each element $x \in U$ a real number $\mu(x)$ in the interval [0.0, 1.0], where the value of $\mu(x)$ at x represents the grade of membership of x in A. Thus, the nearer the value of $\mu(x)$ is unity, the higher the grade of membership of x in A [64].

Table 3.1 Notations used in the clustering algorithms

Notations	Explanation
$X = \{x_j \mid j \in J\}$ $J = \{1, 2, ..., n\}$	X is a dataset in a p-dimensional Euclidean space R^p with its Euclidean norm $\|.\|$, where J is the number of items in the dataset
C	C is a positive integer representing the number of clusters with $C > 1$
$\theta = \{\theta_1, \theta_2, ..., \theta_c\}$	θ represents a set of clusters in which θ_i represents the ith cluster, $i \in I$
$A = \{a_1, a_2, ..., a_C\}$ $I = \{1, 2, ..., C\}$	A denotes a matrix of the centers of all clusters where a_i is the ith cluster center, $i \in I$, where I is a set of indexes from 1 to C
$u_{ij}(x)$	A fuzzy membership of pixel j for cluster i
U_X	$U_X = \{\mu \mid 0 \leq \mu_{ij} \leq 1 \text{ for all } (i, j) \in (I, J)\}$

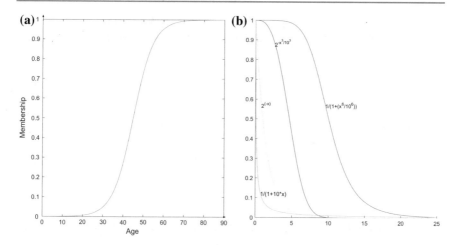

Fig. 3.3 **a** An example of fuzzy membership function of the fuzzy set defined on a set of old residents in a residential area and **b** some functions which can be used as one of fuzzy membership functions

Let us give an example (Example 3.2) to illustrate the concept of fuzzy set and a measure of the membership degree. A monotonically decreasing function (f) of d(x, x_0) with f(0) = 1 and f(+∞) = 0 can be a measurement for membership μ of A as shown in Fig. 3.3a [64]. Figure 3.3b gives some functions that can be used as a fuzzy measure of the membership degree.

Example 3.2 Suppose U is the set of ages of residents in a residential area. The set "old people" in this residential area is a fuzzy set on U, denoted as A. Let the standard of A be $x_0 = 80$ years old, and the dissimilarity between the standard and an element $x \in U$ is defined as

$$d(x, x_0) = \begin{cases} 0 & \text{if } x \geq x_0 \\ x_0 - x, & \text{if } 0 < x < x_0 \end{cases} \tag{3.6}$$

As a basic assumption in fuzzy clustering, each cluster θ_i is supposed to be a fuzzy set with membership function u_i in each iteration, where u_i is defined on the set X by

$$u_i(x_j) = u_{ij} \text{ for each } x_j \in X \tag{3.7}$$

with the u_{ij} representing the degree of compatibility or membership of feature point x_j belonging to fuzzy cluster θ_i. According to the fuzzy set theory, the memberships u_{ij} assigned should satisfy

$$0 \leq u_{ij} \leq 1 \, for \, all \, (i,j) \in (I,J) \tag{3.8}$$

For convenience, we denote the membership matrix by u with

$$u = \begin{pmatrix} u_{11} & \cdots & u_{1n} \\ \cdots & \cdots & \cdots \\ u_{c1} & \cdots & u_{cn} \end{pmatrix} \tag{3.9}$$

and denote the set of all the membership matrices satisfying Eq. 3.8 by U_X with

$$U_X = \{u | 0 \leq u_{ij} \leq 1 \, for \, all \, (i,j) \in (I,J)\} \tag{3.10}$$

where U_X is called the eligible membership matrix set of X. In general, the objective in the fuzzy clustering is to find the optimal membership matrix $u \in U_X$ according to the given data information and some decision criteria from experts' opinions.

The fuzzy C-means (FCM) clustering algorithm is a widely used fuzzy clustering technique. It has been shown that FCM is more stable than the K-means algorithm to avoid the local minima problem [3, 64]. The objective function of FCM is formulated as shown below:

$$J_{FCM}(\mu, A) = \sum_{i=1}^{c} \sum_{i=1}^{n} (\mu_{ij})^m \|x_j - a_i\|^2 \tag{3.11}$$

subject to the constraints $u \in U_X$ and

$$\sum_{i=1}^{c} \mu_{ij} = 1 \quad for \, all \, j \in J$$

The updated equations for both u and A are obtained from the necessary conditions for the minimization of Eq. 3.11:

$$\mu_{ij} = \left(\sum_{k=1}^{c} \frac{\|x_j - a_i\|^{2/(m-1)}}{\|x_j - a_k\|^{2/(m-1)}} \right)^{-1} \quad for \, (i,j) \in (I,\, J) \tag{3.12}$$

$$a_i = \frac{\sum_{j=1}^{n} (\mu_{ij})^m x^j}{\sum_{j=1}^{n} (\mu_{ij})^m} \quad for \, i \in I \tag{3.13}$$

where the weighting exponent m > 1 is called the fuzzifier which has a significant influence on the performance of the FCM [3, 64]. All notations used in Eqs. 3.11–3.13 are similarly defined. If we set m = 0 in the objective function in Eq. 3.11, the K-means algorithm is a special case of the fuzzy C-means algorithm.

FCM starts with arbitrary assignment of the initial cluster centers and randomly generated initial membership values for all the pixels. It then distributes pixels among all the clusters based on the minimum distance metric. In a sense, the FCM is similar to the K-means as an iterative algorithm. However, instead of the winner takes all (i.e., deterministic) in the K-means, a fuzzy technique is used in assigning a membership value for each pixel to each class. The fuzzy membership for each pixel belonging to each class is a real number between zero and one. Hence, an initial fuzzy membership table must be given for all the training pixels in order to run the FCM algorithm. The following illustrates the steps used in the FCM algorithm:

The Fuzzy C-means Algorithm (FCM):

Step 1: Choose C initial cluster centers, a fuzzifier m, an initial U_x which is a collection of μ_{ij}, a small value of δ for the convergence criterion, and a maximum number of iterations (Max-It).

Step 2: Calculate the cluster centers using Eq. 3.13.

Step 3: Update the membership matrix U_x using Eq. 3.12.

Step 4: Increase the iteration count (t) by one and check if it meets Max-It. If not, repeat Steps 2–3 until the clustering converges, i.e.,
$$\left\| u_{ij}(t+1) - u_{ij}(t) \right\| \leq \delta \text{ for all } (i, j) \in (I, J).$$

Step 5: (Clustering) Classify all the pixels using matrix U_x (based on the largest membership to a cluster).

The FCM runs until the convergence criterion is met or the maximum number of iterations is reached. An example of FCM is shown in Example 3.3.

Example 3.3 A same dataset of four pixels is used in Example 3.1 (as shown below) which will be classified to one of two clusters based on the distance similarity using the FCM algorithm. (a) a set of four pixels in two-dimensional space, and (b) the degree of memberships calculated for each pixel belonging to each cluster and the assignment of each pixel to one of two clusters, C_1 and C_2 based on the membership value.

$$\left\{ x_1 = \begin{bmatrix} 1 \\ 0 \end{bmatrix}, x_2 = \begin{bmatrix} 1 \\ 2 \end{bmatrix}, x_3 = \begin{bmatrix} 3 \\ 2 \end{bmatrix}, x_4 = \begin{bmatrix} 3 \\ 3 \end{bmatrix} \right\}$$

(a)

	x_1	x_2	x_3	x_4
u_{1j}	0.81	0.26	0.33	0.13
u_{2j}	0.19	0.74	0.67	0.87
Class assigned	C_1	C_2	C_2	C_2

(b)

3.4 A Fuzzy K-Nearest-Neighbor Algorithm (Fuzzy K-NN)

In the traditional K-NN algorithm, each member of the labeled pixels in the dataset is considered equally important in counting the majority of the class labels for the assignment of a class label to an input pixel. As shown in Fig. 3.1, many samples in a dataset significantly overlap in the distribution. This may create some difficulty for the traditional K-NN algorithm to correctly classify overlapped samples into clusters. Keller et al. [26] pointed out two potential problems associated with the K-NN algorithm: each pixel is given the same weight as those that are representatives of the clusters and there is no degree of the membership for a pixel belonging to a class. This is similar to the K-means problem; there is no weighting used for each sample. Hence, the fuzzy set theory is used in the K-NN algorithm to address those two problems. Keller et al. proposed three different fuzzy nearest algorithms in assigning the fuzzy membership for the training sets [26]. Similar to the fuzzy membership used in the FCM, the membership in the fuzzy K-NN also provides a level of confidence to the assignment of a pixel to a class. The higher the membership value, the more certain of the assignment to the class. We introduce the fuzzy version of the K-NN algorithm below, called the fuzzy K-NN algorithm.

Instead of assigning a pixel to a class as implemented in the traditional K-NN algorithm, the fuzzy K-NN assigns the class membership to a sample pixel. The membership is a function of the distance of the pixel from its K-nearest neighbors and memberships of those neighbors in the possible classes as shown in Eq. 3.14 [26]. Similar to the crisp K-NN algorithm, the fuzzy version still needs to search the K-nearest neighbors in the sample dataset. Please note that $u_{ij} \in U_X$ is an initial fuzzy membership used for calculating $u_i(p)$ for the classification of pixel p.

$$u_i(p) = \frac{\sum_{j=1}^{K} u_{ij} \left(1/\|p - x_j\|^{2/(m-1)} \right)}{\sum_{j=1}^{K} \left(1/\|p - x_j\|^{2/(m-1)} \right)} \qquad (3.14)$$

where μ_{ij} is the membership of jth pixel with respect to ith class. This is very similar to what we do for the FCM initial membership matrix. Unlike FCM, this initial fuzzy membership will be used for the entire procedure without any update. Keller et al. proposed two methods for generating an initial fuzzy membership matrix U_X [26]: the first method is that each pixel will be given a complete membership to the class it belongs and nonmembership to other classes and the second method is to initialize the memberships based on the distance from the cluster mean. Jozwik proposed a scheme for learning the memberships in the fuzzy K-NN rule [25]. The fuzzifier m is similar to that used in the FCM. As stated in [26], the fuzzifier determines how heavily the distance is weighted in calculating the contribution of each neighbor to the membership degree. If the fuzzier is gradually increased, the distance to any neighboring pixel will be treated more equally. In other words, the relative distance will have less effect in calculating the membership degree.

Assume that we use the similar notations defined in Table 3.1, let $X = \{x_1, x_2, \ldots, x_n\}$ be the set of n labeled samples and $u_i(p)$ be the assigned membership of a new pixel p and u_{ij} the membership in the ith class of the jth pixel in the labeled sample set. The fuzzy K-NN algorithm is defined below:

The Fuzzy K-NN Algorithm:

To determine the class of a new pixel p,

Step 1: Initialize K which is usually between 1 and n (number of samples in the training dataset), a fuzzifier m, and the membership values u_{ij} for all $(i, j) \in (I, J)$.

Step 2: Calculate the distance between pixel p and all sample pixels, n, in the training dataset.

Step 3: Select K-nearest sample pixels to p in the training dataset.

Step 4: The new pixel p is assigned the memberships for all classes by computing $u_i(p)$ using Eq. 3.14, where i is a class.

Step 5: Assign p to the most common class among its K-nearest neighbors based on the memberships obtained in Step 4.

3.5 The Fuzzy Weighted C-means Algorithm (FWCM)

The classical fuzzy C-means clustering algorithm (FCM) is an efficient method for partitioning pixels into different categories. The objective function of FCM is defined by the distances from pixels to the cluster centers with their fuzzy memberships. If two distinct clusters have similar mean, then the performance of FCM will not be efficient. To overcome this problem, Li et al. proposed a new fuzzy clustering algorithm, namely, the fuzzy weighted C-means algorithm (FWCM) [33]. In the FWCM, the concept of weighted means used in the nonparametric weighted feature extraction method (NWFE) is employed for calculating the cluster centers in the FWCM. Kuo and Landgrebe proposed nonparametric weighted feature extraction (NWFE) [31, 32] model that is a powerful feature extraction method for dimensionality reduction. The idea of weighted means is an essential part of the NWFE concept used for hyperspectral image classification.

The main idea of NWFE is to give different weights to each pixel for computing the weighted means and defining new nonparametric matrices between- and within-class scatter matrices to obtain more features. Hence, NWFE needs to calculate two scatter matrices: the nonparametric between-class scatter matrix as defined in Eq. 3.15 and the nonparametric within-class scatter matrix as defined in Eq. 3.16:

$$S_b^{NW} = \sum_{i=1}^{c} P_i \sum_{\substack{j=1 \\ j \neq i}}^{c} \sum_{k=1}^{n_i} \frac{\lambda_k^{(i,j)}}{n_i} \left(x_k^{(i)} - M_j\left(x_k^{(i)}\right) \right) \left(x_k^{(i)} - M_j\left(x_k^{(i)}\right) \right)^T \qquad (3.15)$$

$$S_w^{NW} = \sum_{i=1}^{c} P_i \sum_{k=1}^{n_i} \frac{\lambda_k^{(i,j)}}{n_i} \left(x_k^i - M_i\left(x_k^i\right) \right) \left(x_k^i - M_i\left(x_k^i\right) \right)^T \qquad (3.16)$$

where T is the transpose, c is the number of clusters, P_i is a priori probability for class i, n_i is the number of pixels in class i, and $x_k^{(i)}$ is the kth pixel from class i. The scatter matrix weight $\lambda_k^{(i,j)}$ is defined as in Eq. 3.17:

$$\lambda_k^{(i,j)} = \frac{dist\left(x_k^{(i)}, M_j\left(x_k^{(i)}\right) \right)^{-1}}{\sum_{l=1}^{n_j} dist\left(x_l^i, M_j\left(x_k^{(i)}\right) \right)^{-1}} \qquad (3.17)$$

where $dist(x, y)$ denotes the distance from x to y, and $M_j(x_k^{(i)})$ is the weighted mean of $x_k^{(i)}$ in the class j and is defined as

$$M_j\left(x_k^{(i)} \right) = \sum_{l=1}^{N_l} w_l^{(i,j)} x_l^{(j)} \qquad (3.18)$$

where

$$w_l^{(i,j)} = \frac{dist\left(x_k^{(i)}, x_l^j \right)}{\sum_{i=1}^{N_j} dist\left(x_k^i, x_l^j \right)^{-1}} \qquad (3.19)$$

The scatter matrix weight $\lambda_k^{(i,j)}$ will be close to 1 if the distance between $x_k^{(i)}$ and $M_j(x_k^{(i)})$ is small. Otherwise, it will be close to 0. Similarly, the weight $w_l^{(i,j)}$ for computing weighted means will be close to 1 if the distance between $x_k^{(i)}$ and $x_l^{(j)}$ is small. Otherwise, it will be close to 0.

Although NWFE is for supervised learning problems, the concept of weighted means can be extended to unsupervised learning. To extend the weighted means of NWFE to an unsupervised version, it is necessary to develop a method for an unsupervised weighted mean calculation. For any pixel x_j in a class i, the distance from x_j to other pixels is calculated below:

$$\{ \, \|x_j - x_k\| \mid k = 1, 2, \ldots, n, k \neq j \, \} \tag{3.20}$$

In general, if any pixel is close to x_j, the pixel is most likely belonging to the same class of x_j. The corresponding weight should be large. Hence, the reciprocal of the above distance is used for the weighting. If a pixel is close to x_j, but does not belong to the same class, then the influence of this pixel for the weighting must be small. We can solve this problem by multiplying the membership grade. Therefore, the unsupervised weighted mean of x_j in class i is defined in Eq. 3.21.

$$M_{ij} = \sum_{\substack{k=1 \\ k \neq j}}^{n} \frac{\|x_j - x_k\|^{-1} u_{ik}}{\sum_{t=1, t \neq j}^{n} \|x_j - x_t\|^{-1} u_{ik}} \tag{3.21}$$

In the derivation of M_{ij}, we can expect that the unsupervised weighted mean M_{ij} is closer to x_j than the fuzzy cluster center C_i.

Now, the objective function of FWCM is defined as in Eq. 3.22:

$$\bar{J}_{\text{FWCM}} = \sum_{i=1}^{c} \sum_{j=1}^{n} u_{i,j}^{m} \|x_j - M_{ji}\|^2 \tag{3.22}$$

Using the method of Lagrange multipliers, a new objective function of FWCM is formulated as follows in Eq. 3.23:

$$\bar{J}_{\text{FWCM}}(u_{11}, \ldots, u_{1c}, u_{n1}, \ldots, u_{nc}, \xi_1, \ldots, \xi_n)$$
$$= \sum_{i=1}^{c} \sum_{j=1}^{n} u_{i,j}^{m} \|x_j - M_{ji}\|^2 + \sum_{j=1}^{n} \xi_j \left(\sum_{i=1}^{c} u_{ij} - 1 \right) \tag{3.23}$$

where ξ_j are the Lagrange multipliers for the n constraints and the summation of membership grades for each cluster is one.

By differentiating $\bar{J}_{\text{FWCM}}$ in Eq. 3.23 with respect to all the arguments, we obtain the following equations, Eqs. 3.24 and 3.25:

$$\xi_j = \left(\sum_{i=1}^{c} \left(\|x_j - M_{ji}\|^2 \cdot m \sum_{i=1}^{c} u_{ij}^{m-1} \right)^{1/(1-m)} \right)^{1-m} \tag{3.24}$$

$$u_{ij} = \xi_j^{1/(m-1)} \left(\left\| x_j - M_{ji} \right\|^2 \cdot m \sum_{j=1}^{c} u_{ij}^{m-1} \right)^{1/(1-m)} \tag{3.25}$$

The procedure of FWCM is given below. Similar to FCM, FWCM is an iterative algorithm.

The FWCM Clustering Algorithm:

Step 1: Choose a number of clusters C, a fuzzifier m, a small value of δ for the convergence criterion, and a maximum number of iterations (Max-It). Initialize their cluster centers and U_x which is a collection of u_{ij}.

Step 2: Calculate the unsupervised weighted means M_{ij} (Eq. 3.21).

Step 3: Update the Lagrange multipliers ξ_j (Eq. 3.24).

Step 4: Update the membership grade u_{ij} (Eq. 3.25).

Step 5: Increase the iteration count (t) by one and check if it meets Max-It. If not, repeat Steps 2–4 until the clustering converges, i.e.,
$$\left\| u_{ij}(t+1) - u_{ij}(t) \right\| \leq \delta \text{ for all } (i, j) \in (I, J).$$

Step 6: (Clustering) Classify all the pixels using matrix U_x (based on the largest membership to a cluster).

Once the training is complete, assign a pixel to a cluster for calculating the cluster center. Experimental results on both synthetic and real data show that FWCM can generate better clustering results than those of FCM [33]. However, FWCM is quite computationally expensive, in particular, for a large image dataset.

3.6 The New Weighted Fuzzy C-means Algorithm (NW-FCM)

Fuzzy clustering model is a convenient tool for finding the proper cluster structure of given datasets using an unsupervised approach. A new weighted fuzzy C-means (NW-FCM) algorithm was developed to improve the performance of the FWCM model for high-dimensional multiclass pattern recognition problems [16, 21]. The methodology used in NW-FCM is the concept of weighted mean from the nonparametric weighted feature extraction (NWFE) and cluster mean from discriminant analysis feature extraction (DAFE) [44]. These two concepts are combined in the NW-FCM for unsupervised clustering. The main features of NW-FCM, when compared to FCM, are the inclusion of the weighted mean to increase accuracy, and when compared to FWCM, the centroid of each cluster is included to increase the stability. The algorithm gives higher classification accuracy and stability than that of FCM and FWCM.

Comparing DAFE, NAFE, and NWFE methods, DAFE uses the "centroid concept" in the calculation of both within-class and between-class scatter matrices without the weighted mean, NAFE uses a combination of the centroid for within-class scatter matrices and the weighted mean for between-class scatter matrices, and NWFE uses the weighted mean for both within-class and between-class scatter matrices without the centroid. The weighted mean in NWFE was used in FWCM, but not the centroid concept. The weighted mean used in FWCM is very similar to the gradient–weighted inverse concept used in the smoothing filter [54]. In NW-FCM, one can expect that this new unsupervised weighted mean to be even closer to the real cluster center.

The NW-FCM method combines the centroid of each cluster and the weighted mean in deriving the algorithm. The NW-FCM is more stable than FWCM and obtaining higher data classification accuracy than that of FCM. In FWCM, weighted means are calculated based on the point in consideration and all the sample pixels, whereas in NW-FCM it is calculated based on cluster centers and the rest of sample pixels. This makes NW-FCM more precise in assigning a sample pixel to a particular cluster than FWCM. Because the weighted mean is calculated from the cluster centers the NW-FCM algorithm takes computationally less time than FWCM. The NW-FCM algorithm is formulated below.

The NW-FCM clustering algorithm:

Step 1: Choose a number of clusters C, a fuzzifier m, a small value of δ for the convergence criterion, and a maximum number of iterations (Max-It). Initialize their cluster centers and U_x which is a collection of u_{ij} satisfying Eq. 3.26.

$$\sum_{i=1}^{c} u_{ij} = 1, j = 1, 2, \ldots .n \qquad (3.26)$$

Step 2: Calculate the fuzzy cluster center c_i using Eq. 3.27

$$c_i = \sum_{j=1}^{n} \frac{u_{ij}^m}{\sum_{k=1}^{n} u_{ik}^m} x_j, j = 1, 2, \ldots, n \qquad (3.27)$$

Step 3: Calculate the weighted means M_{ij} using Eq. 3.28.

$$M_{ij} = \sum_{\substack{k=1 \\ k \neq j}}^{n} \frac{\|c_i - x_k\|^{-1} u_{ik}}{\sum_{\substack{t=1 \\ t \neq j}}^{n} \|c_i - x_t\|^{-1} u_{it}} x_k \qquad (3.28)$$

Step 4:   Update the Lagrange multiplier ξ_j using Eq. 3.29

$$\xi_j = \left(\sum_{i=1}^{c} \left(\left\| x_j - M_{ij} \right\|^2 m \sum_{i=1}^{c} u_{ij}^{m-1} \right)^{\frac{1}{1-m}} \right)^{1-m} \tag{3.29}$$

Step 5:   Upgrade the membership grade u_{ij} using Eq. 3.30

$$u_{ij} = \xi_j^{\frac{1}{(m-1)}} \left(\left\| x_j - M_{ij} \right\|^2 m \sum_{i=1}^{c} u_{ij}^{m-1} \right)^{\frac{1}{(1-m)}} \tag{3.30}$$

Step 6:   Increase the iteration count (t) by one and check if it meets Max-It. If not, repeat Steps 2–5 until the clustering converges, i.e., $\left\| u_{ij}(t+1) - u_{ij}(t) \right\| \leq \delta$ for all $(i, j) \in (I, J)$.

Step 7:   (Clustering) Classify the pixels based on the largest membership belonging to a cluster using matrix U_x.

Experimental results on both synthetic and real data demonstrate that the NW-FCM clustering algorithm generates better clustering results than those of FCM and FWCM algorithms, in particular, for hyperspectral images [16, 21]. Some results are shown in Fig. 3.4 and Table 3.2. In the classification of Indian Pine images in Table 3.2, four classes including roofs, roads, trails, and grasses with 100 pixels each were used [33]. Table 3.2 shows a statistical comparison for 1000 experiments on the Indian Pine hyperspectral images.

3.7 Possibilistic Clustering Algorithm (PCA)

The memberships generated by the FCM do not always correspond to the intuitive concept of degrees of belongingness or compatibility [28]. This is due to the probabilistic constraints that the summation of the memberships of each data point across classes must be less or equal to one. Hence, the clustering results may be inaccurate for a noisy dataset [28, 29]. To improve this weakness of FCM, Krishnapuram and Keller relax the probabilistic constraints and propose possibilistic clustering algorithms (PCAs), where the memberships provide a better explanation of degrees of belongingness for the data. Since the clustering performance of the PCAs in [28, 29] heavily depends on the parameters used, Yang and Wu [57] suggested a new possibilistic clustering algorithm in which the parameters

Fig. 3.4 a An original image
and **b** clustering results with
FCM, FWCM, and
NW-FCM. The sky is not
properly segmented by using
the FCM with m = 2.5 and 3.0
and FWCM with m = 2, 2.5,
and 3. Five clusters are
assumed in this image

(a)

(b)

FCM	FWCM	NW-FCM
m=2.0		
m=2.5		
m.=3.0		

Table 3.2 A comparison of 1000 experiments for Indian Pine images. The first column lists clustering algorithms and fuzzy indexes, the second column shows the overall accuracy, the third column gives the accuracy distribution, and the fourth column indicates the number of clusters obtained in each run for 1000 runs [16]

Indian pine data set									
Clustering algorithm	Overall accuracy			Accuracy distribution			Variant clusters		
	Highest	Mean	Variance	[0.5, 1]	[0.4, 0.5)	[0, 0.4)	4	3	<3
$m = 2.0$									
FCM	50.25	49.03	0.03	13	987	0	1000	0	0
FWCM	57.75	52.82	1.15	994	4	2	1000	0	0
NW-FCM	61.75	51.41	17.04	644	343	13	1000	0	0
$m = 2.5$									
FCM	51.50	49.42	0.31	84	916	0	1000	0	0
FWCM	61.50	53.53	26.57	803	165	32	889	111	0
NW-FCM	61.75	51.20	18.98	642	336	22	1000	0	0
$m = 3.0$									
FCM	50.25	47.60	0.15	14	986	0	1000	0	0
FWCM	60.50	48.81	20.26	382	578	40	667	332	1
NW-FCM	61.25	51.22	17.09	634	353	13	1000	0	0

can be easily estimated. Compared with FCM, the PCAs are more robust to noise and outliers. Thus, the PCAs have been applied to problems such as function approximations [45, 46].

The PCA is similar to the FCM except the PCA does not have the constraint that the summation of all memberships of a pixel for all clusters must be less or equal to one. To prevent the minimization of the objective function from assigning all memberships to 0, a second term is added in the formulation of the PCA. The possibilistic objective function is given in [28] and formulated in Eq. 3.31. Please note that all the parameters in the objective function are similarly defined as in the FCM except η_i.

$$J = \sum_{j=1}^{N} \sum_{i=1}^{C} u_{ij}^{m} \|x_j - a_i\|^2 + \sum_{i=1}^{C} \eta_i \sum_{j=1}^{N} (1 - u_{ij})^m \qquad (3.31)$$

where η_i is recommended in [57] as shown in Eq. 3.32,

$$\eta_i = K \frac{\sum_{j=1}^{N} u_{ij}^{m} \|x_j - a_i\|}{\sum_{j=1}^{N} u_{ij}^{m}} \qquad (3.32)$$

and K is typically chosen to be 1. The fuzzifier, m, determines the fuzziness of the final possibilistic C-partition and the shape of the possibility distribution [28, 29].

Thus, the membership function for a pixel, j, to a cluster, i, is formulated as in Eq. 3.33:

$$u_{ij} = \frac{1}{1 + \left(\frac{\|x_j - a_i\|^2}{\eta_i}\right)^{1/(m-1)}}$$ (3.33)

The cluster centroid update function for each cluster, a_i, remains the same as FCM. The updated function is listed in Eq. 3.34 for the convenience.

$$a_i = \frac{\sum_{j=1}^{n} (u_{ij})^m x_j}{\sum_{j=1}^{n} (u_{ij})^m} \; for \; i \in C$$ (3.34)

The PCA is run the same way as the FCM. However, PCA is very sensitive to the initial values.

Unlike the FCM, the membership of a pixel in a cluster is not relative to other clusters, but only depends on the distance of the pixel with respect to the cluster center. The new objective function makes the memberships of the representative pixels of clusters to be as high as possible, while the unrepresentative pixels of clusters to be as low as possible [28]. This makes the membership to have more typical interpretation and degree compatibility [28, 29, 57]. In the PCA, the classification result can be interpreted as a possibility classification. The membership values represent the possibility degree of the pixels belonging to the clusters [28, 29, 57]. The PCA clustering algorithm is listed below.

The Possibilistic Clustering Algorithm (PCA):

Step 1: Choose a number of clusters C, a fuzzifier m, a small value of δ for the convergence criterion, and a maximum number of iterations (Max-It). Initialize their cluster centers and U_x which is a collection of u_{ij}.

Step 2: Estimate η_i using Eq. 3.32.

Step 3: Calculate the centroids of clusters using Eq. 3.34.

Step 4: Update the memberships of pixels using Eq. 3.33.

Step 5: Increase the iteration count (t) by one and check if it meets Max-It. If not, repeat Steps 2–5 until the clustering converges, i.e.,

$$\|u_{ij}(t+1) - u_{ij}(t)\| \leq \delta \text{ for all } (i, j) \in (I, \; J).$$

Step 6: (Clustering) Classify the pixels using matrix U_x (based on the largest membership to a cluster).

3.8   A Generalized Approach to Possibilistic Clustering Algorithms (GPCA)

Both FCM and PCAs are iterative algorithms that the update equations for the memberships and cluster centers are derived from the necessary conditions through the minimization of some objective functions. Since each cluster is assumed to be a fuzzy set in fuzzy clustering, it is natural to evaluate the memberships of pixels belonging to clusters directly from the data information based on the fuzzy set theory. Based on this motivation, a new approach of fuzzy clustering for generalizing the existing PCA is developed [64]. In this new approach, the update of cluster centers is performed via a performance index after the calculation of memberships using the fuzzy set theory. Its memberships are estimated directly from the data information. This generalized method leads to an infinite family of possibilistic clustering algorithms (GPCA). Therefore, the existing PCA becomes a member of this new PCA family.

Based on the notations defined in Table 3.1, we can define the measure of dissimilarity between pixel x_j and the cluster center a_i by the distance $\|x_j - a_i\|$ from Example 3.2. Thus, for each fuzzy cluster θ_i, a monotonic decreasing function f_i of the distance can be a good substitution for the membership function. It follows from Example 3.2 that $f_i(0) = 1$ and $f_i(+\infty) = 0$.

In summary, in each iteration of the GPCA, the membership u_{ij} will be evaluated by Eq. 3.35.

$$u_{ij} = f_i(\|x_j - a_i\| \, for \, (i,j) \in (I, J) \tag{3.35}$$

where the membership function f_i satisfies the following three constraints:

(1) f_i is a monotonically decreasing function in the interval of $[0, +\infty)$.
(2) $f_i(0) = 1$
(3) $f_i(+\infty) = 0$

for each $i \in I$. There are many functions satisfying these three constraints [64]. It is straightforward to verify that the membership matrix obtained by Eq. 3.35 is an eligible membership matrix set U_X due to $\|x_j - a_i\| \geq 0$. The cluster centroid update function remains the same as the equation used in the FCM. For the completeness, it is listed in Eq. 3.36.

$$a_i = \frac{\sum_{j=1}^{n} (u_{ij})^m x_j}{\sum_{j=1}^{n} (u_{ij})^m} \, for \, i \in C \tag{3.36}$$

The GPCA is summarized as follows.

The Generalized Possibilistic Clustering Algorithm (GPCA):

Step 1: Choose a number of clusters C, a fuzzifier m, a small value of δ for the convergence criterion, and a maximum number of iterations (Max-It). Initialize their cluster centers.

Step 2: Calculate U_X (which is a collection of u_{ij}) using a function (f_i) which satisfies Eq. 3.35.

Step 3: Update the centroids of clusters using Eq. 3.36.

Step 4: Increase the iteration count (t) by one and check if it meets Max-It. If not, repeat Steps 2–4 until the clustering converges, i.e.,

$$\left\| u_{ij}(t+1) - u_{ij}(t) \right\| \leq \delta \text{ for all } (i, j) \in (I, J).$$

Step 5: (Clustering) Classify the pixels using matrix U_x (based on the largest membership to a cluster).

Table 3.3 A comparison of 1000 experiments for the Iris dataset [64]

Clustering algorithm	Overall accuracy ϕ (%)			Accuracy distribution			Real CluNum c		
	Highest	Mean	Variance	[0.8, 1]	[0.6, 0.8)	[0, 0.6)	3	2	1
$m = 2.0$									
PCA93	92.667	80.005	281.67	618	221	161	778	222	0
PCA96	95.333	77.231	179.36	479	453	68	637	353	10
PCA06	92.000	79.647	263.24	617	224	159	771	229	0
GPCA{f₁}	92.667	80.011	274.04	614	218	168	778	222	0
GPCA{f₂}	92.000	79.277	266.47	606	228	166	772	228	0
FCM	89.333	89.265	1.538	997	3	0	997	3	0
$m = 2.5$									
PCA93	92.000	66.156	4.036	6	994	0	6	994	0
PCA96	95.333	78.634	162.11	538	410	52	771	226	3
PCA06	92.667	79.347	270.01	585	255	160	743	257	0
GPCA{f₁}	93.333	80.979	271.35	624	228	148	770	230	0
GPCA{f₂}	92.000	80.112	251.04	624	238	138	758	242	0
FCM	90.000	89.837	3.788	993	7	0	993	7	0
$m = 3.0$									
PCA93	66.000	66.000	0.000	0	1000	0	0	1000	0
PCA96	95.333	77.007	189.98	526	344	130	792	206	2
PCA06	92.667	80.054	276.65	618	210	172	785	215	0
GPCA{f₁}	94.667	81.763	285.95	617	246	137	752	248	0
GPCA{f₂}	92.667	80.495	278.69	637	187	176	806	194	0
FCM	90.000	89.790	4.861	991	9	0	991	9	0

Note that the only difference among all the members of GPCA is the function vector $f = (f_1, f_2, \ldots, f_c)$, used in Step 2. A series of function vectors $\{f\}$ satisfying three constraints above will establish a corresponding PCA, denoted as GPCA $\{f\}$ [64]. Some specific membership function used in the GPCA and other fuzzy clustering algorithms in this new family were tested on the Iris dataset, and the results showed that the GPCA algorithms are efficient for clustering [64] as illustrated in Table 3.3. The GPCA is straightforward for the implementation. In this experiment, the function, f_i, used for each class, i, is identical. In other words, $f = (f_1 = f_2 = \cdots = f_c)$. Two membership functions in Eqs. 3.37 and 3.38 below were used in the Iris experiments [64].

$$f_1 = \frac{1}{1 + 2x^2} \tag{3.37}$$

$$f_2 = 2^{-x^2} \tag{3.38}$$

3.9 Credibility Clustering Algorithms (CCA)

The GPCA discussed above is not stable due to its sensitivity on parameters initialization. To improve the GPCA, a new clustering algorithm based on credibility theory was developed [62, 63, 65]. It is called the credibilistic clustering algorithm (CCA). Credibility theory is a different measure of fuzzy phenomena [35–37]. The CCA uses a new performance index based on credibility theory for fuzzy clustering. Similar to many fuzzy clustering algorithms, the CCA is an iterative algorithm. Similar to PCA, the CCA also provides a good explanation of degrees of belonging for the data. In

Table 3.4 A comparison of 1000 experiments for the Iris dataset [64]

Clustering algorithm	Overall accuracy (%)			Accuracy distribution			Real CluNum c			Average IterTime
	Highest	Mean	Variance	[0.89, 1]	[0.6, 0.89)	[0, 0.6)	3	2	1	
PCA										
PCA06	92.000	78.884	264.295	589	249	162	751	249	0	25.165
GPCAs										
GPCA (1)	96.667	80.095	274.557	589	6	405	550	443	7	14.578
GPCA (2)	96.667	80.690	180.412	546	34	420	560	429	11	20.150
GPCA (3)	95.333	81.634	272.347	591	150	259	587	393	20	19.735
GPCA (4)	96.667	80.947	280.525	608	117	275	564	429	7	36.898
CCAs										
CCA (1)	92.667	89.707	12.308	868	124	8	1000	0	0	15.150
CCA (2)	92.667	89.789	8.106	856	139	5	1000	0	0	15.168
CCA (3)	92.667	90.869	1.845	964	36	0	1000	0	0	14.558
CCA (4)	92.667	90.870	1.198	970	30	0	1000	0	0	14.829

other words, it represents typicality or compatibility for the data. It has been illustrated that experiments on some randomly generated datasets and real datasets show the effective performance of the CCA [62, 63, 65]. On comparing the results of CCA with those of PCA and GPCA, we incur that CCA improves the performance of similar problems and provides stable classifications in noisy environments with higher accuracies than PCA and GPCA. An experiment on the Iris data is shown in Table 3.4 for a comparison among PCA, GPCAs, and CCAs, where four different membership functions (Eqs. 3.39, 3.40, 3.41, and 3.42) were used in the GPCAs and CCAs which are shown below [65]:

$$f_i^{(1)}(d_{ij}) = \left[1 + (mc)^3 (d_{ij}/\sigma_i^f)^2\right]^{-1} \tag{3.39}$$

$$f_i^{(2)}(d_{ij}) = \left[1 + (mc)^3 (d_{ij}/\sigma_i^\alpha)^2\right]^{-1} \tag{3.40}$$

$$f_i^{(3)}(d_{ij}) = \exp\left\{-\ln 2(mc)^{0.41}\left(\frac{d_{ij}}{\sigma_i^f}\right)^{0.82}\right\} \tag{3.41}$$

$$f_i^{(4)}(d_{ij}) = \exp\left\{-\ln 2(mc)^{0.41}\left(\frac{d_{ij}}{\sigma_i^\alpha}\right)^{0.82}\right\} \tag{3.42}$$

where $d_{ij} = \|x_j - a_i\|$ and the parameters σ_i^f and σ_i^α are defined as in Eqs. 3.43 and 3.44.

$$\sigma_i^f = \sqrt{\frac{\sum_{j=1}^n (\mu_{ij})^m d_{ij}^2}{\sum_{j=1}^n (\mu_{ij})^m}} \tag{3.43}$$

$$\sigma_i^\alpha = \sqrt{\frac{\sum_{\mu_{ij} \geq \alpha} d_{ij}^2}{\sum_{\mu_{ij} \geq \alpha} 1}} \tag{3.44}$$

for each $i \in I$ and α is a value in the interval of [0.1, 0.5]. PCA06 refers to PCA algorithm in [57]. Although the GPCAs can achieve the highest classification accuracy, the CCA algorithm is very stable to obtain three clusters in each of 1000 experiments. A detail about the experiments can be found in [65].

A fuzzy set defined on a set of real numbers is a fuzzy variable [37, 61]. In order to measure a fuzzy event, Zadeh proposed the concept of possibility measure in 1978 [61]. In 2002, Liu and Liu gave the concept of credibility measure [37]. Let v be a fuzzy variable with a membership function u. Then, for any set A of real numbers, we have Eqs. 3.45 and 3.46.

$$\text{Pos}\{v \in A\} = sup_{x \in A} u(x) \tag{3.45}$$

$$\text{Cr}\{v \in A\} = \frac{1}{2}\left(sup_{x \in A} u(x) + 1 - sup_{x \in A^c} u(x)\right) \tag{3.46}$$

where Pos and Cr represent the possibility and credibility measures, respectively, and A^c denotes the complement of set A.

Zhou et al. [65] deduced the credibility measure of fuzzy event $\{x_j \in \theta_i\}$ as shown in Eq. 3.47.

$$Cr_{ij} = \begin{cases} 1 - \frac{1}{2}\sup_{k \neq j} u_{kj}, & \text{if } u_{ij} = 1 \\ \frac{1}{2}u_{ij}, & \text{otherwise} \end{cases} \tag{3.47}$$

It is likely that the memberships u_{ij} calculated using Eq. 3.35 do not satisfy the normalized conditions $sup_{i \in I} u_{ij} = 1$ for all $j \in J$. Therefore, we should normalize the memberships u_{ij} through the transformation using Eq. 3.48.

$$u_{ij}^N = \frac{u_{ij}}{\sup_{k \in I} u_{kj}} \quad \text{for all } (i,j) \in (I,J) \tag{3.48}$$

The credibility measure of the fuzzy event will be rewritten as in Eq. 3.49.

$$Cr_{ij} = \begin{cases} 1 - \frac{\sup_{k \neq j} u_{kj}}{2 u_{kj}}, & \text{if } u_{ij} = \sup_{k \in I} u_{kj} \\ \frac{u_{ij}}{2 \sup_{k \in I} u_{kj}}, & \text{otherwise} \end{cases} \tag{3.49}$$

where u_{ij} can be evaluated using Eq. 3.35.

Zhou et al. also pointed out that the possibility measure defined in [61] lacks the self-dual quality that is an important property for the credibility measure. This is similar to the probability measure, which is self-dual for a random event. The credibility measure is a self-dual. This means that if Cr_{ij} is one, the pixel j belongs to cluster i. If Cr_{ij} is zero, the pixel j is absolutely outside of cluster i.

Similar to the FCM, an objective function is used to deduce the update equation for cluster centers in CCA. The general approach of fuzzy clustering is employed to obtain a new clustering method by setting $u_{ij}= (Cr_{ij})$ for all $(i, j) \in (I, J)$ in the performance index of GPCA. The performance index J_{CCA} used in the credibilistic clustering is shown in Eq. 3.50.

$$J_{CCA}(A) = \sum_{i=1}^{C} \sum_{j=1}^{N} (\text{Cr}_{ij})^m \|x_j - a_i\|^2 \tag{3.50}$$

where Cr_{ij} is defined above as in Eq. 3.49, u_{ij} are evaluated using Eq. 3.35 (it is listed in Eq. 3.51 for the completeness), and $m > 1$ is a fuzzifier same as that defined in the original FCM. The necessary conditions for a minimizer A of J_{CCA} are the following update equation for cluster centers in Eq. 3.52.

$$u_{ij} = f_i(\|x_j - a_i\| \text{ for } (i,j) \in (I, J) \tag{3.51}$$

$$a_i = \frac{\sum_{j=1}^{N} (\text{Cr}_{ij})^m x_j}{\sum_{j=1}^{N} (\text{Cr}_{ij})^m} \text{ for } i \in I \tag{3.52}$$

In the approach of credibilistic clustering, after random initializations of cluster centers and memberships, the membership matrix μ, the credibility matrix $\mathbf{Cr}$, and the cluster center matrix A are updated until the convergence of cluster centers, where $\mathbf{Cr}$ is given in Eq. 3.53.

$$\mathbf{Cr} = \begin{bmatrix} \text{Cr}_{11} & \cdots & \text{Cr}_{1n} \\ \cdots & \cdots & \cdots \\ \text{Cr}_{k1} & \cdots & \text{Cr}_{kn} \end{bmatrix} \tag{3.53}$$

The credibilistic clustering algorithm is described as follows.

The Credibilistic Clustering Algorithm (CCA):

Step 1: Choose a number of clusters C, a fuzzifer m, a small value of δ for the convergence criterion, and a maximum number of iterations (Max-It). Initialize their cluster centers.

Step 2: Calculate the membership matrix U_X (which is a collection of u_{ij}) using a function (f_i) which satisfies three constraints in Eq. 3.35.

Step 3: Calculate Cr_{ij} using Eq. 3.49 to establish a new $\mathbf{Cr}$ (which is a collection of Cr_{ij}).

Step 4: Update the centroids of clusters using Eq. 3.52.

Step 5: Increase the iteration count (t) by one and check if it meets Max-It. If not, repeat Steps 2–4 until the clustering converges, i.e., $\|Cr_{ij}(t+1) - Cr_{ij}(t)\| \leq \delta$ for all $(i, j) \in (I, J)$.

Step 6: (Clustering) Classify the pixels using the matrix $\mathbf{Cr}$ (based on the largest membership to a cluster).

Similar to the GPCAs, the only difference among all the CCAs is the membership functions f_i used in the evaluation equation (Eq. 3.51). By using the four specific membership functions $f(k)(k = 1, 2, 3, 4)$ recommended in [64], we can obtain four corresponding credibilistic clustering algorithms, denoted by CCA(k) ($k = 1, 2, 3, 4$).

3.10   The Support Vector Machine (SVM)

Support vector machine (SVM) is a pattern classification technique proposed by
Vapnik et al. [1, 5, 53]. SVM is a nonparametric classification method that is a
distribution-free algorithm. Unlike many traditional methods that minimize
empirical training errors, the SVM attempts to find an *optimal hyperplane* for
linearly separable patterns [1, 5, 24, 39, 53]. If the patterns are not linearly separable, a kernel function can be used to transform the patterns from the current space
into a new higher dimensional space in which the patterns will become linearly
separable [1]. The SVM also achieves greater empirical accuracy and better generalization capabilities than other standard supervised classifiers [24, 39]. In particular, SVM has shown a good performance on high-dimensional data
classification with a small set of training samples [7]. However, Tuia et al. point out
that the SVM works as a black box model and does not directly obtain the feature
importance from the solution of the model in nonlinear cases [52]. The performance
of SVM can be degraded when some features are uninformative or highly correlated
with other features [30]. The SVM is also frequently used in the image texture
classification [27].

The SVM is designed to maximize the margin around the separating hyperplane
between two classes as shown in Fig. 3.5. This optimal decision function is completely specified by a subset of training samples which is called the *support vectors*.
In a two-dimensional (2-D) pattern space, the optimal hyperplane is a linear
function. This linear programming problem is similar to the perceptron [55]. This
2-D separating function (i.e., hyperplane in 2-D) can be expressed as in Eq. 3.54.

$$ax_1 + bx_2 = c \qquad (3.54)$$

where x_1 and x_2 are elements of a pattern vector and a, b, and c are parameters used
to determine the position of the function. There is an infinite number of solutions of
a, b, and c for Eq. 3.54. Support vectors are the critical elements of the training set
that will change the position of the function if they are removed from the training
set. The problem of finding the optimal hyperplane is an optimization problem. This
can be solved by the optimization techniques using the Lagrange multipliers [1, 5,
53].

Assume that a training dataset $\boldsymbol{D} = \{(\boldsymbol{x}_1, \boldsymbol{y}_1), (\boldsymbol{x}_2, \boldsymbol{y}_2), \ldots, (\boldsymbol{x}_n, \boldsymbol{y}_n)\} \in \boldsymbol{R}^d$ in a
d-dimensional real number space is given, where x_i (i = 1, …, n) is a feature vector
and y_i is the corresponding label. The solution of SVM is to find a separating
hyperplane in the feature (Hilbert) space for a binary classification problem. If we
assume that all dataset have at least a distance of one from the hyperplane, then the
following two constraints (Eq. 3.55) will be satisfied for the training dataset **D**:

$$\boldsymbol{W}^T \boldsymbol{X}_i + b \geq 1 \; if \; y_i = 1$$

$$\boldsymbol{W}^T \boldsymbol{X}_i + b \leq 1 \; if \; y_i = -1 \qquad (3.55)$$

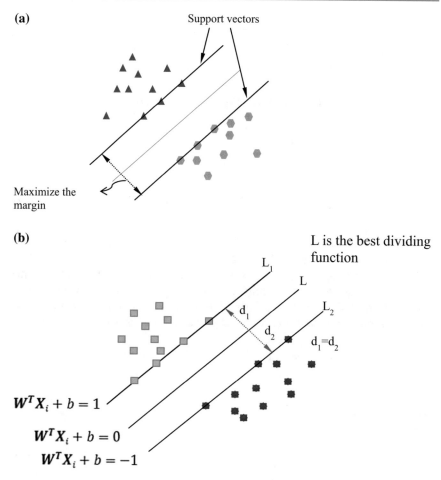

Fig. 3.5 a A diagram shows the maximal margin (same as the sum of d_1 and d_2 in (**b**)) and support vectors between two classes and **b** two alternate functions (i.e., 2-D hyperplanes) lying on the support vectors

Then, since the distance for each support vector from the hyperplane is calculated as in Eq. 3.56,

$$r = y\frac{\mathbf{w}^T\mathbf{x} + b}{\|\mathbf{w}\|} \tag{3.56}$$

both the margin and the hyperplane are expressed as in Eqs. 3.57 and 3.58.

$$\rho = \frac{2}{\|\mathbf{w}\|} \tag{3.57}$$

$$\mathbf{W}^T\mathbf{X} + b = 0 \tag{3.58}$$

This implies that two formulae hold (Eqs. 3.59 and 3.60).

$$\mathbf{w}^T(x_a + x_b) = 2 \tag{3.59}$$

and

$$\rho = \|x_a - x_b\|_2 = \frac{2}{\|\mathbf{W}\|_2} \tag{3.60}$$

where $\|\mathbf{W}\|_2$ is an Euclidean distance. This is shown in Fig. 3.5b. We can formulate the quadratic optimization for the SVM below.

The problem of solving the support vector machine is to find $\mathbf{W}$ and b such that Eq. 3.58 is maximized and all training samples $\{(x_i, y_i)\}$ are met with the constraints in Eq. 3.55. The solution using the quadratic optimization involves constructing a dual problem where a Lagrange multiplier α_i is associated with every constraint in the primary problem:

Find $\alpha_1, \ldots, \alpha_N$ such that Eq. 3.61 is maximized with the following two conditions satisfied:

(1) $\sum \alpha_i y_i = 0$
(2) $\alpha_i \geq 0\, for\, all\, \alpha_i$

$$Q(\boldsymbol{\alpha}) = \sum_{i=1}^{N} \alpha_i - \frac{1}{2}\sum\sum \alpha_i \alpha_j y_i y_j x_i^T x_j \tag{3.61}$$

The solution will have the following form:

$$\mathbf{W} = \Sigma \alpha_i y_i x \text{ and } b = y_k - \mathbf{W}^T x_k \text{ for any } x_k \text{ such that } \alpha_k \neq 0 \tag{3.62}$$

Each nonzero α_i indicates that corresponding x_i is a support vector. The function for the classification will have the following form:

$$f(x) = \sum \alpha_i y_i x_i^T x + b \tag{3.63}$$

where $x_i^T x$ is an inner product of test point x and the support vectors x_i. If slack variables are used in the SVM to prevent the overfitting or the situation where the dataset is not linearly separable [1, 5, 53], a new formulation should be given [1]. A summary of soft margin SVM is given below.

Algorithm of Support Vector Machine (SVM):

Step 1:   To obtain α_i and b using Eqs. 3.61 and 3.62 for the classification function $f(x)$ defined in Eq. 3.63.

Step 2:   (classification) given a new point, we calculate a score on its projection onto the hyperplane normal using $\mathbf{W}^T x + b = \sum \alpha_i y_i x_i^T x + b$ to determine the score (either positive or negative) for the classification.

Since the procedure above is for the binary classification, for the multiple-class classification, the one-against-one strategy (OAO) can be used [1, 5, 53].

3.11   The K-means Clustering Algorithm with the Ant Colony Optimization (K-means-ACO)

The K-means algorithm is a very useful clustering method; however, it may be trapped in a local optimum in exploring the global optimal solution. Several methods for improving the K-means have been proposed and developed in the literature [22, 23, 47]. The K-means algorithm using the ant colony optimization (ACO) for improving the stability of the clustering results will be described in this section. This algorithm is called the K-means-ACO which can be used for the clustering problems similar to the K-means. The ACO algorithm was first introduced to solve the traveling salesman problem (TSP) [10]. The problem of TSP is to find the shortest closed path in a given set of nodes that passes each node once. The ACO algorithm is one of the two main types of swarm intelligence. The other type of swarm intelligent techniques is the particle swarm optimization (PSO) algorithm. Swarm intelligence is inspired by the collaborative behavior of social animals such as birds, fish, and ants and their amazing formation of flocks, swarms, and colonies [4]. By simulating the interactions of these social animals, a variety of optimization problems can be solved with this method. The ACO algorithm consists of a sequence of local moves with a probabilistic decision based on a parameter, called *pheromone* as a guide to the final solution. The learning in the ACO is through the pheromone. The K-means-ACO is less dependent on the initial parameters such as randomly chosen initial cluster centers [47]. Hence, it generates more stable results compared to the K-means.

In the clustering of pixels for the partition of an image, the K-means-ACO heavily depends on the probability used [10]. The probability is formulated based on the distance (i.e., similarity) between the pixel and cluster centers and a variable, τ, representing the *pheromone level*. Pheromone is defined to be dependent on the minimum distance between each pair of cluster centers and inversely dependent on the distances between each pixel and its cluster center. Hence, the pheromone is getting larger when cluster centers are far apart. Therefore, the clusters tend to be more compact. This will have a high probability of assigning a pixel to that cluster. Pheromone evaporation is used to weaken the influence of the previously chosen solutions. In a sense, the K-means-ACO is similar to an ensemble decision as m ants are competing one another and each ant will come up with a solution. A criterion is defined to find the best solution and the pheromone level is updated accordingly for the set of m ants as a leading guide for the next iteration. A termination criterion will stop the iteration of the algorithm and an optimal solution is obtained.

The algorithm starts by assigning a pheromone level τ and a heuristic information η to each pixel. Then, each ant will assign each pixel to a cluster based on the probability obtained from Eq. 3.64 [47]:

$$P_i(x_p) = \frac{(\tau_i(x_p))^\alpha (\eta_i(x_p))^\beta}{\sum_{j=1}^{K}(\tau_j(x_p))^\alpha (\eta_j(x_p))^\beta} \tag{3.64}$$

where $P_i(x_p)$ is the probability of assigning pixel x_p to cluster i, $\tau_i(x_p)$ and $\eta_i(x_p)$ are the pheromone and heuristic information assigned to the pixel x_p for cluster i, respectively, α and β are constant parameters that determine the relative influence of the pheromone and heuristic information, and K is the number of clusters. Heuristic information $\eta_i(x_p)$ is obtained using Eq. 3.65:

$$\eta_i(x_p) = \frac{CONST}{IDist(x_p, ICC_i) * EDist(x_p, ECC_i)} \tag{3.65}$$

where x_p is the pth pixel,

ICC_i is the ith intensity cluster center,

ECC_i is the ith Euclidean cluster center,

$IDist(x_p, ICC_i)$ is the distance in terms of intensity of pixels between x_p and ICC_i,

$EDist(x_p, ECC_i)$ is the Euclidean distance between x_p and ECC_i,

$CONST$ is used to balance the value of τ_i and η_i, and

$*$ denotes the multiplication.

The value for the pheromone level τ_i assigned to each pixel is initialized to one so that it does not have any effect on the probability at the beginning. This pheromone should be getting larger for the better solution. Each ant is exploring its own solution. After m ants have done their exploration for each iteration, the current best solution is chosen and the assigned pheromone to this solution is incremented. In addition, cluster centers are updated by the cluster centers of the current best solution. In other words, in each iteration, each of the m ants finds its solution based on the best solution found by the previous m ants. This procedure will be repeated until reaching a maximum number of iterations or when the overall best solution is achieved.

The best solution in each iteration is chosen according to two factors: *distance between cluster centers* and *sum of the gray scales and physical distances* between each pixel and its cluster center (i.e., similarity and compactness of clusters). The following three conditions should be satisfied:

(1) The distance between cluster centers should be large such that the clusters are well separated,
(2) The sum of grayscale distances between each pixel and its cluster center should be small so that all members in each cluster are similar in the grayscale space (it will be a color space if three images are used), and
(3) The sum of the distances between each pixel and its cluster center should be small so that each cluster becomes more compact.

To achieve the first condition for each ant k ($k = 1, \ldots, m$), the distances between every pair of cluster centers are calculated and sorted to select the minimum distance $Min(k)$. Among all of these minimum distances given by all the ants, we choose the maximum of them ($Min(k')$). To achieve the second and third conditions, for each clustering performed by an ant we compute the sum of the distances between each pixel and its cluster center, and sort these distances. Then, we pick up the maximum for each ant, compare all these maximums, and select the overall minimum. The second maximum and third maximum of the solutions are compared in the same way and the minimum is picked. Solutions are being voted for their leading feature and the solution with the larger vote is selected as the best solution.

After the best solution is found, the pheromone value is updated according to Eq. 3.66 [47]:

$$\tau_i(x_p) = (1 - \rho)\tau_i(x_p) + \sum_i \Delta\tau_i(x_p) \tag{3.66}$$

where ρ is the evaporation factor ($0 \leq \rho \leq 1$) which causes the earlier pheromones to be vanished over the iterations. Therefore, as the solution becomes better, the corresponding pheromones have more effect on the next solution rather than the earlier pheromones in the previous iterations. The quantity of $\Delta\tau_i(x_p)$ in Eq. 3.66 is the amount of pheromone added to the previous pheromone by the succeeded ant, which is obtained from Eq. 3.67:

$$\Delta\tau_i(x_p) = \begin{cases} \frac{Q*Min(k')}{AvgIDist(k',i)*AvgEDist(k',i)} & \text{if } x_p \text{ is a member of cluster } i, \\ 0 & \text{otherwise.} \end{cases} \tag{3.67}$$

In Eq. 3.67, Q is a positive constant which is related to the quantity of the added pheromone by ants, $Min(k')$ is the maximum of all the minimum distances between every two cluster centers obtained by the ant k', $AvgIDist(k', i)$ is the average of the distances in terms of the intensity within cluster i, and $AvgEDist(k', i)$ is the average of the Euclidean distances between all pixels in a cluster i and their cluster center obtained by the ant k'.

When the clusters are falling further apart, $Min(k')$ will make the pheromone larger, and hence it will increase the probability. When the members of a cluster are similar, $AvgIDist(k', i)$ will increase the pheromone level. Similarly, when the cluster is more compact, $AvgEDist(k', i)$ will increase the pheromone level. In other words, if the value of $Min(k')$ is getting larger, it will cause the further apart of the clusters. To achieve a larger pheromone level, $Min(k')$ should be large and both the $AvgIDist(k', i)$ and $AvgEDist(k', i)$ should be small. Next, cluster centers are then updated by the cluster centers of the best solution. The procedure is repeated until a certain amount of time when the best solution is obtained. The algorithm is described below:

The K-means-ACO Algorithm:

Step 1: Initialize the pheromone level to one, and a number of clusters, K, and number of ants to m. Choose a small value of δ for the convergence criterion, a counter of iterations (t), and a maximum number of iterations (Max-It).

Step 2: Initialize each ant with K random cluster centers for m ants.

Step 3: For each ant, assign each pixel $x_i, i \in n$ to one of the clusters based on the probability given in Eq. 3.64. This step will be repeated for each of m ants.

Step 4: Update the Euclidean cluster centers and intensity cluster centers and recalculate the cluster centers. If the difference between each of current cluster centers and previous cluster centers is less than δ, go to next step. Otherwise, repeat Step 3.

$$\text{i.e. } |c_j(t+1) - c_j(t)| \leq \delta \, for \, j = 1, 2, \ldots, K$$

Step 5: Save the best solution among the m solutions found.

Step 6: Update the pheromone level on all pixels according to the best solution using Eq. 3.66.

Step 7: Update cluster centers by the cluster center values of the best solution.

Step 8: If the number of iterations meets Max-It, the procedure stops. Otherwise, the procedure continues and go to Step 3.

Step 9: (Clustering) Classify each of all the pixels to one of clusters based on the minimum distance between the pixel and the clusters (based on the optimal solution obtained).

The stability of the K-means-ACO is illustrated in Figs. 3.6 and 3.7 where different number of iterations of both K-means and K-means-ACO are used. It shows that for a proper selection of the initial cluster centers, both algorithms work well. However, if the initial cluster centers are not suitably selected, the K-means may give unsatisfied results. The experiment shows that the K-means is not a stable algorithm.

(a)   (b)

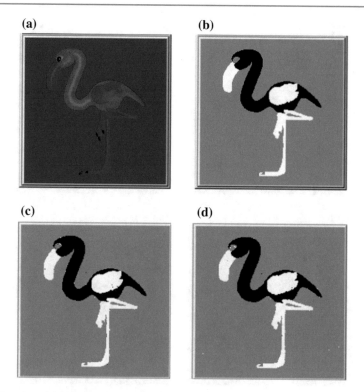

(c)   (d)

Fig. 3.6 **a** An original image, **b** results of K-means with $K = 3$, **c** and **d** results of K-means-ACO with $K = 3$ and different number of iterations (In the experiments, the initial seed values are properly chosen for both algorithms)

3.12   The K-means Algorithm and Genetic Algorithms (K-means-GA)

Genetic algorithm (GA) can improve the performance of K-means algorithm for unsupervised clustering. This has been illustrated in several different applications including color image quantization and image classification [19, 20, 48, 56]. The evolution begins with an initial population. The selected chromosomes (candidate solutions) compete with one another to reproduce based on the Darwinian principle of "survival of the fittest" in each generation of evolution. After a number of generations in the evolution, the chromosomes that survived in the population are the optimal solutions.

Similar to any algorithm which uses GA for the solution evolution, the K-means algorithm needs to generate a set of solutions, P, to form a population for the solution search. This population is shown in Fig. 3.8. A chromosome can be formulated using one of several different representations [12].

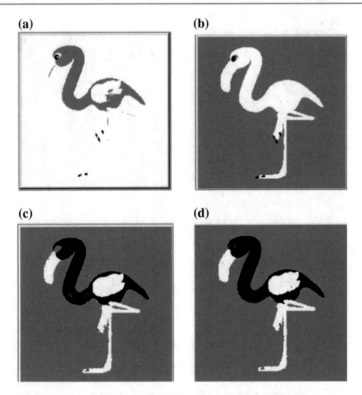

Fig. 3.7 **a** and **b** results of K-means with $K = 3$ and **c** and **d** results of K-means-ACO with $K = 3$ with different number of iterations (In the experiments, the initial seed values are not properly chosen for both algorithms)

String #1	$C_{11}...C_{1L}$	$C_{21}...C_{2L}$	...	$C_{k-1,1}...C_{k-1,L}$	$C_{k1}...C_{kL}$
String #2	$C_{11}...C_{1L}$	$C_{21}...C_{2L}$	...	$C_{k-1,1}...C_{k-1,L}$	$C_{k1}...C_{kL}$
String #3	$C_{11}...C_{1L}$	$C_{21}...C_{2L}$	...	$C_{k-1,1}...C_{k-1,L}$	$C_{k1}...C_{kL}$
⋮	⋮	⋮	...	⋮	⋮
String #P	$C_{11}...C_{1L}$	$C_{21}...C_{2L}$	...	$C_{k-1,1}...C_{k-1,L}$	$C_{k1}...C_{kL}$

Fig. 3.8 A population of P strings with the length of each string, $L \times K$, where L is the dimension of the cluster center and K is the number of clusters

The separability (i.e., distance/similarity) is one of the measures frequently used in the evaluation of classification accuracy. The measure is based on how much of the overlapping is in the intra-class distributions. Among them, Bhattacharya distance, the transformed divergence, and Jeffries–Matusita (JM) distance are widely used. The Bhattacharyya distance has the disadvantage that it will continue to grow even after the classes have become well separated. The transformed divergence has a problem to distinguish two different clusters. To evaluate the effectiveness of the K-means-GA, the JM distance was used as the fitness function [49]. The statistics for each class in the JM distance computation were obtained by distributing the training samples among the classes (a pixel is assigned to the class that is the closest in terms of the Euclidean distance between a class mean and the pixel). The average JM distance is then computed by dividing the sum of pairwise JM distances by the number of pairs. The JM value is in the range of 0 and 2. A higher JM value indicates that the result is better. The formula for calculating the JM distance between classes i and j is listed in Eq. 3.68. Please note that this formula is established assuming that classes are normally distributed.

$$(JM)_{ij} = 2(1 - e^{-B}) \qquad (3.68)$$

where

$$B = \frac{1}{8}(m_i - m_j)^T \left(\frac{Cov_i + Cov_j}{2}\right)^{-1}(m_i - m_j) + \frac{1}{2}\ln\left(\frac{\left|\frac{Cov_i + Cov_j}{2}\right|}{|Cov_i|^{1/2}|Cov_j|^{1/2}}\right)$$

$$(3.69)$$

Equation 3.69 is the Bhattacharyya distance [44, 49]; notations m_i and Cov_i are the mean and covariance of class i, respectively, and ln is a log function.

The K-means with GA algorithm is described below.

The K-means-GA Algorithm:

Step 1:   Determine a number of clusters, K, and their initial cluster centers for a number of chromosomes (strings), say *P*, to form a population. Initialize crossover probability p_c, mutation probability p_m, and a maximum number of iterations (Max-It). This Max-It is the same as the number of generations the algorithm will be evolved.

Step 2:   Distribute the pixels in the training set among K clusters by the minimum distance criterion using the Euclidean distance measure for each string separately and update the centroid of each cluster by calculating the average of pixel values assigned to each cluster. This step is repeated P times for each string.

Step 3:   (**Crossover**) For each string, a one-point crossover is applied with probability p_c. A partner string is randomly chosen for the mating. Both strings are cut into two portions at a randomly selected position between j and j + 1, and the portions are mutually interchanged where j = 1 to N^2.

Step 4:   (**Mutation**) Mutation with probability p_m is applied to an element for each string. In our experiments, either −1 or +1 is selected randomly by comparing with probability p_m (if the random probability is less than p_m,

-1 is selected. Otherwise, +1 is selected) and added to the chosen element. The mutation operation is used to prevent fixation to the local minimum in the search space.

Step 5: (**Reproduction**) The JM distance in Eq. 3.68 is used as the fitness function for each string (i.e., the average of JMs for all pairs of clusters). All strings are evaluated with the fitness function and pairwise compared. In each comparison, the string with the higher JM value will be retained and the other one will be discarded and replaced by a new string generated randomly. In other words, only half of the strings in a population survived and the other half are regenerated by new random strings representing new class means.

Step 6: Repeat Steps 2–5 for several generations defined by the user. If the procedure converges (i.e., exceeds the Max-It), the string with the maximum JM distance will be selected as the best solution.

Step 7: (**Clustering**) Classify each of all the pixels to one of clusters based on the minimum distance between the pixel and the clusters.

3.13   The K-means Algorithm and Simulated Annealing (K-means-SA)

Simulated Annealing (SA) is an optimization technique that is based on the process of annealing metals [55]. When a metal is heated up high enough and slowly cooled down, it will be ultimately in an optimal state which in a sense corresponds to a global minimum energy. This indicates that an optimal solution is obtained. The process of annealing can be simulated with the Metropolis algorithm [40]. The laws of thermodynamics state that at temperature, T, the probability of an increase in energy of magnitude, ΔE, is given by

$$p(\Delta E) = \exp\left(\frac{-\Delta E}{kT}\right) \tag{3.70}$$

where k is a constant known as the Boltzmann's constant [55].

This equation is directly used in the simulated annealing, although it is usual to drop the Boltzmann's constant as this was only introduced into the equation when it is used in the simulation of different materials. Therefore, the probability of accepting a worse state is given by the equation (Eq. 3.71)

$$if\ p = \exp\left(\frac{-\Delta E}{T}\right) > r \tag{3.71}$$

where
ΔE = the change in the cost function between the next state and the current state,
T = the current temperature, and

r = a random number between 0 and 1.

When the temperature T is high, the probability is close to 1. This means that the probability of accepting any move is very high. If the temperature is low, the probability in Eq. 3.71 is close to 0. This indicates that the algorithm will avoid a bad move if the next state is not better. This guarantees that only the most promising solutions will be explored when the temperature is low. This approach allows SA to explore solutions that the K-means is not able to do. Simulated annealing introduces randomness into the selection of the solutions. This will make the algorithm from being trapped in a local optimum. A general SA algorithm is listed below.

A Simulated Annealing (SA) Algorithm:

Step 1: Start with an initial temperature T and a candidate solution randomly.
Step 2: Evaluate this candidate and label it as the current state.
Step 3: Generate a new candidate and evaluate this solution.
Step 4: If this new candidate is better than the current state, accept this as a current state and discard the previous one.
Step 5: If this new candidate is not better than the current state, calculate the probability using Eq. 3.71. If the probability is greater than a random probability, accept this new candidate as the current state.
Step 6: Reduce the temperature and repeat Steps 3–5 until the temperature is cooled down to zero.

An integrated algorithm for simulated annealing with the K-means is sketched below.

The K-means with Simulated Annealing (K-means-SA):

Step 1: Choose a number of clusters, K, and initial cluster centers, i.e., $S = \{C_1, \ldots, C_K\}$ and an initial temperature T.
Step 2: Apply the K-means algorithm to assigning pixels to the clusters and evaluate the performance index for K clusters. Set this as current solution.
Step 3: Produce a new solution (which can be based on the current solution).
Step 4: Apply K-means algorithm to assign pixels and evaluate the performance index for this new solution. For example, the JM distance can be used as a performance index.

Table 3.5 A comparison of JM distance for the algorithms applied to the images shown in Fig. 3.9

Algorithms	JM value (I1)	JM value (I2)	JM value (I3)
K-means	1.8294	1.8065	1.8955
K-means-SA	1.8550	1.8154	1.9059
K-means-GA	1.8550	1.8375	1.9062

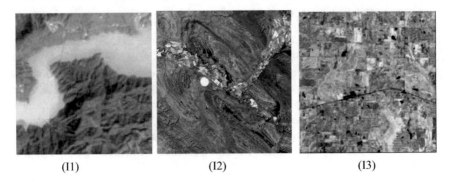

(I1)   (I2)   (I3)

Fig. 3.9 (I1) a satellite image with 3 classes, (I2) a satellite image shown with band 4 only (3 classes), and (I3) a satellite image shown with band 4 only (9 classes)

Step 5: If this new solution is better than the current solution, accept this as the current solution. If not, check if the probability in Eq. 3.71 is greater than the random probability. If it is true, accept this new solution as current solution. Otherwise, reject this new solution.

Step 6: Reduce the temperature T and repeat Steps 3–5 until temperature is equal to 0 or until a stopping criterion is met.

To evaluate the efficiency of the K-means-SA, some of the experimental results are illustrated in Table 3.5. The test images are shown in Fig. 3.9. The JM distance is used as the cost function (energy function) for the K-means-SA. The final average JM distance is then computed as shown in Table 3.5. The higher the average JM distance is, the better the results are. The results shown in this table were obtained with the algorithm which was repeated four times and initial temperature was 20 for

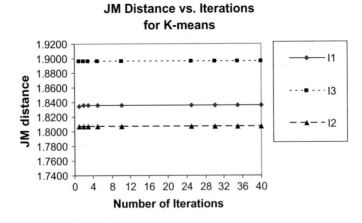

Fig. 3.10 A graph shows the relationship between JM distance and iterations for the K-means for images I1, I2, and I3 shown in Fig. 3.9

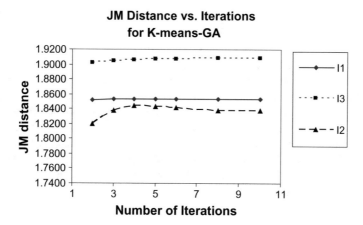

Fig. 3.11 A graph shows the relationship between JM distance and iterations for the K-means-GA with the parameters; the number of clusters is 3, the population is 10, the crossover probability is 0.7, and mutation probability is 0.3 for images I1, I2, and I3 shown in Fig. 3.9

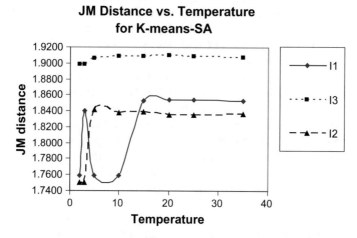

Fig. 3.12 A graph shows the relationship between JM distance and temperatures for the K-means-SA for images I1, I2, and I3 shown in Fig. 3.9

each image. From the experiments, we observed that a high temperature should be given when the image size is large and the number of clusters is small. In other words, a low temperature can be given when the image size is small and the number of clusters is large. The JM distance indicates that the K-means-GA is one of the efficient algorithms.

The graphs in Figs. 3.10 and 3.11 show the relationship between the JM distance and the number of iterations for K-means and K-means-GA, respectively. The graph in Fig. 3.12 shows the relationship between JM distance and the change in temperature for K-means-SA. Figure 3.10 indicates that the JM distance for the K-means does not change significantly. So does the K-means-GA. On the other hand, the JM distance for the K-means-SA increases significantly for some images when the number of iterations is increased. The K-means-SA does not depend much on the diversity of the initialization because the high temperature gives more opportunities for the algorithm to explore more promising solutions. Among these three algorithms tested, the K-means-GA is the most stable algorithm. In the K-means-SA, the algorithm sequentially generates only one solution depending on the temperature. A higher temperature will have a higher probability to accept the new solution although it may not be a good solution temporarily. Thus, the K-means-SA will allow the search going in different directions to avoid being trapped in local optima.

3.14   The Quantum-Modeled K-means Clustering Algorithm (Quantum K-means)

The ability to grouping data naturally and accurately is essential to applications such as image segmentation. Therefore, techniques that enhance accuracy are of keen interest. One such technique involves applying a quantum mechanical system model, such as that of the quantum bit, to generate probabilistic numerical output to be used as variable input for clustering algorithms [38, 41]. It has been demonstrated that by applying a quantum bit model to data clustering algorithms can increase clustering accuracy, as a result of simulating superposition as well as possessing both guaranteed and controllable convergence properties [8]. The quantum model in the form of a string of qubits has been used for the diversity obtained from representing the quantum mechanical superposition of states. Previous works have applied this model to various algorithms [8, 17, 18, 38]. To understand how a qubit works, one needs to acquire a fundamental understanding of quantum state systems. The basis of quantum physics is derived from the Schrodinger equation for matter waves [13].

In this section, we briefly introduce how the quantum concept is combined with the K-means for improving the clustering results of K-means [8]. Quantum properties can be simulated via quantum system modeling algorithms, and used in applications that can benefit from these inherent properties. Quantum bits can be manipulated via quantum operators, such as a rotation gate, which consists of a unitary matrix and can be used to bring algorithmic convergence to fruition. In quantum mechanics, a superposition or linear combination of states can be represented in Dirac notation [42] such that

$$|\psi\rangle = \alpha|0\rangle + \beta|1\rangle \tag{3.72}$$

where ψ represents an arbitrary state vector in Hilbert space, α and β represent probability amplitude coefficients, and $|0\rangle$ and $|1\rangle$ represent basis states. These basis states correspond to spin up and spin down, respectively. The state vector in normalized form can be represented as

$$\langle \psi | \psi \rangle = 1 \tag{3.73}$$

or equivalently

$$|\alpha|^2 + |\beta|^2 = 1 \tag{3.74}$$

where $|\alpha|^2$ and $|\beta|^2$ are the probabilities of quantum particle measurement, yielding a particular state. Moreover, due to the superposition of quantum states, the particle may be in either a single state or multiple states *simultaneously*.

These probability amplitudes are complex numbers, and in matrix form can represent a qubit

$$\begin{bmatrix} \alpha \\ \beta \end{bmatrix} \tag{3.75}$$

Moreover, a series of qubits can form a string such that

$$\begin{bmatrix} \alpha_1 & \alpha_2 & \cdots & \alpha_m \\ \beta_1 & \beta_2 & \cdots & \beta_m \end{bmatrix} \tag{3.76}$$

In addition, states $|0\rangle$ and $|1\rangle$ can be represented in bit form as

$$|0\rangle = \begin{matrix} \mathbf{1} \\ \mathbf{0} \end{matrix} \begin{bmatrix} 1 \\ 0 \end{bmatrix} \tag{3.77}$$

$$|1\rangle = \begin{matrix} \mathbf{0} \\ \mathbf{1} \end{matrix} \begin{bmatrix} 0 \\ 1 \end{bmatrix} \tag{3.78}$$

Likewise, the qubit string can be expressed in the same notation [59]. For instance, the following eight bit string

$$11010010$$

can be represented as

$$\begin{bmatrix} 0 \\ 1 \end{bmatrix} \cdot \begin{bmatrix} 0 \\ 1 \end{bmatrix} \cdot \begin{bmatrix} 1 \\ 0 \end{bmatrix} \cdot \begin{bmatrix} 0 \\ 1 \end{bmatrix} \cdot \begin{bmatrix} 1 \\ 0 \end{bmatrix} \cdot \begin{bmatrix} 1 \\ 0 \end{bmatrix} \cdot \begin{bmatrix} 0 \\ 1 \end{bmatrix} \cdot \begin{bmatrix} 1 \\ 0 \end{bmatrix} \tag{3.79}$$

or in tensor product form

$$|1\rangle \otimes |1\rangle \otimes |0\rangle \otimes |1\rangle \otimes |0\rangle \otimes |0\rangle \otimes |1\rangle \otimes |0\rangle \tag{3.80}$$

In order to simulate the quantum mechanical property of superposition of states, a probabilistic Turing machine must be utilized. The quantum-modeled algorithm will use the output of this state machine as input to the clustering algorithms. Moreover, the probability of obtaining a particular outcome can be controlled by operating on the associated qubits directly with a quantum rotation gate. In order to implement the quantum state machine, for each algorithmic iteration a series of black box quantum *"oracle"* objects are utilized, each of which in this context poses a solution. The qubit string representation previously described represents a superposition of states, and each oracle possesses n qubit strings with m qubits per string. Since m represents the string length in qubits, the value of m for each string is chosen according to the estimated optimal centroid initial value. The total length of each qubit string is the product of m, the number of bands associated with the image being segmented, and the number of clusters chosen beforehand. Once the desired centroid value is determined, the number of qubits is specified accordingly, along with the appropriate number of clusters for the dataset of interest. Moreover, qubit strings may be applied to any random variable, not just cluster centers. We simply apply qubit string values to all desired random variables, obtain some measure of fitness via the inverse of some appropriate cluster validity index, determine the fittest solution thus far, and use the rotation gate and the state information of the best solution to converge the output of the state machine to that of the best solution. The quantum rotation gate is a unitary matrix operator, and can be formulated as follows:

$$G = \begin{bmatrix} \cos\theta & -\sin\theta \\ \sin\theta & \cos\theta \end{bmatrix} \tag{3.81}$$

The angle of rotation θ is determined via a lookup table based upon the variable angle distance method [38]. The rotation gate is only one of a variety of gates that can be applied to the probability amplitude coefficients of each qubit [41].

The quantum K-means (QKM) algorithm [8] begins by initializing a population of quantum oracles, and then a call is made to *Make P(t)*. Following *Make P(t)*, the decoded decimal values are provided as initial centroid input to K-means, and hard partitioning will then ensue until a stopping criterion has been determined. Afterward, the cluster fitness is evaluated, via the Davies–Bouldin (DB) index method [9], and the fitness value is stored in the oracle. The fitness function utilized in the QKM is given in Eq. 3.82.

$$f = \frac{1}{1 + DB} \tag{3.82}$$

The fitness of the oracle is compared to the stored best solution as of yet, and the oracle that posses a superior fitness value is stored as the new best solution. In order to guide the current solution toward the best-stored solution, and hence bring convergence to fruition, subsequent to oracle population fitness evaluation, the quantum rotation gate in Eq. 3.81 is applied to the probability amplitudes α and β,

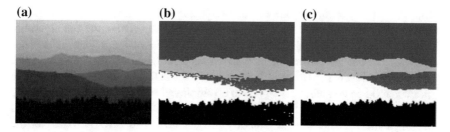

Fig. 3.13 **a** An original image, **b** a segmented result using the K-means, and **c** a segmented result using the quantum K-means [8]. The number of clusters was set to five for both algorithms

respectively, for each qubit in each string. Following quantum gate rotation, quantum crossover and mutation operators are applied to individuals chosen randomly. The previously described process continues for the specified number of iterations. A summary of the algorithm is listed below.

The Quantum K-means Algorithm (QKM):

Step 1: *Initialize Q(t)*—(population initialization).
Step 2: *Make P(t)*—(Observe, encode, decode).
Step 3: Perform the *K-Means Clustering.*
Step 4: *Evaluate P(t)*—(XB Index).
Step 5: *Store B(t)*—(Store best solution).
Step 6: Repeat Steps 3–5 for the entire population.
Step 7: Apply the *Quantum Rotation Gate.*
Step 8: Apply the *Quantum Crossover.*
Step 9: Apply the *Quantum Mutation Inversion.*
Step 10: *Make P(t)*—(Observe, encode, decode).
Step 11: Repeat Steps 3–10 for every iteration.

Some of experimental results shown in Fig. 3.13 gives a visual comparison between the K-means and quantum K-means clustering algorithms. It shows that the quantum K-means gives a more smooth and accurate result than that of K-means.

3.15 The Pollen-Based Bee Algorithm for Clustering (PBA)

Similar to the ant colony, the collective intelligence of social insect groups, including honey bees, presents an appealing model for problem-solving [6]. Many bee algorithms have been developed for data clustering. Among them, bee algorithm (BA), virtual bee algorithm (VBA), artificial bee colony algorithm (ABC), beehive algorithm (BeeHive), bee swarm optimization algorithm (BSO), and bee colony optimization algorithm (BCO) [43, 58]. TheBA developed by Pham et al. has been used in solving the problems in pattern recognition and data clustering

[43]. The bee algorithm is one of solution space search problems which can be formulated as the objective function with constraints. The goal of the bee algorithm is trying to find an optimal solution for the objective function defined. The VBA uses bees and bee interaction intensity to evaluate solution (i.e., food sources) [58]. The bees developed in ABC must know the number of food sources around the hive [6]. Each food source will be assigned to an employed bee (forager) for determining if a better solution can be found in its neighborhood. The beehive algorithm uses foraging behavior and waggle dances in its method. The BSO is based on the foraging behaviors of honey bee swarms. Three different types of bees, foragers, onlookers, and scouts employ different flying patterns for adjusting trajectories in the search space [6]. Each bee embedded in BCO incrementally builds a solution to a problem for a number of iterations [6]. A traditional BA algorithm is listed below to serve as a basic model for clustering [43].

The BA Algorithm:

Step 1:   Initialize the population of solution space.
Step 2:   Evaluate the fitness of each solution in the population.
Step 3:   While (stopping criterion is not true)
Step 3(a): Select sites for the neighborhood search.
Step 3(b): Recruit bees for selected sites (more bees will be recruited for the best sites which are often called elite sites) and evaluate the fitness.
Step 3(c): Select the fittest bee from each site and update the solution space.
Step 3(d): Assign remaining bees for search randomly and evaluate their fitness. End While.
Step 4:   Output the best results.

Based on the BA, a pollen-based bee algorithm (PBA) was developed for the data clustering and image segmentation [6]. The PBA can be considered as a variation of the BA. The PBA embeds bee, hive, environmental interactions, and season change in the design and presents a more precise swarm analogy that allows the PBA model to converge autonomously upon high-quality solutions. The PBA utilizes the natural concept of pollen depletion which, along with creating unique methods of field and honeycomb management, increases optimal solution exploitation. Simultaneously, the PBA tries to reduce the complexity of user input parameters in some bee algorithms.

There are three core conceptualizations behind PBA [6]. First, it is the construction of a bee so that a single bee is a single element of the solution set and is not comprised of the entire solution set (as opposed to "Each bee represents a potential clustering solution as a set of K cluster centers" [43]). Second, the storage of pollen solutions within the hive, as honey, helps define the landscape of active fields, independent of any one bee's ability, so that "source fields" can be rated for suitability of solution. The third conceptualization is the introduction of pollen depletion to model the advancing seasons and mimic the natural changes in the landscape of pollen availability and bee industry, leading to convergence.

In BA, the bees are paramount in their carrying of the solution set and communicating their solution set to other bees. This is not the case in PBA, where the bees are individual elements without any understanding of the solution set required as a whole. This division of the solution as a whole from an individual of the swarm led to the development of the "field" and of "field solution storage" at the hive, in the form of honey which then allows the solution sets to improve by the individual work of the bees and not by the efforts of any single bee alone. The PBA model also takes advantage of particle swarm optimization (PSO) (as does VBA) and thereby considers one bee as one particle of the swarm. PBA does not, however, communicate a global best solution among its bees and instead allows the quality of the pollen gathered from the fields to be rated at the hive in the form of honey in the honeycomb.

PBA does have two types of bees, but, unlike ABC, these bees do not change roles nor are they treated like "generations" where one set of bees is replaced by another later generation. Another similarity between PBA and ABC is the abandonment of food sources (or fields when speaking of PBA) so that our model will abandon a field only if another better field is discovered by the scouts. What beehive algorithm shares in common with PBA is the treatment of the bees as two types, long and short distance agents, in which the agents can be interpreted as individual particles like PSO, and thus like PBA's bees. The long-distance agents would be more comparable to the scout bees in PBA (who explore the landscape to return undiscovered pollen in a random fashion) and the short distance agents as comparable to the forager bees (who return to a given field and pollen location in order to exploit the area around an already given and rated pollen source).

Contrasting PBA with BSO algorithm, by using the pollen depletion method, PBA allows the scouts to search the entire landscape without constriction to a certain radius. Also, the foragers are encouraged to begin their search for better solutions in reverse of that described by BSO, starting in a small area and given enough time (if it is early enough in the harvesting season and there are multiple foragers employed) they are dispersed further and further afield from that solution which allows easy escape from local optima. BCO is most similar to ant colony optimization [4] in its handling of its members. PBA, unlike BCO, does not use a reset strategy as the bees are not able to influence each other in their tasks—the scouts will explore and the foragers will exploit without regard to any particular member finding a better or worse pollen location. The individuals in PBA do their individual best to perform up to the task assigned and so do not change their performance level nor actions based on other individuals of the hive—this allows the swarm as a whole to survive the "missteps" that single individuals can make as they perform their duties.

The PBA algorithm is presented below. The detail is given in [6] for pollen depletion, scouts, fields, landscape, foragers, environment, and interactions.

The PBA Algorithm:

Step 1: Initialize variables.

Step 2: While pollen not depleted and scoutable fields exist, repeat Steps 3–5.

Step 3: Start scout bees loop:
   (1) explore landscape (find pollen),
   (2) create fields (ranked) as found by scout bees, and
   (3) evaluate/replace stored fields with any better found fields.

Step 4: Apply pollen depletion (modifying numbers of bees and viable fields).

Step 5: Start forager bees loop:
   (1) forager bees are assigned a stored field to exploit,
   (2) explore/exploit within the recruited field, and
   (3) evaluate/replace stored pollen source with better returned pollen sources.

Step 6: The value of the best field (having the best honey in the honeycomb) is solution.

For an empirical comparison, PBA is compared with some clustering algorithms previously discussed on the accuracy of the Iris, Glass, and Wine dataset [6, 64]. These algorithms include FCM, FWCM, NW-FCM, PCAs, and GPCAs. Tables 3.6, 3.7 and 3.8 show the results of the accuracy. Different percentages of the pollen depletion were used in the PBA simulation. Except for the results of PBA, others are from results in [64]. Experimental results on two color images for a visual comparison between the BA and PBA are shown in Fig. 3.14 [6]. With different parameters used in both algorithms, the segmentation results will be different.

Table 3.6 A comparison on the classification accuracy of the Iris dataset [6, 63]

Accuracy percentage			
Algorithm	Highest	Mean	Variance
PBA with 28% pollen	98.00	89.20	0.74
FCM	89.33	89.26	1.53
FWCM	92.66	92.42	5.24
NW-FCM	92.66	90.97	19.17
PCA93	92.67	80.00	281.67
PCA96	95.33	77.23	179.36
PCA06	92.00	79.64	263.24
GPCA {f1}	92.66	80.01	274.04
GPCA {f2}	92.00	79.27	266.47

Table 3.7 A comparison on the classification accuracy of the Glass dataset [6, 64]

Accuracy percentage			
Algorithm	Highest	Mean	Variance
PBA with 40% pollen	61.68	52.63	2.79
FCM	55.14	49.12	2.66
FWCM	54.21	44.42	15.22
NW-FCM	47.66	41.11	5.77
PCA93	46.26	38.93	0.97
PCA96	45.79	35.75	6.28
PCA06	62.62	45.62	16.71
GPCA {f3}	55.61	48.82	11.41
GPCA {f4}	56.08	46.20	15.51

Table 3.8 A comparison on the classification accuracy of the Vowel dataset [6, 64]

Accuracy percentage			
Algorithm	Highest	Mean	Variance
PBA with 10% pollen	41.21	35.29	1.06
FCM	32.02	28.00	1.15
FWCM	N/A	N/A	N/A
NW-FCM	N/A	N/A	N/A
PCA93	32.56	23.43	8.17
PCA96	33.64	24.41	5.54
PCA06	40.10	30.48	6.70
GPCA {f5}	39.90	30.54	6.67
GPCA {f6}	40.40	30.78	6.80

3.16 Summary

Techniques for image texture classification and segmentation are very useful for image texture analysis. Clustering methods are frequently used for image texture classification and segmentation. We introduced supervised and unsupervised algorithms which have been widely used in the traditional pattern recognition and machine learning. These algorithms include crisp and fuzzy clustering approaches. The K-means clustering algorithm is a simple and efficient method for the natural grouping of data. Due to its drawback on the local minima problem, several optimization methods have been used to improve the algorithm. Some of them such as ant colony optimization (ACO), particle swarm optimization (PSO), genetic algorithms (GA), and simulated annealing (SA). It has been demonstrated that these methods not only improve the result of the K-means algorithm but also make the algorithm more stable and prevent falling in the local minima. A quantum K-means (QKM) algorithm is also described to compare the performance of the K-means and QKM and show how the quantum model improves the K-means. A nature-inspired

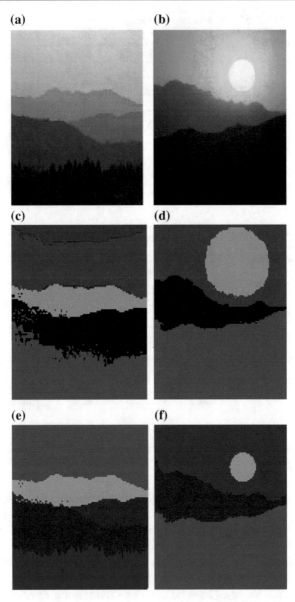

Fig. 3.14 **a** and **b** two original images, **c** and **d** results of the BA, and **e** and **f** results of the PBA [6]

bee algorithm based on the pollen depletion concept is also given to confirm its merits in image segmentation. Some experimental results are given based on testing on the datasets used. Although not all of them are image textures in the experiments, these algorithms can be used in image texture analysis.

Artificial neural networks and their deep models have been primarily used in pattern and image classification [34]. These neural computation platforms are parallel and frequently used to construct computing systems that are more complex.

3.17 Exercises

A hypothetical color image is given below (Red, Green, and Blue), and two initial cluster centers are $\begin{bmatrix} 0 \\ 1 \\ 3 \end{bmatrix}$ and $\begin{bmatrix} 1 \\ 2 \\ 2 \end{bmatrix}$.

0	1	2	3
1	2	3	0	(Red)
2	3	0	1
3	0	1	2

1	2	3	3
3	2	1	1	(Green)
1	3	2	1
1	2	3	2

3	2	2	3
0	1	3	2	(Blue)
1	3	1	2
1	3	2	1

1. Apply the K-means clustering algorithm to classify the image into two clusters with two initial cluster centers given.
2. Use the fuzzy C-means algorithm (FCM) to classify the image into two clusters with two initial cluster centers given.
3. Apply the fuzzy weighted C-means algorithm (FWCM) to classify the image into two clusters with two initial cluster centers given.
4. Perform the new weighted fuzzy C-means algorithm (NW-FCM) to classify the image into two clusters with two initial cluster centers given.
5. Apply the PCA algorithm to classify the image into two clusters with two initial cluster centers given.

References

1. Abe S (2010) Support vector machines for pattern recognition, 2nd edn. Springer
2. Ahalt SC, Krishnamurthy AK, Chen P, Melton DE (1990) Competitive learning algorithms for vector quantization. Neural Netw 3:277–290
3. Bezdek JC (1981) Pattern recognition with fuzzy objective function algorithms. Plenum Press, New York
4. Bonabeau E, Dorigo M, Theraulaz G (1999) Swarm intelligence: from natural to artificial systems. Santa Fe institute studies on the sciences of complexity. Oxford University Press
5. Boser BE, Guyon IM, Vapnik VN (1992) A training algorithm for optimal margin classifiers. In: Proceedings of the fifth annual workshop on computational learning theory, pp 144–152
6. Bradford D, Hung C-C (2012) Pollen-based bee algorithm for data clustering—a computational model. Prog Intell Comput Appl (PICA) 1(1):16–36
7. Camps-Valls G, Bruzzone L (2005) Kernel-based methods for hyperspectral image classification. IEEE Trans Geosci Remote Sens 43(6):1351–1362
8. Casper E, Hung C-C (2013) Quantum modeled clustering algorithms for image segmentation. Prog Intell Comput Appl (PICA) 2(1):1–21
9. Davies DL, Bouldin DW (1976) A cluster separation measure. IEEE Trans Pattern Anal Mach Intell PAMI-1(2):224–227
10. Dorigo M, Maniezzo V, Colorni A (1996) Ant system: optimization by a colony of cooperating agents. IEEE Trans Syst Man Cyber Part B 26:29–41
11. Fukunaga K (1990) Statistical pattern recognition, 2nd edn. Morgan Kaufmann
12. Goldberg E (1989) Genetic algorithms in search, optimization, and machine learning. Addison-Wesley, Reading, MA
13. Griffiths D (2005) Introduction to quantum mechanics. Pearson, Upper Saddle River
14. Hart P (1968) The condensed nearest neighbor rule. IEEE Trans Inf Theory IT-14:515–516
15. Hertz J, Krogh A, Palmer RG (1991) Introduction to the theory of neural computation. Addison-Wesley, Redwood City
16. Hung C-C, Kulcarni S, Kuo B-C (2011) A new weighted fuzzy C-means clustering algorithm for remotely sensed image classification. IEEE J Sel Top Signal Process 5(3):543–553
17. Hung C-C, Casper E, Kuo B-C, Liu W, Jung E, Yang M (2013) A quantum-modeled fuzzy C-means clustering algorithm for remotely sensed multi-band image segmentation. In: Proceedings of the IEEE international geoscience and remote sensing symposium (IGARSS '13) (In press)
18. Hung C-C, Casper E, Kuo B-C, Liu W, Jung E, Yang M (2013) A quantum-modeled artificial bee colony clustering algorithm for remotely sensed multi-band image segmentation. In: Proceedings of the IEEE international geoscience and remote sensing symposium (IGARSS '13) (In press)
19. Hung C-C, Coleman T, Scheunders P (1998) The genetic algorithm approach and K-means clustering: their role in unsupervised training in image classification. In: Proceedings of the international conference on computer graphics and imaging, Halifax, Canada, June 1998
20. Hung C-C, Fahsi A, Coleman T (1999) Image classification. In: Encyclopedia of electrical and electronics engineering. Wiley, pp 506–521
21. Hung C-C, Jung E, Kuo B-C, Zhang Y (2011) A new weighted fuzzy C-means algorithm for hyperspectral image classification. In: The 2011 IEEE international geoscience & remote sensing symposium (IGARSS), Vancouver, Canada, 25–29 July 2011
22. Hung C-C, Saatchi S, Pham M, Xiang M, Coleman T (2005) A comparison of ant colony optimization and simulated annealing in the K-means algorithm for clustering. In: Proceedings of the 6th international conference on intelligent technologies (InTech'05), Phuket, Thailand, 14–16 Dec 2005
23. Hung C-C, Xu L, Kuo B-C, Liu W (2014) Ant colony optimization and K-means algorithm with spectral information divergence. In: The 2014 IEEE international geoscience & remote sensing symposium (IGARSS), Quebec, Canada, 13–18 July 2014

24. John ST, Nello C (2004) Kernel methods for pattern analysis. Cambridge University Press
25. Jozwik A (1983) A learning scheme for a fuzzy k-NN rule. Pattern Recognit Lett 1:287–289
26. Keller JM, Gray MR, Givens JA Jr (1985) A fuzzy K-nearest neighbor algorithm. IEEE Trans Syst Man Cybern SMC-15(4):580–585
27. Kim KI, Jung K, Park SH, Kim HJ (2002) Support vector machines for texture classification. IEEE Trans Pattern Anal Mach Intell 24(11):1542–1550
28. Krishnapuram R, Keller JM (1993) A possibilistic approach to clustering. IEEE Trans Fuzzy Syst 1(2):98–110
29. Krishnapuram R, Keller JM (1996) The possibilistic c-means algorithm: insights and recommendations. IEEE Trans Fuzzy Syst 4(3):385–393
30. Kuo B-C, Landgrebe DA (2004) Nonparametric weighted feature extraction for classification. IEEE Trans Geosci Remote Sens 42(5):1096–1105
31. Kuo B-C, Ho H-H, Li C-H, Hung C-C, Taur J-S (2013) A kernel-based feature selection method for SVM with RBF kernel for hyperspectral image classification. IEEE J Sel Top Appl Earth Obs Remote Sens 317–326. https://doi.org/10.1109/JSTARS.2013.2262926
32. Landgrebe DA (2003) Signal theory methods in multispectral remote sensing. Wiley
33. Li CH, Huang WC, Kuo BC, Hung C-C (2008) A novel fuzzy weighted C-means method for image classification. Int J Fuzzy Syst 10(3):168–173
34. Lippmann RP (1987) An introduction to computing with neural nets. I.E.E.E. A.S.S.P. Mag 27(11):4–22
35. Liu B (2004) Uncertainty theory: an introduction to its axiomatic foundations. Springer, Berlin
36. Liu B (2006) A survey of credibility theory. Fuzzy Optim Decis Mak 5(4):387–408
37. Liu B, Liu YK (2002) Expected value of fuzzy variable and fuzzy expected value models. IEEE Trans Fuzzy Syst 10(4):445–450
38. Liu W, Chen H, Yan Q, Liu Z, Xu J, Yu Z (2010) A novel quantum-inspired evolutionary algorithm based on variable angle-distance rotation. In: IEEE congress on evolutionary computation (CEC), pp 1–7
39. Melgani F, Bruzzone L (2004) Classification of hyperspectral remote sensing images with support vector machines. IEEE Trans Geosci Remote Sens 42(8):1778–1790
40. Metropolis N, Rosenbluth AW, Rosenbluth MN, Teller AH, Teller E (1953) Equations of state calculations by fast computing machines. J Chem Phys 21:1087–1091
41. Mohammed AM, Elhefhawy NA, El-Sherbiny MM, Hadoud MM (2012) Quantum crossover based quantum genetic algorithm for solving non-linear programming. In: The 8th international conference on informatics and systems (INFOS), pp BIO-145–BIO-153, 14–16 May 2012
42. Nielsen M, Chung I (2010) Quantum computation and quantum information. Cambridge University Press, New York
43. Pham DT, Otri S, Afify A, Mahmuddin M, Al-Jabbouli H (2007) Data clustering using the bees algorithm. In: Proceedings of the 40th CIRP international manufacturing systems seminar, Liverpool
44. Richards JA, Jia X (2006) Remote sensing digital image analysis: an introduction, 4th edn. Springer
45. Runkler TA, Bezdek JC (1999) Function approximation with polynomial membership functions and alternating cluster estimation. Fuzzy Sets Syst 101:207–218
46. Runkler TA, Bezdek JC (1999) Alternating cluster estimation: a new tool for clustering and function approximation. IEEE Trans Fuzzy Syst 7:377–393
47. Saatchi S, Hung C-C (2005) Hybridization of the ant colony optimization with the K-means algorithm for clustering. Lecture notes in computer science (LNCS 3540, pp 511–520) SCIA 2005: image analysis. Springer
48. Scheunders P (1997) A genetic C-means clustering algorithm applied to color image quantization. Pattern Recognit 30(6):859–866
49. Swain PH, Davis SM (eds) (1978) Remote sensing: the quantitative approach. McGraw-Hill

50. Tao JT, Gonzalez RC (1974) Pattern recognition principles. Addison-Wesley
51. Tomek I (1976) A generalization of the K-NN rule. IEEE Trans Syst Man Cybern SMC-6 (2):121–126
52. Tuia D, Camps-Valls G, Matasci G, Kanevski M (2010) Learning relevant image features with multiple-kernel classification. IEEE Trans Geosci Remote Sens 48(10):3780–3791
53. Vapnik VN (2001) The nature of statistical learning theory, 2nd edn. Springer, New York
54. Wang X (1982) On the gradient inverse weighted filter. IEEE Trans Signal Process 40 (2):482–484
55. Wasserman PD (1989) Neural computing: theory and practice. Van Nostrand Reinhold, New York
56. Xiang M, Hung C-C, Kuo B-C, Coleman T (2005) A parallelepiped multispectral image classifier using genetic algorithms. In: Proceedings of the 2005 IEEE international geoscience & remote sensing symposium (IGARSS), Seoul, Korea, 25–29 July 2005
57. Yang M-S, Wu K-L (2006) Unsupervised possibilistic clustering. Pattern Recognit 39 (1):5–21
58. Yang X-S (2010) Nature-inspired metaheuristic algorithms, 2nd edn. Luniver Press
59. Yanofsky NS, Mannucci MA (2008) Quantum computing for computer scientists. Cambridge University Press, New York
60. Zadeh LA (1965) Fuzzy sets. Inf Control 8:338–353
61. Zadeh LA (1978) Fuzzy sets as a basis for a theory of possibility. Fuzzy Sets Syst 1:3–28
62. Zhou J, Wang Q, Hung C-C, Yang F (2017) Credibilistic clustering algorithms via alternating cluster estimation. J Intell Manuf 28(3):727–738
63. Zhou J, Wang Q, Hung C-C, Yi X (2015) Credibilistic clustering: the model and algorithms. Int J Uncertain Fuzziness Knowl Based Syst 23(4):545–564
64. Zhou J, Hung C-C (2007) A generalized approach to possibilistic clustering algorithms. Int J Uncertain Fuzziness Knowl Based Syst 15(Supp. 2):117–138
65. Zhou J, Hung C-C, Wang X, Chen S (2007) Fuzzy clustering based on credibility measure. In: Proceedings of the sixth international conference on information and management sciences, Lhasa, China, pp 404–411, 1–6 July 2007

Dimensionality Reduction and Sparse Representation

4

Nature does not hurry, yet everything is accomplished.

—Lao Tzu

Image representation is a fundamental issue in signal processing, pattern recognition, and computer vision. An efficient image representation can lead to the development of effective algorithms for the interpretation of images. Since Marr proposed the fundamental principle of the *primary sketch* concept of a scene [28], many image representations have been developed based on this concept. The primary sketch refers to the edges, lines, regions, and others in an image. These are also called *parts of objects*. These are characteristic features which can be extracted from an image by transforming an image from the pixel-level to a higher level representation for image understanding. This step is usually considered as a low-level transformation.

Many different techniques of transformation have been developed in the literature for signal and image representation. Those techniques can be used for image transformations which will result in efficient representation of characteristic features (or called intrinsic dimension). Dimensionality reduction (DR) and sparse representation (SR) are two representative schemes frequently used in the transform for reducing the dimension of a dataset. These transformations include principle component analysis (PCA), singular value decomposition (SVD), non-negative matrix factorization (NMF), and sparse coding (SC). The study of the mammal brain suggests that only a small number of active neurons encode sensory information at any given point [26, 30]. This finding has led to the rapid development of sparse coding which refers to a small number of nonzero entries in a feature vector. Due to many zeros or small nonzeros in a feature vector, it is called the sparsity of the feature vector. Hence, it is important to represent the sparsity for the dataset by eliminating the data redundancy for applications [6, 34]. The ultimate goal is to have a compact, efficient, and compressed representation of the input data.

© Springer Nature Switzerland AG 2019
C.-C. Hung et al., *Image Texture Analysis*,
https://doi.org/10.1007/978-3-030-13773-1_4

In the following sections, we will introduce the Hughes effect in the classification of images. Due to this effect, dimensionality reduction is frequently used to solve this problem. We will then present the basis vector concept from linear algebra. Based on this concept, the principle component analysis (PCA), singular value decomposition (SVD), non-negative matrix factorization (NMF), and sparse coding (SC) will be introduced. The PCA is one of the dimensionality reduction methods developed earlier and is widely used in pattern recognition and remote sensing image interpretation. Please note that since a basis image can be represented as a basis vector, we use both terms interchangeably in the following discussions.

4.1　The Hughes Effect and Dimensionality Reduction (DR)

In a high-dimensional space, we usually encounter the problem of shortage of training samples for a model. For example, assume that the number of dimensions (i.e., features) for the multispectral images is d and the number of training samples is s. If s is much smaller than d (i.e., $s \ll d$), s may be too small for accurate parameter estimation for a classification model. Most of the classification algorithms for hyperspectral images which usually have hundreds of dimensions run into the Hughes phenomenon [12]. When the training samples are fixed and the spatial dimensions are increased, the classification accuracy reaches a maximum value for a given size and then decreases, even the number of dimensions are continuously increased. The Hughes phenomenon is shown in Fig. 4.1a where mean recognition accuracy represented in the vertical axis is plotted versus measurement complexity in the horizontal axis.

Because of this Hughes effect, dimensionality reduction (DR) is an important technique in reducing the number of dimensions. If we consider that a dimension is a feature, DR becomes the problem of feature selection (FS) or feature extraction (FE). Feature selection method is to determine a subset of the original features. It is a critical issue for a feature selection algorithm to find a subset of features that is

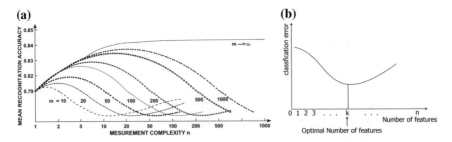

Fig. 4.1　a The Hughes phenomenon shows that even the number of dimensions represented in the horizontal axis increased, the recognition accuracy (denoted by the vertical axis) is still decreased; **b** the classification error will be the minimum if an optimal number of features can be found

still discriminative for classification after a reduction on the number of features. Feature extraction is to transform the original feature space to a low-dimensional subspace [18]. In addition, some new features can be reconstructed based on the original set of features, and then it is used for the classification. The objective of feature selection and feature extraction is to find an optimal number of features so that the classification error is minimized as shown in Fig. 4.1b. The optimality refers to a minimum set of features that are discriminative when used in the classification. In the pattern recognition and remote sensing image interpretation, principal component analysis (PCA) has been a widely used dimensionality reduction technique [3, 4, 33]. Nonparametric weighted feature extraction (NWFE) is a widely used supervised dimensionality reduction method for hyperspectral image data [19]. A number of techniques have been developed for both feature selection and feature extraction to identify the most informative features [33].

Mathematically, dimensionality reduction such as the PCA can be regarded as solving a matrix which is replaced by a low-rank matrix. If we denote the original matrix as A, a low-rank approximation for matrix A is another matrix L with a rank lower than that of matrix A. Here, rank is defined as the maximum number of linearly independent vectors in a matrix, which is equal to the number of nonzero rows if we use elementary row operations on the matrix [17]. The objective is to minimize the error of difference between these two matrices using Eq. 4.1 in order to have a good approximation.

$$Minimize \|A - L\|_m, m \text{ is a matrix norm} \tag{4.1}$$

If the rank of A is n, we are looking for the rank of L which will be satisfied with the relationship $m \ll n$. This means that if we need n basis vectors to span A, only m basis vectors needed to span L. In other words, we try to find a set of the best basis vectors with size m so that we can produce a good approximation of matrix A. Therefore, we use a linear combination of the basis vectors with a coefficient vector of size m to replace the original vector of size n. In doing so, we reduce the original dimensions from n to m with m is much smaller than n.

However, the problem with such a minimization formulated in Eq. 4.1 is that there is no guarantee that the technique will preserve and generate the discriminative features for the optimal classification. In a sense, the minimization should be optimal for image classification.

4.2 The Basis and Dimension

The concept of dimensionality reduction (and sparse coding), perhaps, can be traced back to the study of the structure of a vector space in linear algebra in which we can determine a set of basis vectors that completely describes (spans) a vector space. In doing so, any vector on that space can be represented as a linear combination of a set of basis vectors. PCA is an example of this type of transformation. However, a basis vector obtained in the linear algebra is not sparse. A square matrix can be used to denote a set of basis vectors. Similarly, in the computation of a set of basis vectors for sparse coding, we model the data vectors as the sparse linear combination of basis vectors, called *dictionary*. Each of basis vectors, which form the dictionary, is called *atom*. Such a dictionary is also represented as a matrix. This matrix is usually derived through the dictionary learning [6, 34]. Unlike the matrix used for the basis vectors in linear algebra, the matrix for the dictionary is over-complete (this means that the matrix is not square). The difference between the basis vectors in linear algebra and the sparse coding is that the atoms in a dictionary may have a higher dimensional length in the basis vector than the input signal vector and most of the components in each atom are zero.

To lay out a foundation for representing an image with a set of basis images, we will review the basis and dimension with some examples in the vector space. Linear algebra provides us a rich groundwork for the relationship of the basis and dimension [17]. In a vector space V $(V \subseteq R^n)$, a set of vectors in V can be determined to completely describe V. The notation R^n represents an n-dimensional real number space. We give the definition of a set of basis vectors from [17].

Definition 4.1 A set of vectors $S = \{X_1, X_2, \ldots, X_n\}$ in a vector space V is called a *basis* for V if S spans V and S is linearly independent.

Based on Definition 4.1, any vector X in a vector space V $(V \subseteq R^d)$ can be represented as in Eq. 4.2.

$$X = a_1 X_1 + a_2 X_2 + \cdots + a_n X_n \qquad (4.2)$$

Therefore, some properties associated with the definition of the basis vectors can be summarized below:

(1) If $S = \{X_1, X_2, \ldots, X_n\}$ is a basis for a vector space V, then every vector in V can be written in one and only one way as a linear combination of the basis vectors in S [17].
(2) A set of basis vectors in S is linearly independent (i.e., orthogonal). Hence, it is also called a set of orthogonal basis vectors.
(3) If the magnitude of each basis vector is unity, it is called a set of orthonormal basis vectors.
(4) A vector space has many different bases and all bases have the same number of vectors.

The dimension of a vector space V is defined in the following [17]:

Definition 4.2 Let V be a subspace of $\mathbf{R}^d$ for some d. The number of vectors in a basis for a vector space $V \subseteq \mathbf{R}^d$ is called the *dimension* of V. We often write dim V for the dimension of V.

Examples 4.1, 4.2, and 4.3 given below show that a vector is represented by a set of basis vectors.

Example 4.1 The set $S = \{X_1, X_2, X_3\}$ with $X_1 = (1, 0, 0)$, $X_2 = (0, 1, 0)$, and $X_3 = (0, 0, 1)$ is a *basis* for R^3 where 3 is a dimension.

Example 4.2 A general vector $X = (6, 7, 8)$ can be represented as $X = 6X_1 + 7X_2 + 8X_3$ using the basis given in Example 4.1.

Example 4.3 If a set of the basis $S = \{X_1, X_2, X_3, X_4\}$ with $X_1 = \begin{bmatrix} 1 & 0 \\ 0 & 0 \end{bmatrix}$, $X_2 = \begin{bmatrix} 0 & 1 \\ 0 & 0 \end{bmatrix}$, $X_3 = \begin{bmatrix} 0 & 0 \\ 1 & 0 \end{bmatrix}$, and $X_4 = \begin{bmatrix} 0 & 0 \\ 0 & 1 \end{bmatrix}$. Then, a matrix $A = \begin{bmatrix} 2 & 1 \\ 6 & 1 \end{bmatrix}$ is a linear combination of all of 2×2 matrices. It is represented as

$$A = 2 \times X_1 + 1 \times X_2 + 6 \times X_3 + 1 \times X_4 \tag{4.3}$$

4.3 The Basis and Image

As an analogy to the basis vectors for coordinate systems in which a vector is expressed as a linear combination of the orthogonal basis vectors (Eq. 4.2), the standard basis for any image is a set of basis (images) as shown in Eq. 4.4 in the following. A simple numerical example is given in Example 4.4. This example is exactly the same as Example 4.3 since an image can be represented in a matrix format.

Example 4.4 A general image of $\begin{bmatrix} 2 & 1 \\ 6 & 1 \end{bmatrix}$ is described by the following linear combination of four basis images of $\left\{ \begin{bmatrix} 1 & 0 \\ 0 & 0 \end{bmatrix}, \begin{bmatrix} 0 & 1 \\ 0 & 0 \end{bmatrix}, \begin{bmatrix} 0 & 0 \\ 1 & 0 \end{bmatrix}, \begin{bmatrix} 0 & 0 \\ 0 & 1 \end{bmatrix} \right\}$.

$$I = \begin{bmatrix} 2 & 1 \\ 6 & 1 \end{bmatrix} = 2 \begin{bmatrix} 1 & 0 \\ 0 & 0 \end{bmatrix} + 1 \begin{bmatrix} 0 & 1 \\ 0 & 0 \end{bmatrix} + 6 \begin{bmatrix} 0 & 0 \\ 1 & 0 \end{bmatrix} + 1 \begin{bmatrix} 0 & 0 \\ 0 & 1 \end{bmatrix} \tag{4.4}$$

Similar to the basis in linear algebra, the standard basis (images) is not the only one which we can use to describe a general image. Example 4.5 gives a set of basis images to a 2×2 image $\begin{bmatrix} 2 & 1 \\ 6 & 1 \end{bmatrix}$ used in Example 4.4. This set of basis images is called the Hadamard basis.

Fig. 4.2 Hadamard basis
images are used in
Example 4.5

Example 4.5 The Hadamard basis (basis images shown here for a 2×2 image, where white represents a pixel of $+1$ and black represents a pixel of -1. The basis images consist of $\left\{ \begin{bmatrix} 1 & 1 \\ 1 & 1 \end{bmatrix}, \begin{bmatrix} -1 & 1 \\ -1 & 1 \end{bmatrix}, \begin{bmatrix} -1 & -1 \\ 1 & 1 \end{bmatrix}, \begin{bmatrix} 1 & -1 \\ -1 & 1 \end{bmatrix} \right\}$. Their image representation is shown in Fig. 4.2.

Similar to Example 4.4, we can express a general image of $\begin{bmatrix} 2 & 1 \\ 6 & 1 \end{bmatrix}$ using the following linear combination of this new set of basis images as

$$I = \begin{bmatrix} 2 & 1 \\ 6 & 1 \end{bmatrix} = \frac{1}{2} \left\{ 5 \begin{bmatrix} 1 & 1 \\ 1 & 1 \end{bmatrix} - 3 \begin{bmatrix} -1 & 1 \\ -1 & 1 \end{bmatrix} + 2 \begin{bmatrix} -1 & -1 \\ 1 & 1 \end{bmatrix} - 2 \begin{bmatrix} 1 & -1 \\ -1 & 1 \end{bmatrix} \right\}$$
(4.5)

The coefficient in each basis image is the projection of $\begin{bmatrix} 2 & 1 \\ 6 & 1 \end{bmatrix}$ onto the corresponding basis image using the dot product operation. In fact, these are the coordinates of the image in the Hadamard space [4]. In other words, the image of $\begin{bmatrix} 2 & 1 \\ 6 & 1 \end{bmatrix}$ has been mapped to a new space using the Hadamard transform.

This example shows that an image can be expressed as a linear combination by multiplying each basis image by a coefficient. Many discrete image transform methods can achieve this purpose by using the forward transform. Based on the examples given above, we can see that the forward transform is a process of breaking an image into its elemental components in terms of a set of the basis images. This set of basis images forms the so-called *transformation matrix* (also called the forward transformation matrix). In other words, it is a projection of an image onto the corresponding basis image using the dot product operation. There exist some image transforms which are frequently used including the Fourier transform, wavelet transform, and sinusoidal transform [8]. To obtain the original image from the transformed domain, the so-called *inverse transformation matrix* is used. In other words, the inverse transformation is a process of reconstructing the original image in terms of its elemental components (i.e., a set of basis images used in the forward transform) through the linear combination of multiplications and summations. Example 4.6 shows the forward and inverse discrete Fourier transform for an image.

Example 4.6 The forward and inverse discrete Fourier transform for a two-dimensional image, $f(k, l)$ with a size of N × N where variables u and v denote the Fourier domain and variables k and l represent the spatial image domain. The function $F(u, v)$ is the transformed image (is usually called frequency) in the Fourier domain.

The forward transform is

$$F(u,v) = \frac{1}{N} \sum_{k=0}^{N-1} \sum_{l=0}^{N-1} f(k,l) e^{-j2\pi\left(u\frac{k}{N} + v\frac{l}{N}\right)} \tag{4.6}$$

The inverse transform is

$$f(k,l) = \frac{1}{N} \sum_{u=0}^{N-1} \sum_{v=0}^{N-1} F(u,v) e^{j2\pi\left(k\frac{u}{N} + l\frac{v}{N}\right)} \tag{4.7}$$

In the literature, the matrix factorization techniques are often used to obtain the basis functions (i.e., vectors or images). For example, the singular value decomposition (SVD) and non-negative matrix factorization (NMF) are widely used techniques [10]. Mathematically, if the image is represented by a matrix $\mathbf{X} = \{x_1, x_2, \ldots, x_n\} \in \mathbf{R}^{m\times n}$, the matrix factorization can be defined as finding two matrices $\mathbf{U} \in \mathbf{R}^{m\times k}$ and $\mathbf{A} \in \mathbf{R}^{k\times n}$ such that Eq. 4.8 holds.

$$\mathbf{X} \cong \mathbf{UA} \tag{4.8}$$

The formula shows that the product of two decomposed matrices $\mathbf{U}$ and $\mathbf{A}$ should be equal or appropriate to $\mathbf{X}$ [3]. In general, the basis functions of $\mathbf{U}$ should capture the intrinsic features which are hidden in the image (i.e., $\mathbf{X}$) and each column of $\mathbf{A}$ should be sparse which give weights in the linear combination of the basis functions of $\mathbf{U}$ [3]. The factorization concept can be represented as shown in Fig. 4.3:

$$U = \begin{bmatrix} u_{11} & 0 & \cdots & 0 \\ u_{21} & u_{22} & \cdots & 0 \\ \vdots & \vdots & \ddots & \vdots \\ u_{m1} & u_{m2} & \cdots & u_{mm} \end{bmatrix} \quad A = \begin{bmatrix} a_{11} & a_{12} & \cdots & a_{1m} \\ 0 & a_{22} & \cdots & a_{2m} \\ \vdots & \vdots & \ddots & \vdots \\ 0 & 0 & \cdots & a_{mm} \end{bmatrix}$$

Fig. 4.3 An illustration of matrix factorization; X = UA. We assume that X is a nonsingular square matrix with m x m. Matrix X can be decomposed into two matrices U and A where U is a lower triangular matrix and A is an upper triangular matrix

4.4 Vector Quantization (VQ)

Vector quantization (VQ) is an encoding technique that has been used in speech and image encoding and pattern recognition [21]. VQ is one of the compressed representations developed in the early days for data encoding. Conceptually, an image is divided into a number of distinct blocks and a representative vector is learned for each block. A set of possible representative vectors is called the *codebook* of the quantizer, and each member is called *codeword*. Hence, the vector quantization can be regarded as one of the sparse representations. The Linde–Buzo–Gray (LBG) algorithm is a popular method for the generation of the codebook, which results in a low distortion rate based on the peak signal-noise-ratio (PSNR) measure [1]. As a codebook determines the quality of encoding, it is important to choose an appropriate codebook. The optimization technique can be used for generating an optimal codebook [9]. Figure 4.4 represents an example of the vector quantization to an image input.

The LBG algorithm is given below in a step-by-step procedure [21]. The algorithm is a type of competitive learning method. It is quite similar to the k-means algorithm and the Kohon's self-organizing map neural networks as we discussed in Chap. 3.

The LBG algorithm for Vector Quantization:

Step 1: Initialize the number of codewords from codebook, K, their initial codewords (same as the cluster centers), the convergence criterion, ε, and the maximum number of iterations (Max-It). In addition, set an initial distance $D_0 = 0$ and the iteration number k = 0.

Repeat the following steps for each vector in the training dataset. Assume that the training vectors of $S = \{x_i \in R^d | i = 1, 2, \ldots, n\}$ and an initialization of a codebook $C = \{c_j \in R^d | j = 1, 2, \ldots, n\}$.

Step 2: Each vector is assigned to a cluster based on the minimum distance to the cluster centers. Mathematically, it is expressed as in Eq. 4.9.

$$x_i \in c_q \text{ if } \left\| x_i - c_q \right\|_p \leq \left\| x_i - c_j \right\|_p \text{ for } j \neq q \qquad (4.9)$$

where the notation $\|.\|_p$ represents the Minkowski distance.

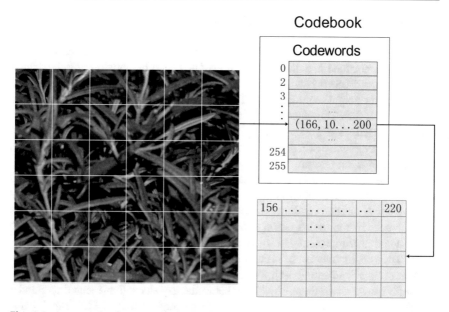

Fig. 4.4 An example of vector quantization by dividing an image into several pieces of blocks. Each block is represented by a codeword from the codebook

Step 3: Each of the cluster centers is updated by calculating the average of the vectors assigned to each cluster. Mathematically, it is updated as in Eq. 4.10.

$$c_j = \frac{1}{|S_j|} \sum_{x_i \in S_j} x_i | j = 1, 2, \ldots, K \qquad (4.10)$$

Step 4: Increase the number of iterations k by one (i.e., $k \leftarrow k + 1$) and calculate the distortion (difference) as below:

$$D_k = \sum_{j=1}^{K} \sum_{x_i \in S_j} \left\| x_i - c_j \right\|_p \qquad (4.11)$$

Step 5: If $\frac{D_{k-1} - D_k}{D_k} > \epsilon$, or the number of iterations, k is less than Max-It, repeat Steps 2–5.

Step 6: Output the codebook $C = \{c_j \in R^d | j = 1, 2, \ldots, n\}$.

4.5   Principal Component Analysis (PCA)

Principal component analysis (PCA) is a linear transformation that removes the correlation embedded in a dataset. This is accomplished by transforming the dataset to a new coordinate system [3, 4]. This new set of coordinates represents the orthogonal principal components. The PCA was developed by Pearson and Hotelling [11, 32]. Therefore, it is also called the Hotelling transform. The PCA is frequently used as a dimensionality reduction method in pattern recognition to reduce the complexity of a dataset. If we stack several (say k) multispectral images with a size of n x n (assuming they are registered and properly aligned), each pixel will then be a vector with k components. Hence, a matrix of $n^2 \times k$ can be formed where n^2 is the number of rows and k is the number of columns. Those elements in each vector are called random variables and each variable is a dimension in this vector space. In the multispectral and hyperspectral image analysis, the PCA will create a compact representation of multiple images based on the principal components. Those components are orthogonal and hence uncorrelated [15]. Figure 4.5a illustrates a stack of multispectral images are cascaded for the transformation and Fig. 4.5b shows a two-dimensional dataset in the x-y space (represented as Band 1 and Band 2) is transformed into the x'-y' space (represented as PCA Band 1 and PCA Band 2). The PCA transforms a correlated dataset into an uncorrelated dataset in a different coordinate system.

The transformation results of the PCA on the most discriminative information will be concentrated on the first few principal components. In other words, the first principal component creates maximum possible variation in the images, and each succeeding component obtains as much of the remaining variability as possible. In general, most of the information will be kept in a few principal components. If we discard the principal components with low variances, we will have the minimal information loss.

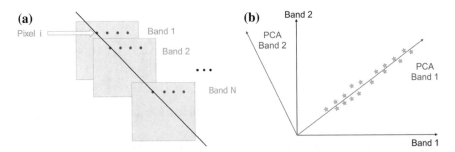

Fig. 4.5 An illustration of the principal component analysis (PCA); **a** a stack of multispectral images (i.e., bands) to be formed for the PCA transformation and **b** demonstrates a set of pixel vectors are transformed into uncorrelated pixel vectors in the space of multispectral images. Please note that a pixel vector with only two bands are shown here

The PCA reduces feature vector space from a large number of dimensions (variables) to a smaller number of dimensions of each feature vector. It is an unsupervised learning algorithm to discover the intrinsic features embedded in a dataset. The PCA assumes that the relationships among variables in the dataset are linear. If the structure of the dataset is nonlinear, the principal components obtained will not be an effective representation of the dataset. The PCA has been proved as an effective transformation method for an image classification algorithm to improve the classification accuracy [13]. The PCA is widely used in the remote sensing image interpretation [33].

Similar to the linear transformation in linear algebra, the PCA is formulated as in the following: if the K original variables are represented as $X = \{x_1, x_2, \ldots, x_k\}$ and the output of the transformation is $Y = \{y_1, y_2, \ldots, y_k\}$. We will have the following expressions (Eq. 4.12):

$$
\begin{aligned}
y_1 &= a_{11}x_1 + a_{12}x_2 + \cdots + a_{1k}x_k \\
y_2 &= a_{21}x_1 + a_{22}x_2 + \cdots + a_{2k}x_k \\
&\cdots \\
y_k &= a_{k1}x_1 + a_{k2}x_2 + \cdots + a_{kk}x_k
\end{aligned}
\tag{4.12}
$$

Equation 4.12 can be expressed in the matrix format below:

$$
Y = AX \tag{4.13}
$$

where A is the transformation matrix which is the collection of coefficients a_{ij} in Eq. 4.12. The PCA transformation is to make the output $\{y_1, y_2, \ldots, y_{k-1}, y_k\}$ uncorrelated (i.e., orthogonal). Each of the variables is called *principal component*. The procedure for the PCA transformation is listed below.

Principal Component Analysis (PCA) Algorithm:

Step 1: Let m be the mean vector (taking the mean of all feature vectors from the original dataset X).

$$
m = \frac{1}{K} \sum_{k=1}^{K} X_k \tag{4.14}
$$

Step 2: Adjust the original data X by subtracting the mean (i.e., $X' = X - m$) for each feature vector.

Step 3: Compute the covariance matrix C of adjusted X'.

$$
C = \frac{1}{K} \sum_{k=1}^{K} X'_k X'^{T}_k \tag{4.15}
$$

Step 4: Find the eigenvectors and eigenvalues of C.

Step 5: Select the first p eigenvectors e_i where p is the number of eigenvalues that are ranked from the largest eigenvalues to form a new set of the feature vectors (principal components).

A numerical example to illustrate the PCA transformation is given in Example 4.7.

Example 4.7 Assume that we have the following dataset.

$$\begin{bmatrix} 1 \\ 2 \\ 3 \end{bmatrix} \quad \begin{bmatrix} 4 \\ 5 \\ 6 \end{bmatrix} \quad \begin{bmatrix} 7 \\ 8 \\ 9 \end{bmatrix}$$

Step 1:   Calculate the mean for all the feature vectors.

$$\begin{bmatrix} 4 \\ 5 \\ 6 \end{bmatrix}$$

Step 2:   Subtract the mean vector from each feature vector.

$$\begin{bmatrix} -3 \\ -3 \\ -3 \end{bmatrix} \quad \begin{bmatrix} 0 \\ 0 \\ 0 \end{bmatrix} \quad \begin{bmatrix} 3 \\ 3 \\ 3 \end{bmatrix}$$

Step 3:   Calculate the covariance matrix.

$$\begin{bmatrix} 9 & 9 & 9 \\ 9 & 9 & 9 \\ 9 & 9 & 9 \end{bmatrix}$$

Step 4:   Calculate the eigenvectors and eigenvalues of the covariance matrix: each eigenvector is arranged as a row in the following matrix and eigenvalues are also shown in a matrix.

$$Eigenvectors = \begin{bmatrix} -5.77350269\mathrm{e}{-01} & 8.04908467\mathrm{e}{-01} & 1.09446620\mathrm{e}{-16} \\ -5.77350269\mathrm{e}{-01} & -5.21162995\mathrm{e}{-01} & 7.07106781\mathrm{e}{-01} \\ -5.77350269\mathrm{e}{-01} & -2.83745472\mathrm{e}{-01} & -7.07106781\mathrm{e}{-01} \end{bmatrix}$$

$$Eigenvalues = \begin{bmatrix} 2.70000000\mathrm{e}{+01} & 0 & 0 \\ 0 & -2.05116020\mathrm{e}{-15} & 0 \\ 0 & 0 & 1.76986475\mathrm{e}{-32} \end{bmatrix}$$

Step 5: Once eigenvectors are arranged based on the corresponding eigenvalues from the largest to the smallest, we can discard the eigenvectors corresponding to the smaller eigenvalues which represent the least information. If the eigenvector corresponding to the smallest eigenvalue is discarded, the first and second principal components will be retained for the PCA transformation matrix as shown below.

$$PCA = \begin{bmatrix} -5.77350269\mathrm{e}{-01} & 8.04908467\mathrm{e}{-01} & 1.09446620\mathrm{e}{-16} \\ 5.77350269\mathrm{e}{-01} & -5.21162995\mathrm{e}{-01} & 7.07106781\mathrm{e}{-16} \end{bmatrix}$$

Step 6: Derive the new dataset by multiplying the transformation matrix PCA from Step 5 with each original vector. The transformed vectors are given below:

$$\begin{bmatrix} 1.03 \\ -1.62 \end{bmatrix} \quad \begin{bmatrix} 1.72 \\ -4.92 \end{bmatrix} \quad \begin{bmatrix} 2.40 \\ -8.21 \end{bmatrix}$$

The PCA provides us a reduced dimensional representation while the sparse coding produces a high-dimensional representation in which only a few elements are nonzero. In PCA, the basis vectors derived from its square matrix are orthonormal. On the other hand, in sparse coding, an overcomplete set of basis vectors are used. Hence, its matrix is usually not square where an L_1 regularized optimization is needed for solving the sparse coding.

4.6 Singular Value Decomposition (SVD)

In image analysis, the singular value decomposition (SVD) is a technique which uses a rank-reduced approximation of intrinsic features embedded in a dataset for the generalization [10]. Similar to the PCA, the SVD is also used for the dimensionality reduction in machine learning. The SVD not only eliminates the collinearity in the original dataset but also reduces the number of features for better generalization in the machine learning.

Given an m × n matrix **A** of rank r, there exists a factorization (SVD) as follows:

$$\mathbf{A} = \mathbf{UDV}^t \tag{4.16}$$

where the columns of $\mathbf{U_{m \times m}}$ and $\mathbf{V_{n \times n}}$ are the orthonormal eigenvectors of $\mathbf{AA^t}$ and $\mathbf{A^tA}$, respectively. $\mathbf{D_{m \times n}}$ is a diagonal matrix with the *singular values* of **A**. This means

$$U^T U = I \tag{4.17}$$

$$\text{and } V^T V = VV^T = I \tag{4.18}$$

$$\text{also if } m = n, \text{ then } U^T U = UU^T = I. \tag{4.19}$$

SVD matrices are illustrated in Eq. 4.20 below. In general, *rank*(**A**) equals to the number of nonzero σ_i.

$$[A] = [U] \begin{bmatrix} \sigma_1 & 0 & 0 \\ 0 & \ddots & 0 \\ 0 & 0 & \sigma_n \end{bmatrix} [V]^T \tag{4.20}$$

where σ_i for i = 1, ..., n are singular values. If λ_i is an eigenvalue of A^TA (or AA^T), then $\lambda_i = \sigma_i^2$. Two important properties of the SVD are listed below:

(1) A square (n × n) matrix A is singular if at least one of its singular values σ_1, ..., σ_n is zero.
(2) The rank of matrix A is equal to the number of nonzero singular values σ_i.

Example 4.8 gives a numerical matrix and its SVD results.

Example 4.8 An example of a numerical matrix, A and its SVD results.

$$A = \begin{bmatrix} 1 & 2 & 3 \\ 4 & 5 & 6 \\ 7 & 8 & 9 \end{bmatrix}$$

Result of SVD: A = UDV^T

$$U = \begin{bmatrix} -0.21483724 & 0.88723069 & 0.40824829 \\ -0.52058739 & 0.24964395 & -0.81649658 \\ -0.82633754 & -0.38794278 & 0.40824829 \end{bmatrix}$$

$$D = \begin{bmatrix} 1.68481034e+01 & 0 & 0 \\ 0 & 1.06836951e+00 & 0 \\ 0 & 0 & 3.33475287e-16 \end{bmatrix}$$

$$V = \begin{bmatrix} -0.47967118 & -0.57236779 & -0.66506441 \\ -0.77669099 & -0.07568647 & 0.62531805 \\ -0.40824829 & 0.81649658 & -0.40824829 \end{bmatrix}$$

with the singular values arranged in the decreasing order.

One common definition for the norm of a matrix is the Frobenius norm shown in Eq. 4.21.

$$\|A\|_F = \sum_i \sum_j a_{ij}^2 \tag{4.21}$$

where a_{ij} are elements in the matrix A.

Frobenius norm can be computed from SVD by adding all σ_i as shown in Eq. 4.22 from the diagonal matrix **D**.

$$\|A\|_F = \sum_i \sigma_i^2 \tag{4.22}$$

If we want to find a best rank of k approximation to A, we may set all elements but the largest k singular values to zero. This will form compact representations (i.e., sparse representations) by eliminating columns of **U** and **V** corresponding to σ_i which is zero.

SVD can be used to compute optimal low-rank approximations that can be obtained by minimizing a matrix A of rank k using Eq. 4.23.

$$A_k = \min\|A - X\|_F, \text{ the rank of } X \text{ is } k \tag{4.23}$$

Both A_k and X are m × n matrices with the expected k ≪ r (assuming the number of diagonal elements is r). The solution of Eq. 4.23 is

$$A_k = U \, diag(\sigma_1, \ldots, \sigma_k, 0, \ldots, 0) V^T \tag{4.24}$$

where (r − k) smallest singular values are set to zero in Eq. 4.24.

Summary of the SVD Method

Step 1:   Any real m × n matrix A can be decomposed uniquely as shown in
             Eq. 4.16:

$$\mathbf{A} = \mathbf{UDV}^t$$

Step 2   The columns of $\mathbf{U}$ are eigenvectors of $\mathbf{AA}^t$ and the columns of V are
             eigenvectors of $\mathbf{A}^t\mathbf{A}$.

Step 3:   Calculate eigenvalues of $\mathbf{AA}^t$ (or $\mathbf{A}^t\mathbf{A}$) to form the diagonal matrix $\mathbf{D}$.

4.7   Non-negative Matrix Factorization (NMF)

Nonnegative matrix analysis is a low-rank approximation method of the matrix [22, 31]. The non-negative matrix factorization (NMF) technique decomposes an m x n matrix **A** to two matrices as shown in Eq. 4.25:

$$\mathbf{A}_{mxn} = \mathbf{W}_{mxr}\mathbf{H}_{rxn} \tag{4.25}$$

where m denotes nonnegative scalar variables, n denotes measurements forming the columns of matrix **A**, **W** a matrix of *basis vectors*, $r < \min(m, n)$, and **H** represents a matrix of coefficients. The matrix **H** is used for describing how strongly each building block (i.e., basis images from **W**) is present in the measurement vectors. Each column of **H** is also called *encoding*. Each basis image is a representation of localized features. Hence, a representation using the NMF is called *parts*-based structure [22, 31].

The **W** and **H** can be obtained by solving the optimization problem below (Eq. 4.26) [16]:

$$\min_{W,H} f_r(\mathbf{W}, \mathbf{H}) \equiv \frac{1}{2}\|\mathbf{A} - \mathbf{WH}\|_F^2 \; where \; \mathbf{W}, \mathbf{H} \geq 0 \tag{4.26}$$

where W and H are nonnegative matrices and r is the reduced dimension. Similar to some of the clustering algorithms, the NMF does not have a unique solution. Since the objective of the NMF is to find the parts-based structure (i.e., localized features), the NMF has been used as a clustering algorithm [16, 37]. It has been shown that the NMF produces a better characteristic structure (i.e., basis images) for a dataset than other matrix factorizations such as PCA [22, 31]. There are many NMF algorithms which can be used for obtaining the reduced matrices. These include: (1) basic NMF, (2) constrained NMF, (3) structured NMF, and (4) generalized NMF [38]. To optimize Eq. 4.26, an algorithm using the alternating nonnegative least squares (ANLS) for obtaining **W** and **H** was proposed by Paatero and Tapper [31]. The algorithm is listed below.

The NMF Algorithm Using Alternating Nonnegative Least Squares (ANLS):

Step 1:   Initialize $W \in R^{mxk}$ or $H \in R^{nxk}$ with nonnegative values and scale the columns of W to unit L_2-norm.

Step 2:   Iterate Eqs. 4.27 and 4.28 until both converge.

$$(a)\ \text{Solve } \min\|WH - A\|_F^2 \ for\ H(H \geq 0)\ \text{and } W \text{ is fixed} \qquad (4.27)$$

$$(b)\ \text{Solve } \min\|H^T W^T - A^T\|_F^2 \ for\ W(W \geq 0)\ \text{and } H \text{ is fixed} \qquad (4.28)$$

Step 3:   The columns of W are normalized to L_2-norm and the rows of H are scaled accordingly.

A fast NMF algorithm using the ANLS method has been developed by Kim and Park based on the nonnegative least squares [31]. Although the NMF is suitable for the square matrices, Eggert and Korner combined the concepts of NMF and sparse conditions to improve the NMF [5]. Their method is efficient compared to the standard NMF and is applicable to the overcomplete cases which will be discussed in the next section.

4.8   Sparse Representation—Sparse Coding

Sparse representation (SR) is an efficient model for representing and compressing high-dimensional images. Sparse representation is to mimic the topology of the underlying manifolds in the image [20, 25, 27, 35, 39]. Sparse coding has been used in image texture classification for the local sparse description of contents [7]. Similar to the principal component analysis (PCA), the SR is a compact representation for an image. However, unlike the PCA which is a representation by obtaining the orthonormal basis vectors, the SR uses an overcomplete set of basis vectors for sparse coding [20, 27, 35, 39]. A sparse coding algorithm learns a new representation of the input data and in that, it only has a few components which are significantly nonzeros. Hence, it is called sparse representation.

Traditionally, the analytic basis functions derived from a dataset based on the mathematical formulation have been used in the pattern recognition and image analysis. These analytic basis functions can be generated using the Fourier, Wavelet, and Discrete Cosine transforms. Unlike the analytic basis functions, sparse coding attempts to find those basis functions directly from the dataset. This is data-driven generated basis functions similar to the PCA. Strictly speaking, the PCA is usually not a sparse coding although some sparse PCA has been developed. It has been demonstrated that an overcomplete basis functions learned from the dataset for sparse representation mimics the human vision system [29]. For natural image analysis, predefined dictionaries (consisting of analytic basis functions) based on various types of transforms such as wavelets [24] have been used. However, learning the dictionary is illustrated to dramatically improve signal reconstruction [6, 34].

The foundation of sparse representation is to construct a dictionary which can represent a vector as a sparse linear combination of the training vectors [2, 6, 21, 30, 34]. If we denote a feature vector by x in the n-dimensional real number space, $\mathbf{R^n}$, the vector x is a sparse approximation over an overcomplete dictionary $\mathbf{D}$ in $\mathbf{R^{n \times m}}$ ($n \ll m$) which composes of m columns. Each column is called *atom*. In other words, we can find a linear combination of a few atoms from $\mathbf{D}$ that is close to the original vector X [6, 34]. In the matrix format, given a vector $X \in \mathbf{R^n}$ and a matrix $\mathbf{D} \in \mathbf{R^{n \times m}}$, we try to find a vector $\alpha \in \mathbf{R^m}$ such that Eq. 4.29 is satisfied.

$$X \approx \sum_{i=1}^{n} \sum_{j=1}^{m} d_i \alpha_j = \mathbf{D}\alpha \text{ where } d_i \in D. \tag{4.29}$$

In this formulation, the matrix $\mathbf{D}$ is called the *dictionary* and α is the sparse vector which contains the representation coefficients (α_j) of the vector. Figure 4.6 gives a diagram showing the decomposition of the SR scheme.

Let us take an example to clarify the concept of sparse representation and sparse approximation using a randomly generated vector and matrix [2] as shown below.

Example 4.9: Let x be an original feature vector, D dictionary, and α a sparse vector as shown below.

Fig. 4.6 A diagram shows the decomposition of the SR scheme

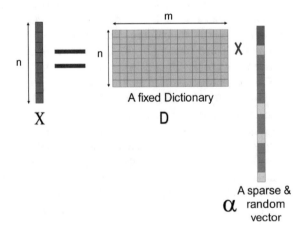

$$x = \begin{bmatrix} 0.3133 \\ 0.9635 \\ 0.4964 \\ 0.8721 \end{bmatrix}$$

$$D = \begin{bmatrix} 0.6579 & 0.7948 & 0.2346 & 0.8273 & 0.1276 \\ 0.9376 & 0.1298 & 0.3627 & 0.1432 & 0.8374 \\ 0.1425 & 0.8475 & 0.2982 & 0.1983 & 0.2934 \\ 0.1749 & 0.1938 & 0.1827 & 0.9238 & 0.9384 \end{bmatrix}$$

$$\alpha = \begin{bmatrix} 0 \\ 0 \\ 0.9283 \\ 0 \\ 0.7485 \end{bmatrix}$$

We will have the following equation: $x = D \times \alpha$. Hence, α is a sparse vector.

$$\begin{bmatrix} 0.3133 \\ 0.9635 \\ 0.4964 \\ 0.8721 \end{bmatrix} = \begin{bmatrix} 0.6579 & 0.7948 & 0.2346 & 0.8273 & 0.1276 \\ 0.9376 & 0.1298 & 0.3627 & 0.1432 & 0.8374 \\ 0.1425 & 0.8475 & 0.2982 & 0.1983 & 0.2934 \\ 0.1749 & 0.1938 & 0.1827 & 0.9238 & 0.9384 \end{bmatrix} \times \begin{bmatrix} 0 \\ 0 \\ 0.9283 \\ 0 \\ 0.7485 \end{bmatrix}$$

4.8.1 Dictionary Learning

Considering a finite training set of vectors $\mathbf{X} = \{x_1, x_2, \ldots, x_n\} \in \mathbf{R}^{m \times n}$ which can be represented by a dictionary $\mathbf{D}$ and a set of sparse coefficients $\boldsymbol{\alpha}$ using Eq. 4.30 [7]

$$\min_{D,\alpha} \sum_{i=1}^{m} \left(\frac{1}{2} \|X_i - D\alpha_i\|_2^2 + \lambda \varphi(\alpha_i) \right) \tag{4.30}$$

where λ is a regularization parameter and $\varphi(.)$ is a sparsity function. The most common used sparsity function is l_1-norm. Hence, Eq. 4.30 is rewritten as Eq. 4.31 by using the l_1-norm. This equation can be solved using the Lasso method [8].

$$\min_{D,\alpha} \sum_{i=1}^{m} \left(\frac{1}{2} \|X_i - D\alpha_i\|_2^2 + \lambda \|\alpha_i\|_1 \right) \tag{4.31}$$

To prevent obtaining very large values of $\mathbf{D}$ which may lead to very small values of α_i, a constraint is imposed on the columns of $\mathbf{D}$ such that they have unit l_2-norm [25]. The dictionary $\mathbf{D}$ and sparse coefficients α_i will be obtained by solving Eq. 4.31 using the K-SVD [1, 36] among several methods developed for the solutions. If the dictionary $\mathbf{D}$ is fixed by using all the training dataset $\mathbf{X} = \{x_1, x_2, \ldots, x_n\} \in \mathbf{R}^{m \times n}$, we just need to solve the sparse coefficients α_i by Eq. 4.31.

K-SVD is an algorithm to learn a dictionary for sparse signal representations. K-SVD is a generalization of the k-means clustering method using the SVD, hence, it is called K-SVD. The SVD refers to the singular value decomposition method. The K-SVD works by iteratively alternating between sparse coding the dataset based on the current dictionary, and updating the atoms in the dictionary to better fit the dataset [6]. Given a training dataset, we look for the dictionary that is potentially the best representation for each member in this dataset, under strict sparsity constraints as formulated in Eq. 4.31. The dictionary is updated by solving Eq. 4.32.

$$\min_{D} \sum_{i=1}^{n} \|x_i - D\alpha_i\|_2^2 \tag{4.32}$$

Equation 4.32 is rewritten as Eq. 4.33 as below:

$$\min_{D} \sum_{i=1}^{n} \|x_i - D\alpha_i\|_2^2 = \min_{D} \left\| X - \sum_{j=1, j \neq k}^{n} D_j \alpha^j - d_k \alpha^k \right\|_2^2 = \|E_k - d_k \alpha^k\|_F^2 \tag{4.33}$$

where d_k is obtained by solving the SVD of $E_k = U \sum V$, $d_k = U(:, 1)$ and α^k is the kth row of $\alpha \in R^{k \times n}$.

K-SVD is widely used in applications such as pattern recognition and image classification. The K-SVD dictionary learning algorithm is outlined below.

K-SVD Dictionary Learning Algorithm [36]:

Step 1: Initialize the dictionary, D, the convergence criterion, δ, and the maximum number of iterations (Max-It). In addition, set an initial distance $D_0 = 0$ and the iteration number $k = 0$.

Repeat the following steps for each vector in the training dataset.

Step 2: *Sparse code update*: while the dictionary is kept fixed, we update the sparse vector α_i using Eq. (4.30).

Step 3: *Dictionary update*: while the sparse code is kept fixed, we update each column of the dictionary D using Eq. 4.32. Specifically, Steps 2 and 3 are to solve the following equations formulated in 4.32 and 4.33:

$$\min_{D} \sum_{i=1}^{N} \|x_i - D\alpha_i\|_2^2$$

$$\min_{d_k} \|E_k - d_k \alpha^k\|_F^2 \ \forall k$$

4.9 Experimental Results on Dimensionality Reduction of Hyperspectral Image

Hyperspectral image data is a progression of spectral bands collected over visible and infrared of the electromagnetic spectrum. These datasets hold relevant information as well as accommodate noise and redundancy leading to sparseness. Correlation between the bands is inversely proportional to sparseness. It is imperative to preprocess hyperspectral data to efficiently extract meaningful information.

Hence, dimensionality reduction techniques including PCA, NMF, Independent component analysis (ICA), and SVD were used in this experiment for reducing the number of hyperspectral bands [23]. ICA is an extension of PCA [14]. The experiment explores the dependency of the standard PCA, NMF, ICA, and SVD algorithms on the selected number of dimensions (L). Unsupervised clustering algorithms Fuzzy C-means (FCM) was utilized to identify the influence of L on the dimensionality reduction techniques through classification accuracy. As L value increases, each algorithm yields different accuracy. Indian Pines hyperspectral images with a size of 145×145 and 200 bands were used for dimensionality reduction and then for classification. Experimental results are shown in Table 4.1 and Fig. 4.7. Table 4.1 is a summary of classification accuracy using the FCM algorithm with dimensionality reduction methods of PCA, NMF, ICA, and SVD and FCM. Their variances and deviations for each chosen dimension L are presented for each dimensionality reduction method. Figure 4.7 shows the classified images for the visualization.

Table 4.1 FCM clustering results of Indian Pines dataset; the first column shows different dimensionality reduction methods, second, third, and fourth columns give the minimum, maximum, and average classification accuracy over 10 iterations, respectively. Here, κ represents the overall accuracy. The fifth, sixth, and seventh columns give the variance, standard deviation, and the number of bands obtained with dimensionality reduction methods, respectively

Algorithm	κ Min over 10 iters (%)	κ Max over 10 iters (%)	κ Average over 10 iters (%)	κ Variance x 10^{-5} over 10 iters	Deviation	L
PCA	85.15	85.65	85.37	0.209806	0.00144	3
NMF	84.47	85.11	84.76	0.510506	0.00225	
ICA	85.08	85.71	**85.41**	0.475800	0.00218	
SVD	84.12	84.93	84.62	0.451861	0.00212	
PCA	81.66	84.33	83.63	5.90619	0.00768	5
NMF	84.75	85.26	85.02	0.267256	0.00163	
ICA	83.13	84.48	83.74	3.01680	0.00549	
SVD	85.01	85.40	**85.21**	0.170667	0.00130	
PCA	61.07	77.77	71.26	290.638	0.05391	15
NMF	73.20	79.94	**78.32**	34.0453	0.01845	
ICA	61.86	76.01	70.62	152.749	0.03908	
SVD	55.75	73.47	62.83	286.098	0.05348	

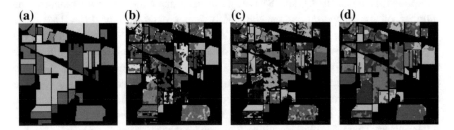

Fig. 4.7 Classified images of Indian Pines dataset using the FCM algorithm with dimensionality reduction techniques. These classified images corresponding to the maximum accuracy, which was taken from Table 4.1 for each reduced dimension, L, of 3, 5, and 15. **a** Ground Truth; **b** ICA (κ = 85.71%, L = 3); **c** SVD (κ = 85.40%, L = 5); **d** NMF (κ = 79.94%, L = 15)

4.10 Summary

Although both dimensionality reduction (DR) and sparse representation (SR) techniques give a compressed representation of images, there exist similarity and difference between them. DR techniques such as PCA provide us methods to select a low-dimensional space from the orthogonal dimensional representations obtained through matrix manipulation. The SR gives us the sparse basis vectors to select the nonzero elements obtained from an overcomplete set of basis vectors by solving an L1-regularized optimization problem such as Lasso method. For a given matrix, which represents an original dataset, the optimization of a low-rank approximation for the given matrix is the goal for many dimensional reduction techniques. However, the problem in this optimization is that there is no guarantee that the technique will preserve and generate the discriminative features for the optimal classification. In other words, the optimization may be good just for the image and signal reconstruction.

Sparse representation (SR) is to construct a dictionary which can represent a vector as a sparse linear combination of the original training vectors. It is an efficient method to reduce the complexity of the dataset. Each feature vector using SR can be represented with a few atoms. The sparse coding is a more general approach compared with other methods such as the PCA. However, the foundation of principal component analysis (PCA), NMF, and singular value decomposition (SVD) is still widely used in many applications. For example, the SVD is used in the K-SVD algorithm for the learning of dictionary in the sparse coding. The NMF is a family of dimensionality reduction techniques for matrix factorization. The NMF assumes that all hidden variables are nonnegative.

4.11 Exercises

A hypothetical color image is given below (Red, Green, and Blue):

0	1	2	3
1	2	3	0
2	3	0	1
3	0	1	2

(Red)

1	2	3	3
3	2	1	1
1	3	2	1
1	2	3	2

(Green)

3	2	2	3
0	1	3	2
1	3	1	2
1	3	2	1

(Blue)

1. Apply the principal component analysis (PCA) to the color image into a new set of images.
2. Use the singular value decomposition (SVD) technique to one of three bands.
3. Perform the non-negative matrix factorization (NMF) technique to the images.
4. Apply the sparse coding to the images.

References

1. Aharon M, Elad M, Bruckstein A (2006) K-SVD: an algorithm for designing overcomplete dictionaries for sparse representation. IEEE Trans Signal Process 54(11):4311–4322. https://doi.org/10.1109/TSP.2006.881199
2. Breen P (2009) Algorithms for sparse approximation. University of Edinburgh, School of Mathematics
3. Cai D, Bao H, He X (2011) Sparse concept coding for visual analysis. CVPR 2011:20–25
4. Castleman KR (1996) Digital image processing, Prentice Hall, New Jersey
5. Eggert J, Korner E (2004) Sparse coding and NMF. In: Proceedings of IEEE international joint conference on Neural Networks 2004, vol 4, pp 2529–2533
6. Elad M (2006) Sparse and redundant representations: from theory to applications in signal and image processing. Springer, Berlin
7. Gangeh MJ, Ghodsi A, Kamel MS (2011) Dictionary learning in texture classification. In: Kamel M, Campilho A (eds) Image analysis and recognition. ICIAR 2011. Lecture notes in computer science, vol 6753. Springer, Berlin
8. Hastie T, Tibshirani R, Friedman J (2009) The elements of statistical learning: data mining, inference, and prediction, 2nd edn. Springer, Berlin
9. Horng MH (2009) Honey bee mating optimization vector quantization scheme in image compression. In: Deng H, Wang L, Wang FL, Lei J (eds) Artificial intelligence and computational intelligence (AICI 2009). Lecture notes in computer science, vol 5855. Springer, Berlin
10. Horn RA, Johnson CR (1985) Matrix Analysis, Cambridge. Cambridge University Press, England
11. Hotelling H (1933) Analysis of a complex of statistical variables into principal components. J Educ Psychol, 24: 417–441 and 498–520
12. Hughes GF (1968) On the mean accuracy of statistical pattern recognitions. IEEE Trans Inf Theory, IT-14(1)
13. Hung CC, Fahsi A, Tadesse W, Coleman T (1997) A comparative study of remotely sensed data classification using principal components analysis and divergence. In: Proceedings of IEEE international conference on systems, man, and cybernetics, Orlando, FL, 12–15 Oct 1997, pp 2444–2449
14. Hyvärinen A, Oja E (2000) Independent component analysis: algorithms and applications. Neural Netw 13(4–5):411–430
15. Jolliffe IT (2002) Principal component analysis, 2nd edn. Springer, New York
16. Kim H, Park H (2007) Sparse non-negative matrix factorizations via alternating non-negativity-constrained least squares for microarray data analysis. Bioinformatics 23 (12):1495–1502
17. Kolman B (1980) Introductory linear algebra with applications, 2nd edn. Macmillan Publishing Company Incorporated, New York
18. Kuo B-C, Ho H-H, Li C-H, Hung C-C, Taur J-S (2013) A kernel-based feature selection method for SVM with RBF kernel for hyperspectral image classification. IEEE J Sel Top Appl Earth Obs Remote Sens, 7(1):317–326
19. Kuo B-C, Landgrebe DA (2004) Nonparametric weighted feature extraction for classification. IEEE Trans Geosci Remote Sens 42(5):1096–1105
20. Lee H, BattleA, Raina R, Ng AY (2006) Efficient sparse coding algorithms. Advances in neural information processing systems, pp 801–808
21. Linde Y, Buzo A, Gray RM (1980) An algorithm for vector quantizer design. IEEE Trans Commun, COM-28(1):84–95
22. Lee DD, Seung HS (1999) Learning the parts of objects by non-negative matrix factorization. Nature 401:788–791

23. Mallapragada S, Wong M, Hung C-C (2018) Dimensionality reduction of hyperspectral images for classification. In: Proceedings of the ninth international conference on information, pp 153–160
24. Mallat SG (1989) A theory for multiresolution signal decomposition: the wavelet representation. IEEE Trans Pattern Anal Mach Intell 2(7):674–693
25. Marial J, Bach F, Ponce J, Sapiro G (2010) Online learning for matrix factorization and sparse coding. J Mach Learn Res 11:19–60
26. Mairal J, Bach F, Ponce J, Sapiro G (2009) Online dictionary learning for sparse coding. In: Proceedings of the 26th international conference on machine learning, montreal, Canada
27. Mairal J, Bach F, Sapiro G, Zisserman A (2008) Supervised dictionary learning. INRIA
28. Marr D (1982) A computational investigation into the human representation and processing of visual information. MIT Press, Cambridge
29. Olshausen BA, Field DJ (1996) Emergence of simple cell receptive field properties by learning a sparse code for natural images. Nature 381(6583):607–609
30. Olshausen BA, Field DJ (2004) Sparse coding of sensory inputs. Curr Opin Neurobiol 14:481–487
31. Paatero P, Tapper U (1994) Positive matrix factorization: a non-negative factor model with optimal utilization of error estimates of data values. Environmentrics 5(2):111–126
32. Pearson K (1901) On lines and planes of closest fit to systems of points in space. Philos Mag 2 (11):559–572 (series 6)
33. Richards JA, Jia X (2006) Remote sensing digital image analysis, 4th edn. Springer, Berlin
34. Rish I, Grabarnik GY (2015) Sparse modeling: theory, algorithms, and applications. Chapman & Hall/CRC
35. Rubinstein R, Bruckstein AM, Elad M (2010) Dictionaries for sparse representation modeling. Proc IEEE 98(6):1045–1057. https://doi.org/10.1109/JPROC.2010.2040551
36. Sarkar R (2017) Dictionary learning and sparse representation for image analysis with application to segmentation, classification and event detection. Ph.D. Dissertation, University of Virginia
37. Turkmen AC (2015) A review of nonnegative matrix factorization methods for clustering. Allen Institute for Artificial Intelligence, 31 Aug 2015
38. Wang Y-X, Zhang Y-J (2013) Nonnegative matrix factorization: a comprehensive review. IEEE Trans Knowl Data Eng 25(6):1336–1353
39. Yang J, Yu K, Gong Y, Huang T (2009) Linear spatial pyramid matching using sparse coding for image classification. In IEEE conference on computer vision and pattern recognition, pp 1794–1801

Part II
The K-views Models and Algorithms

Basic Concept and Models of the K-views

5

In this chapter, we introduce the concepts of "view" and "characteristic view". This view concept is quite different from those of gray-level co-occurrence matrix (GLCM) and local binary pattern (LBP). We emphasize on how to precisely describe the features of a texture and how to extract texture features directly from a sample patch (i.e., sub-image), and how to use these features to classify an image texture. The view concepts and related methods work with a group of pixels instead of a single pixel. Three principles are used in this work for developing the model: (1) texture features from a view should carry as much information as possible for image classification; (2) the algorithm should be kept as simple as possible; and (3) the computational time to distinguish different texture classes should be the minimum. The view-related concepts are suitable for textures that are generated by one or more basic local patterns and repeated in a periodic manner over some image region. The set of characteristic views is a powerful feature extraction and representation to describe an image texture. As different textures show different patterns, the patterns of a texture also show different views. If a set of characteristic views is properly defined, it is possible to use this set of characteristic views for texture classification. The K-views template is an algorithm that uses many characteristic views, denoted by K, for the classification of images. The K-views algorithm is suitable for classifying image textures that have basic local patterns repeated periodically. Several variations of the basic K-views model are given in Chaps. 6, 7 and 8.

© Springer Nature Switzerland AG 2019
C.-C. Hung et al., *Image Texture Analysis*,
https://doi.org/10.1007/978-3-030-13773-1_5

5.1   View Concept and a Set of Views

Human beings are capable of using the texture in the interpretation of a photograph for the targets of interest. It is very natural for a machine to use the same feature of texture for the recognition. Researchers in image texture analysis have proposed many innovative methods for image texture classification. These methods can be divided into two major categories: the first category is based on the features with a high degree of spatial localization, which can use edge detection operations for recognition. The major problem with this approach is that it is challenging to distinguish the texture boundaries and the micro-edges located in the same texture. The second category is based on the discrimination function using several texture features. The classification accuracy in this category depends upon the discriminative power of the extracted texture features. Many methods have been developed to extract features either using statistical or other algorithms as discussed in Chap. 2. In most cases, the feature is represented numerically by a vector, which is composed of real numbers (vector components) derived from a neighborhood of the corresponding class. In this chapter, we present a different framework for representing texture features for the classification. We describe how to extract texture features directly from a sample sub-image of a texture and how to use them to classify an image. As each texture class has a characteristic feature that can distinguish this class from others, this characteristic feature may show different "views". When we determine if a pixel belongs to a specific texture class during the classification, if the spatial neighborhood of the pixel (which is a small image patch) is considered, we may be able to look up for a set of the "views" of texture classes to determine the categorization of this image patch [7, 12]. In other words, one can observe that any local patch of a texture consists of only a few patterns, which are called views in this context.

In the following, we illustrate the concept of the view by using a simple image as shown in Fig. 5.1 that contains two different texture classes. One texture class consists of parallel vertical lines. The other consists of two intersected sets of diagonal lines. These two arrangements show two different textures. This type of pattern structure can be taken as the basic element of measure for image textures. Figure 5.1 also indicates that an image texture not only depends on the values of its composed pixels but also on the spatial arrangement of those pixels. Please note

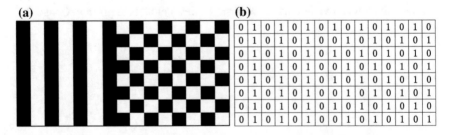

Fig. 5.1 **a** An image shows two texture classes and **b** the corresponding pixel values

that it is impossible for a per-pixel-based classification method to classify this texture image correctly. To classify this image into two different texture classes, we can use a correlation matching method. The following steps are used to illustrate the correlation matching method.

The Correlation Matching Method:

Step 1: Select randomly in the area of the texture class a sample sub-image for each texture class from the original image. An example of selected sample sub-images, sample 1 and sample 2, are shown in Fig. 5.2a and b. Note that, the size of these two sample sub-images do not have to be the same.

Step 2: Take a small image template (we can call this template a patch) from the original image being classified as shown in Fig. 5.2c and d. The small patch should be much smaller than any of the sample sub-image. Then, find the best match between this small image patch and the sample sub-images.

Step 3: If the best match occurs in sample sub-image **k**, classify all the pixels (in the original image) corresponding to this small image patch into class **k**. (or if the small image patch is regarded as a neighborhood of one pixel, classify only that pixel to class **k**).

Step 4: Repeat Steps 2 and 3 until the entire original image is classified.

In Steps 2 and 3, when we perform the classification of an image, a small patch is taken and looks up a set of sub-images extracted from the sample image to determine which texture class this small patch belongs. These steps will be repeated for each pixel in a neighborhood of the patch size in the original image. In a sense, this operation is very similar to how we apply the spatial filter to an image.

The correlation matching method, which measures the similarity between a small image patch and a sample sub-image, can be defined in several ways. A straight-forward method is to use Euclidean distance. Suppose that a small image patch is

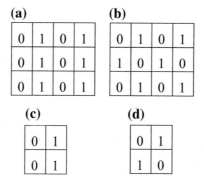

Fig. 5.2 a and **b** Show sample sub-images with a size of 3 × 4 from two different textures, respectively, from Fig. 5.1 and **c** and **d,** a small patch (size of 2 × 2) is taken from **a** and **b,** respectively

Fig. 5.3 A sample sub-image with a size of M × N which contains (M − m + 1)*(N − n + 1) small patches of size m × n with overlapping

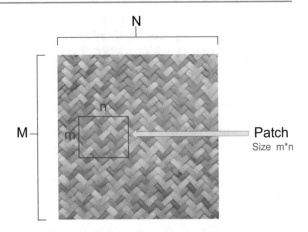

taken from an original image which has a size of m × n. A sample sub-image with a size of M × N will contain (M − m + 1)*(N − n + 1) small patches of size m × n with overlapping. This is illustrated in Fig. 5.3.

If we use V_o to denote a small patch taken from an original image and V_i (i = 1 to (M − m + 1)*(N − n + 1)) to denote a small image patch taken from a sample sub-image representing a textural class and d_i denote the Euclidean distance between V_o and V_i. We assume that both V_o and V_i have the same size. The similarity which is measured by the Euclidean distance, say $S_{V_o V_i}$, between V_o and a patch V_i, can be expressed by the following equation:

$$S_{V_o V_i} = \min\{d_1, d_2, d_3, \ldots, d_k, \ldots, d_{(M-m+1)*(N-n+1)}\} \qquad (5.1)$$

Please note that Eq. 5.1 will be repeated for each sample sub-image taken from a textural class. The textural class i (from 1 to C) to which V_o belongs can be determined by Eq. 5.2.

$$S_{V_i} = \min\{S_{V_1}, S_{V_2}, \ldots, S_{V_i}, \ldots, S_{V_C}\} \qquad (5.2)$$

where C is the total number of textural classes.

This method can accurately classify an image such as the one shown in Fig. 5.1. If the small image patch has a size of 2 × 2, this method can classify this image well into two texture classes. Lee and Philpot described a similar approach in their work [8].

Here, we call each small image patch, V, a "view". There are two different views in Fig. 5.2a, if the view size is 2 × 2: $\begin{pmatrix} 0 & 1 \\ 0 & 1 \end{pmatrix}$ and $\begin{pmatrix} 1 & 0 \\ 1 & 0 \end{pmatrix}$. In total, there are six views in this sample sub-image (i.e., $(3 - 2 + 1) * (4 - 2 + 1)$). Among a total of six views, there are four identical views of $\begin{pmatrix} 0 & 1 \\ 0 & 1 \end{pmatrix}$ and two identical views of

$\begin{pmatrix} 1 & 0 \\ 1 & 0 \end{pmatrix}$. A view is of a size of m × n, where m > 0 and n > 0. When m = 1 and n = 1, a view is just a single pixel.

For a simple representation, a view with a size of m by n can be denoted by a vector:

$$(x_{11}, x_{12}, \ldots, x_{1n}; x_{21}, x_{22}, \ldots, x_{2n}; \ldots; x_{m1}, x_{m2}, \ldots, x_{mn})^T \qquad (5.3)$$

where T is the transpose. In Eq. 5.3, a group of values separated from others by semicolons corresponds to a row in the view. Each value in this group corresponds to a pixel value in the view. Hence, $\begin{pmatrix} 1 & 0 \\ 1 & 0 \end{pmatrix}$ can be expressed by $(1, 0; 1, 0)^T$. All of these views from a sample sub-image form a set called a *view set*. A view set is an exemplary set for an image texture class.

Now, it is clear that the correlation matching method is, in fact, a method to compare a view with those in the view sets formed from different sample sub-images (i.e., textures).

5.2 Set of Characteristic Views and the K-views Template Algorithm (K-views-T)

Although the correlation matching method can accurately classify a textural image, it is a computationally intensive algorithm. To have a representative set of views, a large sample sub-image has to be chosen. A large sample sub-image indicates that it will increase the computation time. In fact, it is not necessary to compare a view (from an image being classified) with the entire set of views extracted from a sample sub-image in the matching process because this original view set may contain several identical views, and some views are very similar. It will be more efficient if a representative set of views can be chosen from an original set of views which has similar or identical views. In doing so, it will not affect the matching result. If a small representative set of views can be derived from the entire large view set of a sample sub-image, the computation time for the matching method will be dramatically reduced. This representative set of views derived from an original set of views will be called the set of *characteristic views*. A view in the set of characteristic views is called the *characteristic view* and denoted by V_{cs}.

An original set of views (abbreviation *view set* and denoted by V_s) can be formulated as

$$V_s = D@V_{cs} \qquad (5.4)$$

where V_s denotes an original set of views, V_{cs} a set of all different views from a sample sub-image, and D the relative frequency (or distribution) of the views (i.e., elements) in the set of different views (V_{cs}). The notation @ is the operator that we have chosen to relate the datagram to the frequency of each characteristic view in V_{cs}. The datagram will be explained later.

For example, with the sample sub-image in Fig. 5.2a and the view with a size of 2×2, the *view set*, V_s, of sample sub-image is

$$\left\{ \begin{pmatrix} 0 & 1 \\ 0 & 1 \end{pmatrix}, \begin{pmatrix} 1 & 0 \\ 1 & 0 \end{pmatrix}, \begin{pmatrix} 0 & 1 \\ 0 & 1 \end{pmatrix}, \begin{pmatrix} 0 & 1 \\ 0 & 1 \end{pmatrix}, \begin{pmatrix} 1 & 0 \\ 1 & 0 \end{pmatrix}, \begin{pmatrix} 0 & 1 \\ 0 & 1 \end{pmatrix} \right\} \quad (5.5)$$

or

$$\{(0, 1; 0, 1), (1, 0; 1, 0), (0, 1; 0, 1), (0, 1; 0, 1), (1, 0; 1, 0), (0, 1; 0, 1)\} \quad (5.6)$$

please note that the transpose T for each vector in Eq. 5.6 is omitted for simplicity. Similarly, notation T will be omitted in the following vector representations.

In this view set, there are four views of the pattern $(0, 1; 0, 1)$ and two views of the pattern $(1, 0; 1, 0)$. The distribution can be represented as

$$V_s = (4, 2)@\{(0, 1; 0, 1), (1, 0; 1, 0)\} \quad (5.7)$$

where $(4, 2)$ is the datagram, $\{(0, 1; 0, 1), (1, 0; 1, 0)\}$ is the set of characteristic views. If we choose to use only one characteristic view, V_s can be further simplified as

$$V_s = (6)@((0.3, 0.7; 0.3, 0.7)) \quad (5.8)$$

where the value 6 is the total number of views in the view set V_s, 0.3 is the average value of the distribution in the first component of all vectors in Eq. 5.6, 0.7 is the average value of the distribution in the second component, and so on. If the size of the sample sub-images is getting larger, the average of the distribution is closer to 0.5 in this case, then $Vs \approx (6)@\{(0.5, 0.5; 0.5, 0.5)\}$. Similarly,

the View Set of the sample sub - image in Figure 5.2 b
$$= \{(0, 1; 1, 0), (1, 0; 0, 1), (0, 1; 1, 0), (1, 0; 0, 1), (0, 1; 1, 0), (1, 0; 0, 1)\}$$
$$= \{3@(0, 1; 1, 0), 3@(1, 0; 0, 1)\}$$
$$= (3, 3)@\{(0, 1; 1, 0), (1, 0; 0, 1)\}$$
$$= (6)@\{(0.5, 0.5; 0.5, 0.5)\}$$

$$(5.9)$$

The correlation matching method now will use the set of characteristic views to classify an image texture. We call this method the **K-views Template Algorithm (K-views-T)**, as the characteristic view is similar to a "template". The procedure of the K-views template algorithm based on the modification of correlation matching method is described in the following.

The K-views Template Algorithm (K-views-T)

Step 1:   Select randomly a sample sub-image in the area of the textures for each textural class from the original image. In other words, N sample sub-images will be selected for N textural classes. The size of each sub-image can be different.

Step 2:   Extract a view set, V_s from each sample sub-image.

Step 3:   Determine the value of K for each view set, and derive K-views for each characteristic view set from each sample sub-image using the K-means algorithm or fuzzy C-means algorithm. The number of views, K, may vary for each texture class (i.e., sample sub-image).

Step 4:   In the matching process, each view (a small image patch), say V, of the original image being classified will be compared with each characteristic view in each set of the characteristic views and find the best match (a high correlation). Please note that the size of each view is the same.

Step 5:   If the best matching characteristic view belongs to the characteristic view set j, classify all pixels in the view V to class j where $j = 1, …, N$. (If the view is regarded as a neighborhood of one pixel, classify only that pixel to class j).

Step 6:   Repeat Steps 4 and 5 for each view in the original image being classified.

The procedure sketched above leaves two parameters undefined. One is the size of the view and the other is the number of the characteristic views, K. If a specific pattern repeated in the texture class frequently, the size of the view can be small. Otherwise, the size of the view should be large. The larger the size of the view is, the more information about the texture the view can carry. The number of the characteristic views should depend on both the texture structure in the image and the similarity between texture classes. The smaller K of the characteristic views is, the less powerful the characteristic views can describe for the texture. For the image shown in Fig. 5.1, if K is set to 1, the classification result will not be satisfied.

Deriving the representative characteristic views from a view set of a sample sub-image is a simple and straightforward process. As long as the number of characteristic views (K) is determined, most clustering methods described in Chap. 3 can be used to select a representative set of characteristic views and obtain K cluster centers [9]. It can be proved that the cluster centers derived from these methods are those representative characteristic views of the view set by minimizing the objective function.

If the size of the view is selected appropriately, the K-views template method can have optimal performance in texture classification. However, if the size of the view is very small, different view sets may have some views in common. Hence, different sets of characteristic views may also have some same or similar characteristic views. For example, if the size of the view is 1×2 for the sample sub-images shown in Fig. 5.2a and b, we will have the following set of views:

the set of views for sample sub-image-1
$$= \{(0,1),(1,0),(0,1),(0,1),(1,0),(0,1),(0,1),(1,0),(0,1)\} \qquad (5.10)$$
$$= (6,3)@\{(0,1),(1,0)\},$$

and

the set of views for sample sub-image-2
$$= \{(0,1),(1,0),(0,1),(1,0),(0,1),(1,0),(0,1),(1,0),(0,1)\} \qquad (5.11)$$
$$= (5,4)@\{(0,1),(1,0)\}$$

These two sets of characteristic views for two different textural samples are almost the same. In this situation, we cannot solely depend on these sets of characteristic views to obtain a correct classification. One solution to this problem is to increase the size of the view. However, before we do that, we should ask one question: are the sample sub-images really good representatives for textures? Is it likely that a sample sub-image contains a part that is similar to another texture class? This leads us to a second solution. The information from the distribution in the datagram can be used. Suppose that two characteristic views in two different sets are identical (or similar). If 40% of sample sub-image-1 can be classified by this characteristic view and only 5% of the sample sub-image-2 can be classified by the same characteristic view, we can just remove this characteristic view from the second set of characteristic views.

In our experiments, the size of the view is set to between 10×10 and 15×15. If a view size of 10×10 is chosen, a sample sub-image of size 50×50 has at most 41 * 41 different views. It is unlikely that these sets of characteristic views for different texture classes will have an identical characteristic view. In the empirical study, it shows that some of the views coming from sample sub-image class i may be classified into class j. In such a situation, the third solution is to increase K of the characteristic views in a set so that more characteristic views can be used to accurately describe the characteristics of a texture class. In summary, three solutions to this problem can be used: (1) the first solution is to increase the size of the view, (2) the second solution is to use both the information from the distribution in the datagram and the set of characteristic views, and (3) the third solution is to increase the number of characteristic views in each set for a texture class.

Besides the above three solutions, there exists another solution from the perspective of the histogram point of view. Assume that there are two sets of characteristic views for two textural classes and arranged as histograms (we will call this datagram [12]) shown in Fig. 5.4: class 1 is $(1,1,2,7,2)@(V_4, V_5, V_6, V_7, V_8)$ and class 2 is $(1,3,6,3,1)@(V_1, V_2, V_3, V_4, V_5)$. Characteristic view 7 frequently appears in texture class 1 and only occurs in class 1. Similarly, characteristic views 2 and 3 frequently appear in texture class 2 and only occurs in class 2. If we take an image patch containing characteristic view 7, we can say that this image patch belongs to texture class 1 since characteristic view 7 is the most distinguished view

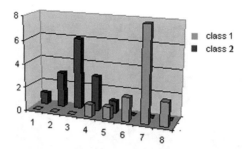

Fig. 5.4 Two textural classes have some characteristic views in common. As shown in Eq. 5.3, i.e., $V_s = D@V_{cs}$ y-coordinate represents D and x-coordinate represents V_{cs} which has five views $(V_4, V_5, V_6, V_7, V_8)$ for class 1 and $(V_1, V_2, V_3, V_4, V_5)$ for class 2 in the histogram

in this set. If it contains characteristic view 2 or 3, the entire patch will be classified into class 2 because these two characteristic views are the prominent features in this set. If the image patch consists of characteristic views 3 and 7, or, 2 and 7, that indicates that the patch is in the boundary of these two textural classes.

In a grayscale image, if the view size is set to 1 × 1, there will be at most 256 different characteristic views. The possible values are 0, 1, 2, 3, ..., and 255. If two texture classes have the same set of characteristic views, the classification should totally depend on the view distribution in the datagram instead of the set of characteristic views. As defined in Eq. 5.3, our texture classification model has been focusing on V_{cs}, instead of D. This is in contrast with most other texture classification algorithms.

The K-views template algorithm is suitable for textures that have periodically repeating patterns. For image texture that possesses some random structures, the K-views template may not be effective to distinguish them. In this situation, both the datagrams and sets of characteristic views can be used in the image texture classification algorithms. Characteristic views are powerful and simple to describe the characteristics of textures. A datagram is also a useful feature for image classification [12]. The algorithm, which uses the datagram, will be discussed in Chap. 6.

5.3   Experimental Results Using the K-views-T Algorithm

The K-views template algorithm was tested on satellite images in the experiments [7]. Figure 5.5a shows an original image that contains three texture classes, which are smooth land, ocean, and mountain. Figure 5.5b shows the classified result using one characteristic view for each texture class. From Fig. 5.5c to f, the same K value was used for all the three texture classes. The value K was set to 2, 5, 10, and 20, respectively, for Fig. 5.5c, d, e, and f. If a larger K is used for a set of characteristic views, the better the classification result one can achieve. Each texture class does not necessarily have the same number of characteristic views. This means that K

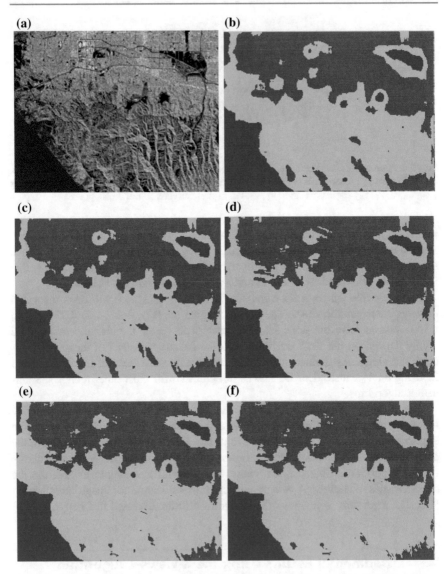

Fig. 5.5 Classification results using the K-views template algorithm. We assume that there are three texture classes in the image. **a** an original image, and the results of **b**, **c**, **d**, **e**, and **f** are obtained using the same K value (i.e., same number of characteristic views for each class) for all the three texture classes. The value K was set to 1, 2, 5, 10, and 20 for **b**, **c**, **d**, **e**, and **f**, respectively

may vary for each set of characteristic views of a texture class. For example, the ocean class and the smooth land can have much fewer characteristic views than that of the mountain class. Figure 5.6 shows five sets with a varying number of

Fig. 5.6 Five sets with a varying number of characteristic views (K-views) for mountain texture class; the K, from the first row, was set to 1, 2, 5, 10, and 20, until the last row

characteristic views (i.e., K-views) for the mountain class. We can see that the more number of characteristic views used in a set, the set of characteristic views is more close to the real image.

Figure 5.7 shows the classification results on another remotely sensed image. The original image in Fig. 5.7a is a region of Atlanta city in Georgia. The image is classified into the residential area (red), the lawns (green), the commercial area (blue), and the undeveloped area (black) in Fig. 5.7b. Figure 5.8 illustrates some classified results of animal images taken from the Berkeley website (http://sunsite. berkeley.edu/ImageFinder/) and compared with the results of the color region method. Figure 5.9 shows an image consisting of four different texture classes taken from Brodatz texture album and their classification results using the K-views-T algorithm. When the number of K-views increases, the classification accuracy is improved. Each texture class has a size of 100 × 100.

(a)   **(b)**

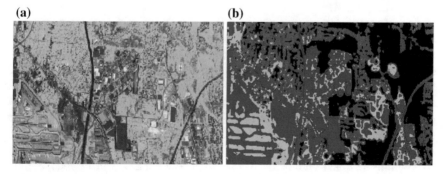

Fig. 5.7 **a** A sub-image of Atlanta city in Georgia, USA and **b** the classified image using the K-views template algorithm: residential area (red), lawns (green), commercial areas (blue), and undeveloped area (black)

(a)   **(b)**   **(c)**

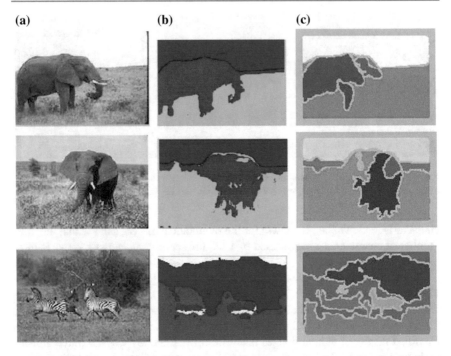

Fig. 5.8 **a** Three images of animals, **b** classified results using the K-views template algorithm, and **c** classified results using the color region method. (images in the column of (**a**) and segmented results in the column of (**c**) are taken from the Berkley website (http://sunsite.berkeley.edu/ImageFinder/)

5.4   Empirical Comparison with GLCM and Gaussian MRF (GMRF)

Spatial models are frequently used for image texture classification [1–6, 11]. These models exploit the contextual information by utilizing spatial features for the classification. These spatial features capture the spatial relationships encoded in the image. As described in Chap. 2, the gray-level co-occurrence matrix (GLCM) is a statistical method which calculates properties of the relationship of pairwise of pixels [5, 6]. The spatial relationships between a pixel and its neighbors are recorded into the GLCM and then used for calculating the statistics for features [5]. The statistics that produce independent features are preferred such as dissimilarity (D), entropy (E), and correlation (C) [5, 6]. These features will be mapped into corresponding feature vectors, and the k-means and other clustering algorithms can be used to cluster these vectors.

Geostatistics has been used to measure spatial properties. Car and Miranda [2] proposed a method which is based on the geostatistics (called the variogram), which is also a second-order statistics, to extract the texture features from the image. Unlike the GLCM, the variogram is to capture average gray-level spatial dependence. The

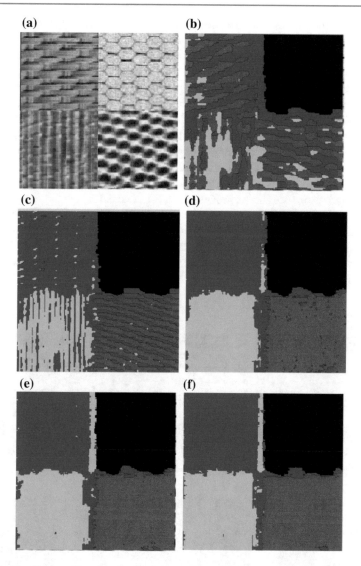

Fig. 5.9 Classified results using the K-views template algorithm on a grayscale texture image with four different textures. **a** an original image with the size of 200×200, **b, c, d, e,** and **f** are classified results obtained with the number of K-views from 1, 2, 8, 15, and 25, respectively

variogram can be computed with particular spatial directions. Four directions, E-W, N-S, NE-SW, NW-SE, are usually used for the spatial directions and statistics calculation [1]. Markov random field (MRF) models are stochastic processes which define the local spatial characteristics of an image. They are used to model the textural content of the observed image. The models characterize the statistical relationships between a pixel and its neighbors [3, 10].

Experimental results were performed on some of the Brodatz texture images to show the effectiveness of the models [11]. There are four different patterns of textures in images as shown in Figs. 5.10 and 5.12 and five different patterns of texture image in Fig. 5.11. In the experiments for the K-views-T model, the size of the K-views (i.e., characteristic view), the number of characteristic views and the statistics size (kernel size) are randomly selected for testing three different texture images. Although a variety of GLCM techniques are used in the literature, a simple GLCM is developed for the comparison. The classified results using the GLCM depend on the parameters such as distance, angle, and the number of gray levels. In this experiment, the distance $\delta = 1$ and the angle $\alpha = 0, 45, 90, 135, 180$ and 225 degrees were used. Since the gray level of 256 causes some overhead, the image is quantized to 16 gray levels. The experimental results are shown in Figs. 5.10, 5.11 and 5.12.

Experimental results demonstrate that the K-views-T model is effective in the classification of image texture. By increasing the size of K-view template and the number of K-views, it will improve the classification result in the K-views-T model. The K-views-T model has shown a significant improvement in the texture classification.

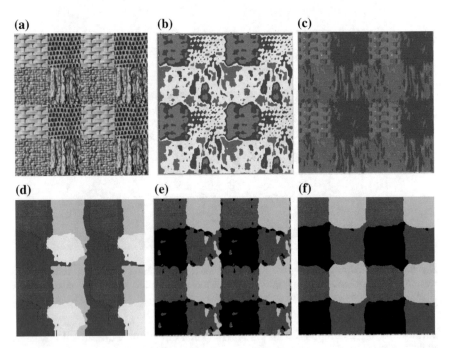

Fig. 5.10 Classified results of an image texture using different spatial models. **a** an original image, **b** the GLCM with the gray level of 16, a window size of 13, distance 1, and the average of all directions, **c** the Variogram with the window size of 9 and the average of all directions, **d** the GMRF with the window size of 16 and the fourth-order neighborhood structure, **e** K-views-T results (the size of K-views is 10, the number of characteristic views K is 20, and the sample sub-image size M is 20), and **f** K-views-T results (the size of K-views is 10, the number of characteristic views K is 30, and the sample sub-image size M is 30) [11]

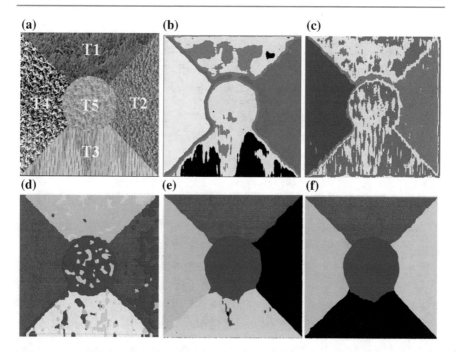

Fig. 5.11 Classified results of an image texture using different spatial models. **a** an original image, **b** the GLCM result with the gray level of 16, a window size of 32, distance 1 and the average of all directions, **c** the Variogram with the window size of 11 and the average of all directions, **d** the GMRF with window size of 8 and fourth-order neighborhood structure, **e** K-views-T results (the size of K-views is 6, the number of characteristic views K is 20, and the sample sub-image size M is 30), and **f** K-views-T results (the size of K-views is 6, the number of characteristic views K is 40, and the sample sub-image size M is 40)

5.5   Simplification of the K-views

The concept of K-views has illustrated the capability to distinguish different texture classes. The view set consisting of characteristic views is used to describe this relationship. The K-views template algorithm was developed for texture image classification based on the set of characteristic views.

If we simplify and reduce the size of K-views, some interesting results can be obtained. A K-views template with a size of 1×1 is equivalent to a pixel. Hence, a view with any size can be simplified as a line, a surface or represented by using the normal. If the view size is 1×2, and assuming that the set of characteristic views has a size of 256 * 256 for an 8-bit pixel in an image, a view distribution in the datagram is equivalent to a horizontal gray-level co-occurrence matrix (GLCM) with the distance of 1. Similarly, If the view size is 2×1, a view distribution in the datagram is equivalent to a vertical co-occurrence matrix with the distance of 1. However, the K-views are derived based on a sample sub-image while the GLCM is derived based on a matrix with the arrangement of gray levels.

(a)   (b)   (c)

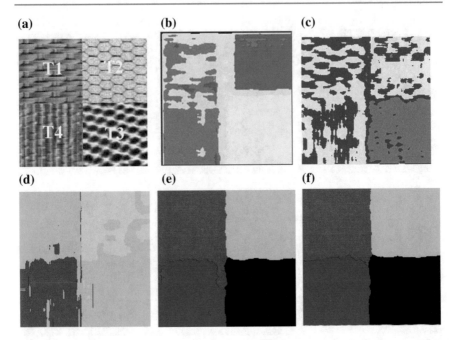

(d)   (e)   (f)

Fig. 5.12 Classified results of an image texture using different spatial models. **a** An original image **b** GLCM result with the gray level of 16, a window size of 32, distance 1, and the average of all directions, **c** the Variogram with the window size of 11 and the average of all directions, **d** GMRF with the window size of 8 and fourth-order neighborhood structure, **e** K-views-T results (with characteristic views are 4, the number of characteristic views k is 20, and the sample sub-image size M is 20), and **f** K-views results (with characteristic views are 4, the number of characteristic views k is 25, and the sample sub-image size M is 25)

If we are only interested in the two-end pixels of views with a size of $1 \times n$, the view can be denoted as a vector, $(x_1, x_2, \ldots, x_n)^T$. The distribution in a datagram would be equivalent to the horizontal co-occurrence matrix with the distance of n-1. This similarity can also be found between the distribution in a datagram and other different co-occurrence matrices. In general, the view distribution in a datagram contains more messages because the information of all pixels is preserved. In the image texture classification literature, the features of image textures can be described by the surface, normal, and basic textural unit. Some of these are discussed in Chap. 2. Compared with those features, characteristic views keep the original messages and information for the classification.

5.6 Summary

The set of characteristic views is a powerful feature extraction method to describe an image texture. Different textures show different patterns. The patterns of a texture also show different views. If the size of K-views and the number of K-views in a set of characteristic views are properly defined, it is feasible to use a set of characteristic views for texture classification. The K-views template method (K-views-T) is an algorithm that uses a set of characteristic views for image texture classification. The K-views-T algorithm is suitable for classifying image textures that have basic local patterns repeated in a periodic manner.

The performance of K-views algorithm is related to the size of K-views template and the number of characteristic views (i.e., K-views) in each set. Increasing the view size and the number of characteristic views will generally improve the classification result at the expense of processing time. However, an issue remains to be explored in determining the relationship between the view size and the number of characteristic views in a set. This means that it is necessary to develop an algorithm which can automatically determine the view size and the number of characteristic views so that the K-views-T algorithm will have optimal performance in terms of computation time and classification accuracy. The proposed classification method needs to select the sample sub-images for each class interactively. It would be useful to develop an unsupervised learning approach without human interaction by using view-related features.

5.7 Exercises

For a numerical image shown below, assume that there are two different textures; one texture in the first four columns and the other in the remaining of the image.

0	1	2	3	4	5	6	3
1	2	3	0	5	6	7	6
2	3	0	1	5	4	7	7
3	0	1	2	4	6	5	6
3	2	1	0	4	5	6	3
2	3	2	3	6	5	5	4
1	2	3	0	4	5	6	7
3	0	2	1	7	6	4	5

1. Develop a set of views with a template size of 2×2 and 3×3.
2. Develop a set of characteristic K-views from Exercise #1 using the K-views-T algorithm.

3. Compare the performance of the K-views-T algorithm with different K values.
4. Implement the K-views-T algorithm using a high-level programming language and apply the algorithm to an image with different textures.

References

1. Carr JR (1999) Classification of digital image texture using variograms. In: Atkinson PM, Tate NJ (ed) Advances in remote sensing and GIS analysis. Wiley, New York, pp 135–146
2. Carr JR, Miranda FP (1998) The semivariogram in comparison to the co-occurrence matrix for classification for image texture. IEEE Trans Geosci Remote Sens 36(6):1945–1952
3. Chellappa R, Chatterjee S (1985) Classification of textures using gaussian markov random fields. IEEE Trans Acoust Speech Signal Process 33(4):959–963
4. Gurney CM, Townshend JRG (1983) The use of contextual information in the classification of remotely sensed data. Photogramm Eng Remote Sens 49(1):55–64
5. Haralick RM, Shanmugam K, Dinstein I (1973) Textural features for image classification. IEEE Trans Syst Man Cybern 3(6):610–621
6. Hung CC, Yang S, Laymon C (2002) Use of characteristic views in image classification. In: Proceedings of 16th international conference on pattern recognition, pp 949–952
7. Hung CC, Karabudak D, Pham M, Coleman T (2004) Experiments on image texture classification with K-views classifier, markov random fields and cooccurrence probabilities. In: Proceedings of the 2004 IEEE international geoscience & remote sensing symposium (IGARSS), Anchorage, Alaska, 20–24 Sept 2004
8. Lee JH, Phipot WD (1991) Spectral texture pattern matching: a classifier for digital imagery. IEEE Trans Geosci Remote Sens 29(4):545–554
9. Tou JT, Gonzalez RC (1974) Pattern recognition principles. Addison-Wesley, Reading
10. Woods JW (1972) Two-dimensional discrete Markovian fields. IEEE Trans Inf Theory 18:232–240
11. Xiang M, Hung CC, Pham M, Coleman T (2005) Spatial models for image texture classification: an experiment. In: Proceedings of the 4th international conference on information and management sciences, Kunming, China, 1–10 July 2005, pp 341–343, ISSN 1539-2023
12. Yang S, Hung CC (2003) Image texture classification using datagrams and characteristic views. In: Proceedings of the 18th ACM symposium on applied computing (SAC), Melbourne, FL, 9–12 March 2003, pp 22–26. https://doi.org/10.1145/952532.952538

Using Datagram in the K-views Model

6

> *Truthful words are not beautiful; beautiful words are not truthful. Good words are not persuasive; persuasive words are not good.*
>
> — Lao Tzu

It is feasible for us to use only characteristic views (i.e., the basic K-views template algorithm) to classify different image textures. The performance of the K-views template (K-views-T) algorithm is related to the size of a view template and the number of characteristic views in the set of characteristic views. If the size of a view template and the number of characteristic views are increased, the classification accuracy will be improved at the expense of the time complexity. To reduce the time complexity of the K-views-T algorithm and maintain the high classification accuracy, the algorithm can utilize the *datagram* in which the frequencies of characteristic views are cumulated and distributed in a histogram. Due to the use of frequency, a smaller size of the view can be used for maintaining similar classification accuracy. In a sense, this is very similar to the approach used in the LBP and Textural Unit in which a histogram depicting the distribution of all the frequency (i.e., number) for a texture patch is used for the classification. In the basic K-views-T algorithm, the decision is made by a single characteristic view whose center is located at the current pixel being classified. By using this new datagram in the K-views model, the decision is made by the distribution of all the views contained in a large patch (i.e., block) in which the current pixel is the center of the block. Hence, a new K-views datagram algorithm (the K-views-D) is developed based on the datagram concept. Due to the spatial template used for the view, the pixels located in the boundary between texture classes are needed to be taken care of for a complete classification. This problem is similar to spatial smoothing filters applied to the boundary areas among different textures in an image. Therefore, a boundary-refined method is described to improve the boundary pixel classification.

© Springer Nature Switzerland AG 2019
C.-C. Hung et al., *Image Texture Analysis*,
https://doi.org/10.1007/978-3-030-13773-1_6

6.1   Why Do We Use Datagrams?

The K-views template is based on the assumption that an image texture has a specific pattern that distinguishes it from other textures, and this particular pattern reveals different characteristic views. If an image has random structures, we must choose both a large K and a reasonable size of view in order to have high classification accuracy. A larger K value means that it is necessary to increase the computation time to derive sets of characteristic views for the classification. To reduce the computation time, the datagram can be used for this purpose [7, 11, 13]. The datagram concept is very similar to the histograms used for the distribution of local binary patterns (LBP) and textural spectrum (TS) [4, 5, 10, 12]. As discussed in Chap. 5, a full set of views (abbreviation *view set*) can be formulated as

$$V_s = D@V_{cs} \tag{6.1}$$

where V_s denotes an original set of views, V_{cs} a set of all different views from a sample sub-image, and D the relative frequency (or distribution) of the views (i.e., elements) in the set of different views (i.e., V_{cs}). The notation @ is the operator that we have chosen to relate the datagram to the frequency of each characteristic view in V_{cs}.

Although an image texture may show a random structure in a macroscope, it may consist of small nonrandom "micro structures" (small views). Random structured textures also have stable statistical values. For example, reducing the size of view template to 1×1, any 8-bit gray-level image has only at most 256 characteristic views. These are gray levels 0, 1, 2,..., and 255. In such a case, different textures may have different datagrams (in this case, the datagram is equivalent to the histogram), and the important features of different image textures are shown in their datagrams. Hence, we can develop an algorithm to classify image textures based on the datagrams. This is a similar idea behind the histogram-based methods. An algorithm, which uses the datagram, has an advantage: a smaller size of the view can be used. Due to the frequency of views used, it will maintain a similar classification accuracy as a large size of view used in the K-views-T algorithm. This datagram approach is very similar to those used in the LBP and Textural Unit in which a histogram depicting the distribution of all the frequency (i.e., a feature index extracted from the image) for a texture patch is used for the classification [1, 2, 4–6, 10, 12].

Let us take the same textures used for the K-views template in Chap. 5 and create datagrams for the K-views extracted from the sub-image as shown in Fig. 6.1. Datagrams of Fig. 6.1 with two texture classes are illustrated in Example 6.1; texture-1 with vertical lines in parallel and texture-2 with diagonal lines crossed each other.

(a)   **(b)**

0	1	0	1	0	1	0	1	0	1	0	1	0	1	0
0	1	0	1	0	1	0	0	1	0	1	0	1	0	1
0	1	0	1	0	1	0	1	0	1	0	1	0	1	0
0	1	0	1	0	1	0	0	1	0	1	0	1	0	1
0	1	0	1	0	1	0	1	0	1	0	1	0	1	0
0	1	0	1	0	1	0	0	1	0	1	0	1	0	1
0	1	0	1	0	1	0	1	0	1	0	1	0	1	0
0	1	0	1	0	1	0	0	1	0	1	0	1	0	1

Fig. 6.1 a An image shows two texture classes and **b** the corresponding pixel values

Example 6.1 Datagrams of Fig. 6.1 with two texture classes (texture-1 and texture-2). Assume that the following two view templates in a set of *Vcs* are used to extracting the frequency from these two texture classes. These two view templates can be denoted as *Vcs*1 and *Vcs*2.

0	1
0	1

*Vcs*1

0	1
1	0

*Vcs*2

By using Eq. 6.1, for texture-1, $D = 12$ @ *Vcs*1 and $D = 0$ @ *Vcs*2. Similarly, for texture-2, $D = 0$ @ *Vcs*1 and $D = 8$ @ *Vcs*2. The datagram is shown below:

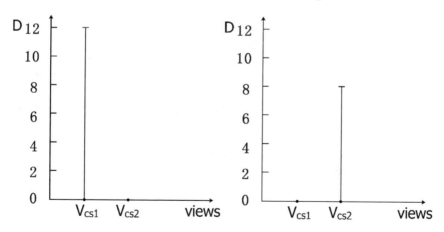

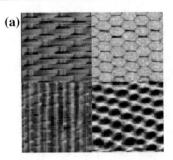

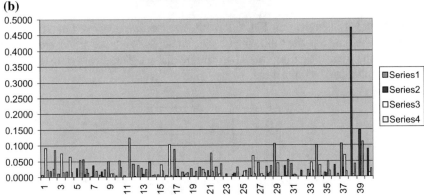

Fig. 6.2 **a** An image with four different textures and **b** a datagram of four different textures

The datagrams are obtained by using Eq. 5.1 in Chap. 5 (for the convenience, it is listed below in Eq. 6.2),

$$S_{V_o V_i} = \min\{d_1, d_2, d_3, \ldots, d_k, \ldots, d_{(M-m+1)*(N-n+1)}\} \qquad (6.2)$$

Please note that the similarity, $S_{V_o V_i}$, between V_o and a patch V_i, is measured by the Euclidean distance.

Based on the set of characteristic views, V_{cs}, we can calculate a datagram (D) for each of the N sample sub-images. According to Eq. 6.2, each datagram D can be normalized to become a normalized datagram D_N using Eq. 6.3. We call each of these N normalized datagrams coming from sample sub-image as the sample datagrams D_S which is identical to D_N. Hence, $D_S = D_N$ in Eq. 6.3.

$$D = (d_1, d_2, d_3, \ldots, d_K)$$

$$T = \sum_{i=1}^{k} d_i \tag{6.3}$$

$$D_N = (d_{n1}, d_{n2}, d_{n3}, \ldots, d_{nK}) = (d_1/T, d_2/T, d_3/T, \ldots, d_K/T)$$

where d_i is the number of views in the corresponding distribution of the datagram.

A datagram for each texture in the image from Fig. 6.2a is shown in Fig. 6.2b. The characteristic views of the texture image in Fig. 6.2a is classified into 40 clusters using the K-means algorithm. These 40 clusters are equivalent to the set of characteristic views. Then, for each texture, a normalized datagram is obtained from the statistics of the characteristic views. The datagrams are shown as four series (Series1, Series2, Series3, and Series4) in Fig. 6.2b. An index number is assigned to each characteristic view. The index number indicates a different characteristic view. These numbers are shown on the horizontal axis in Fig. 6.2b. The vertical axis shows the appearance probability of each characteristic view in the datagram. For example, the first yellow column has a probability of 0.09. It means that characteristic view 1 has an appearance probability of 9% in the third texture class. This datagram shows that, if we take any small image patch from the first texture class, its datagram should be like series 1 in Fig. 6.2b.

If different image textures have the same characteristic views, we can still use the datagrams for classification as we are using the distribution instead of the view template. Since a small size of views is used, compared with K-views template, the time to calculate the set(s) of characteristic views is reduced. But the datagram-based algorithm will use the extra time on constructing the datagram.

6.2 The K-views Datagram Algorithm (K-views-D)

Similar to the LBP and Textural Unit, a histogram depicting the distribution of all the frequency of all characteristic views in a set for a texture sub-image can be used for the classification. Such a histogram is called a datagram. The algorithm which uses datagrams for classification is described in the following steps:

Step 1: Select a sample sub-image for each texture class from the original image. In other words, N sample sub-images will be selected for N texture classes.

Steps 2–4 will be repeated for each texture class.

Step 2: Determine the size of the view template (m × n) and extract views from each sample sub-image and form a view set V_S.

Step 3: Determine a value (i.e., K) for K-views and use the K-means (or Fuzzy C-means) to derive a set of characteristic views (C_{VS}) with K groups of characteristic views from the view set V_S.

Step 4: Based on the set of characteristic views C_{VS}, calculate a datagram (D) for each of the N sample sub-images. According to Eq. 6.3, each datagram D is normalized to obtain a normalized datagram (D_N). We call each of N normalized datagrams (for each sample sub-image) as a sample datagram (D_S).

Step 5: Scan the image from top-left to top-right and top to bottom using a window of $M \times M$ pixels ($M \times M$ should be much larger than the view size. We have tested different view sizes of 3×3, 4×4, and 5×5, and M value from 20 to 30 in this datagram algorithm), and derive the corresponding normalized datagram for each window.

Step 6: Calculate the difference between the normalized datagram and each of the N sample datagrams (D_S), and classify the central pixel of the windows to the class, such that the difference between the sample datagram of this class and the normalized datagram of the window is the minimum. The difference (*Diff*) in Eq. 6.4 between a normalized datagram for each window, W, as D_{NW} (in Eq. 6.5) and a sample datagram D_S (from Eq. 6.3) can be derived.

$$Diff = \sum_{i=1}^{K} |d_{Si} - d_{Ni}| \qquad (6.4)$$

$$D_{NW} = (d_{S1}, d_{S2}, d_{S3}, \ldots, d_{SK}) \qquad (6.5)$$

Figure 6.3 shows the classification result by using the K-views-D algorithm described above. Table 6.1 shows the experimental results conducted on 55 pairs of images randomly taken from the Brodatz gallery. The average classification

Fig. 6.3 a Classified result by applying the K-views-D algorithm on the image shown in Fig. 6.2a

Table 6.1 Classification accuracy on the experimental results using the K-views-D algorithm. Please note that (1) the images tested are randomly selected from the Brodatz Gallery, (2) the sample sub-image size is 40 × 40; the view size is 3 × 3; K = 60; M = 30. The notation v1\v2 means the classification accuracy to different texture classes. For example, 96\99 (in row 2 and column 2) means 96% of the pixels of D9 and 99% of the pixels of D12 are correctly classified

	D12	D15	D24	D29	D38	D68	D84	D92	D94	D112
D9	96\99	93\100	100\100	99\100	100\100	100\99	100\100	100\100	100\100	100\100
D12		99\96	100\96	90\100	100\100	91\94	100\100	90\100	97\90	99\95
D15			100\100	94\100	100\100	99\89	96\100	87\100	86\99	100\97
D24				94\97	97\100	100\96	95\99	95\98	95\91	100\87
D29					100\100	100\95	100\100	84\100	96\78	100\96
D38						100\87	100\100	100\100	100\80	100\100
D68							86\100	86\100	85\96	99\100
D84								88\98	100\98	100\99
D92									98\77	100\97
D94										100\99

accuracy is 96.6% (when we calculate the classification accuracy, the pixels on the image boundaries are not taken into consideration). The K–views datagram algorithm was used in this experiment. The size of sample sub-image is 40 × 40, the view size is 3 × 3, the number of K-views is K = 60, and M is set to 30 for the K-views datagram algorithm. Sample sub-images are selected randomly. If sample sub-images are carefully chosen, the classification accuracy can be improved. From these experimental results, we observed that the K-views-D algorithm takes less time than the K-views-T algorithm to achieve the same classification accuracy. The K-views-D algorithm does not show a good performance on image D94 versus other images as shown in Table 6.1. The reason is that D94 is not uniform in the distribution of pixels. The left bottom part of the image is much darker than the right top portion in D94. Note that both the K-views-T and K-views-D algorithms are not invariant to texture rotation. This is why the experimental results on D15 versus other images in Table 6.1 do not show high classification accuracy.

6.3 Boundary Refined Texture Segmentation Based on the K-views-D Algorithm

If we do not consider the pixels on the boundary among different texture classes, the K-views-D algorithm can achieve good segmentation results on most natural images and remotely sensed images [8, 9, 11]. But in some applications such as

Fig. 6.4 a An original image
and **b** an initial segmentation
result of **a** using the
K-views-D algorithm

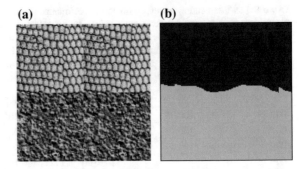

medical image segmentation, an exact segmentation on the boundary areas is needed. Existing K-views algorithms cannot provide satisfactory results for the boundary discrimination among different texture classes.

Figure 6.4 shows an example of the initial segmentation on a pair of image textures taken from the Brodatz Gallery. We can observe from Fig. 6.4 that the misclassifications are near the boundary of two texture classes. This is because the K-views-D method requires a large scanning window. This large window will cover multiple texture classes.

We introduce a new texture segmentation method to improve the segmentation of boundary pixels [6]. We define a boundary set for an image and then apply a modified K-views-T method with a small scanning window to the boundary set to improve the accuracy of the segmentation. The boundary set (B) is defined as a set of pixels which includes all the pixels P with more than half of its neighboring pixels being classified into different classes other than those of P itself by the initial segmented result of K-views-D algorithm. Here the neighboring pixel means a pixel within the $n \times n$ square window around the center pixel, where n is an odd integer. Figure 6.5 shows the misclassified pixels from Fig. 6.4 and the boundary set, B, of the image.

Fig. 6.5 a Misclassified
pixels from Fig. 6.4 and **b** the
boundary set B of the image

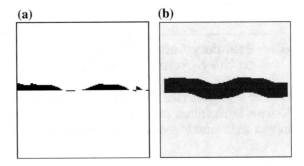

It can be observed in Fig. 6.5 that almost all the misclassified pixels are included in the boundary set. The boundary-refined algorithm consists of three steps in the following:

Step 1: To apply the K-views-D algorithm to the image to obtain an initial segmentation.

Step 2: To find a boundary set which includes the pixels with high probabilities which were misclassified by the initial K-views-D algorithm.

Step 3: To apply the K-views-T method with a small scanning window to the boundary set to refine the segmentation.

The algorithm was tested on the benchmark images which are randomly selected from Brodatz Gallery [3] to evaluate the effectiveness of the algorithm. For the initial K-views-D segmentation, a large K value and reasonable kernel size and view size must be chosen in order to have high segmentation accuracy in the non-boundary areas. We chose $K = 60$, which is the number of views in each characteristic view set. The size of the kernel was chosen as 40×40 ($L = 40$), the size of view was chosen as 10×10 ($m = 10$), the size of the scanning window was chosen as 30×30 ($M = 30$), which is smaller than the size of kernel but is still large enough. At the boundary set searching stage, $n = 11$ is chosen. It means that we consider the pixels in the square block of size 11×11 around a pixel as its neighboring pixels. At the refinement stage, for the K-views-T algorithm, a different K value and a smaller view size are chosen to achieve high segmentation accuracy in the boundary set. We chose $K = 30$, and the size of view was set to 7×7 ($m = 7$) for this stage.

Figure 6.6 shows the boundary refined segmentation result for a combined image consists of five benchmark texture images. As shown in Fig. 6.6, it can be seen that the result shown in **b** is improved with the result shown in **e**.

The most common technique for the diagnosis of prostate cancer is core biopsy using ultrasound images [11]. Many researchers have investigated methods for improving the accuracy of biopsy protocols. Automatic or interactive segmentation of the prostate in ultrasonic prostate images is an important step in these techniques [10]. This boundary refined algorithm provides an automatic method for improving the segmentation of medical images. The experimental results show that this algorithm gives satisfactory segmentation accuracy. Figure 6.7 shows an initial experimental result for an axial ultrasonic prostate image.

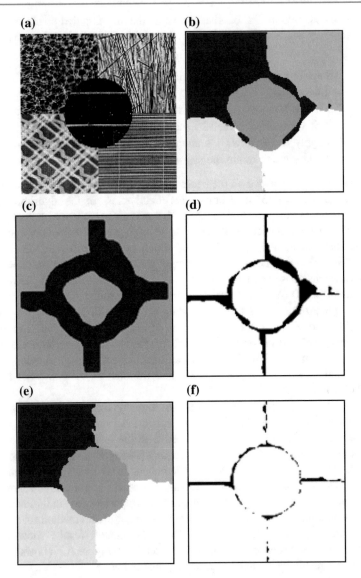

Fig. 6.6 **a** An original image with five different textures, **b** the initial segmentation result, **c** the boundary set, **d** pixels misclassified by the initial segmentation, **e** the refined segmentation result, and **f** pixels still misclassified after the refinement of the segmentation

(a)   **(b)**

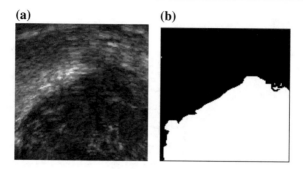

Fig. 6.7 **a** An original ultrasonic prostate image and **b** final segmentation result: white: prostate and black: other tissues [11]

6.4 Summary

A set of characteristic views is a useful feature set to describe image textures. It is possible for us to use only a set of characteristic views to classify different image textures. However, the performance of the K-views template method is related to the view size and the number of characteristic views in each set. Increasing the view size and number of characteristic views will generally improve the classification result at the expense of processing time. The algorithm using datagrams allows us to use a smaller view size, but still, achieve high classification accuracy. When the K-views datagram (K-views-D) algorithm is used for classifying image textures which have random structures, it generally takes much less time than the K-views template (K-views-T) algorithm to achieve the same classification accuracy in the empirical study.

For random image structures, sometimes, it is difficult for us to derive a robust set of characteristic sets. Hence, the normalized datagrams of textures are acquired to replace the K-views feature set. A K-views datagram algorithm is then developed for texture classification by using the datagrams. By testing on textural images, the K-views datagram algorithm can achieve promising classification results. Both the K-views-T and K-views-D algorithms described are the supervised models. In the supervised models, sample sub-images are manually selected. The development for automatic image classification models can be done based on the set of characteristic views and datagrams. Those models should include the semi-automatic model, which can be used to create a database of image textures for unsupervised learning, an automatic model based on the datagram, and an automatic model based on the set of characteristic views.

6.5 Exercises

For a numerical image shown below, assume that there are four different textures in the image; each texture occupies one quadrant.

0	1	2	3	100	90	100	90
1	2	3	0	100	90	100	90
2	3	0	1	100	90	100	90
3	0	1	2	100	90	100	90
200	200	200	200	4	5	6	3
210	190	200	200	6	5	5	4
190	205	210	200	4	5	6	7
205	209	200	210	7	6	4	5

1. Develop a set of views with a template size of 2×2 and 3×3.
2. Develop a set of characteristic K-views from Exercise #1 using the K-views-T algorithm.
3. Compare the performance of the K-views-T algorithm with different K values.
4. Develop the datagram of K-views with different K values.
5. Implement the K-views-D algorithm using a high-level programming language and apply the algorithm to an image consisting of different textures.
6. Compare the performance of K-views-D algorithm, Local Binary Patterns (LBP) and Texture Spectrum (TS) on image textures.

References

1. Arasteh S, Hung C-C (2006) Color and texture image segmentation using uniform local binary pattern. Mach Vis Graph 15(3/4):265–274
2. Arasteh S, Hung C-C, Kuo B-C (2006) Image texture segmentation using local binary pattern and color information. In: The proceedings of the international computer symposium (ICS 2006), Taipei, Taiwan, 4–6 Dec 2006
3. Brodatz P (1966) Textures: a photographic album for artists and designers. Dover Publications, New York
4. He D-C, Wang L (1989) Texture unit, texture spectrum, and texture analysis. In: Proceedings of IGARSS' 89/12th Canadian symposium on remote sensing, vol 5. pp 2769–2772
5. He D-C, Wang L (1990) Texture unit, texture spectrum, and texture analysis. In: IEEE transactions on geosciences and remote sensing, vol 28, issue 4
6. Hung C-C, Yang S, Laymon C (2002) Use of characteristic views in image classification. In: Proceedings of 16th international conference on pattern recognition, pp 949–952
7. Hung C-C, Pham M, Arasteh S, Kuo B-C Coleman T (2006) Image texture classification using texture spectrum and local binary pattern. In: The 2006 IEEE international geoscience & remote sensing symposium (IGARSS), Denver, Colorado, USA, 31 July–4 Aug 2006
8. Lan Y, Liu H, Song E, Hung C-C (2010) An improved K-view algorithm for image texture classification using new characteristic views selection methods. In: Proceedings of the 25th

association of computing machinery (ACM) symposium on applied computing (SAC 2010)–Computational intelligence and image analysis (CIIA) track, Sierre, Swizerland, 21−26 March 2010, pp 960−964. https://doi.org/10.1145/1774088.1774288

9. Lan Y, Liu H, Song E, Hung C-C (2011) A comparative study and analysis on K-view based algorithms for image texture classification. In: Proceedings of the 26th association of computing machinery (ACM) symposium on applied computing (SAC 2011)−computational intelligence, signal and image analysis (CISIA) track, Taichung, Taiwan, 21−24 March 2011. https://doi.org/10.1145/1982185.1982372

10. Ojala T, Pietikainen M, Maenpaa T (2002) Multiresolution gray-scale and rotation invariant texture classification with local binary patterns. In: IEEE transaction on pattern recognition and machine intelligence, vol 24, issue 7

11. Song E, Jin MR, Hung C-C, Lu Y, Xu X (2007) Boundary refined texture segmentation based on K-Views and datagram method. In: Proceedings of the 2007 IEEE international symposium on computational intelligence in image and signal processing (CIISP 2007), Honolulu, HI, USA, 1−6 April 2007, pp 19−23

12. Wang L, He D-C (1990) A new statistical approach for texture analysis. Photogramm Eng Remote Sens 56(1):61–66

13. Yang S, Hung C-C (2003) Image texture classification using datagrams and characteristic views. In: Proceedings of the 18th ACM symposium on applied computing (SAC), Melbourne, FL, 9−12 March 2003, pp 22−26. https://doi.org/10.1145/952532.952538

Features-Based K-views Model

7

> *Now the general who wins a battle makes many calculations in his temple ere the battle is fought. The general who loses a battle makes but few calculations beforehand. Thus do many calculations lead to victory and few calculations to defeat: how much more no calculation at all! It is by attention to this point that I can foresee who is likely to win or lose.*
>
> —Sun Tzu

This chapter describes a new K-views algorithm, the K-views rotation-invariant features (K-views-R) algorithm, for texture image classification using rotation-invariant features. These features are statistically derived from a set of characteristic views for each texture. Unlike the basic K-views model such as K-views-T method, all the views used are transformed into rotation-invariant features, and the characteristic views (i.e., K-views) are selected randomly. This is in contrast to the basic K-views model that uses the K-means algorithm for choosing a set of characteristic views (i.e., K-views). In this new algorithm, the decision of assigning a pixel to a texture class is made by considering all those views, which have the pixel (being classified) located inside the boundary of their views. To preserve the primitive information of a texture class as much as possible, the new algorithm randomly selects K-views of the view set from each sample sub-image as the set of characteristic views.

7.1 Rotation-Invariant Features

Although the K-views datagram (K-views-D) algorithm performs better than the K-views template (K-views-T) algorithm, the classification accuracy in the boundary areas are still a challenging problem for the K-views model. In addition, the "characteristic views" extracted for the K-views-T algorithm are not rotation-invariant, which leads to the recognition of different texture classes cannot be correctly classified when the image is rotated. A new K-views algorithm is developed in order to extract the rotation-invariant features of texture images and

© Springer Nature Switzerland AG 2019
C.-C. Hung et al., *Image Texture Analysis*,
https://doi.org/10.1007/978-3-030-13773-1_7

use them for improving the classification [5]. In this new algorithm, the K-views are randomly selected from the view set of each texture class as the "characteristic views", which is different from the existing K-views-T and K-views-D algorithms. Then, we extract the rotation-invariant features from the "characteristic views". In the process of classification, the decision that a pixel belongs to which texture class is made by considering all the views which consist of the pixel being classified. The rotation-invariant features of each of these corresponding views in the image being classified are also calculated.

To develop a new K-views algorithm, a set of rotation-invariant features will be extracted from all the characteristic views, which are obtained using the K-views-T algorithm as described in Chap 5. The rotation-invariant features are then used in the new K-views algorithm which will be coined as the K-views rotation-invariant features (K-views-R) algorithm. Let us define the feature vector of a view as in Eq. 7.1:

$$f_K = [x_1, x_2, \ldots, x_C]^T \tag{7.1}$$

where C is the dimension of the feature vector which is obtained by stacking all the rows in a (characteristic) view forming a vector and the subscript K is the index representing one of the characteristic views. If a view size is m × n, then C = m × n. Without loss of generality, a normalization process can be applied to the feature vector. The normalized feature vector of the corresponding Kth view is described as in Eq. 7.2:

$$x_{Ki} = \begin{cases} 0, & \text{if } x_{Ki} \le (x_{Oi})_{min} \\ 1, & \text{if } x_{Ki} \ge (x_{Oi})_{max} \\ \dfrac{x_{Ki} - (x_{Oi})_{min}}{(x_{Oi})_{max} - (x_{Oi})_{min}}, & \text{otherwise} \end{cases} \tag{7.2}$$

where $i = 1, \ldots, C$, K is the Kth view and $(x_{Oi})_{min}$ and $(x_{Oi})_{max}$ are defined in Eq. 7.3.

Let S be the total number of characteristic views obtained from a sample sub-image for each texture class. For each sample sub-image with a size of M × N, a set of characteristic views of (M − m + 1)*(N − n + 1) can be extracted if the view size is m × n. Hence, the total number of characteristic views, S = (M − m + 1)*(N − n + 1)*N_{tc}, if we assume that there are N_{tc} texture classes in an image. Now, the $(x_{Oi})_{min}$ and $(x_{Oi})_{max}$ can be defined as in Eqs. 7.3 and 7.4, respectively.

$$(x_{Oi})_{min} = \left\{ \min_{l=1}^{S} x_{l1}, \min_{l=1}^{S} x_{l2}, \ldots, \min_{l=1}^{S} x_{lC} \right\} \tag{7.3}$$

$$(x_{Oi})_{max} = \left\{ \max_{l=1}^{S} x_{l1}, \max_{l=1}^{S} x_{l2}, \ldots, \max_{l=1}^{S} x_{lC} \right\} \tag{7.4}$$

In other words, the minimum and maximum values are chosen for each component across all the feature vectors for the normalization. The subscript Oi in Eqs. 7.3 and 7.4 means for the overall views (i.e., feature vectors) and i refers to a component in a feature vector. Example 7.1 illustrates the concept described above.

Example 7.1 Assume that three characteristic views, $Vcs1$, $Vcs2$, and $Vcs3$, are obtained from a sample sub-image;

0	1	2
1	8	3
2	3	7

4	5	6
6	5	5
4	5	6

10	9	10
10	9	10
10	9	10

Their corresponding feature vectors are

$$f_{v_{cs1}} = [0, 1, 2, 1, 8, 3, 2, 3, 7]^T$$

$$f_{v_{cs2}} = [4, 5, 6, 6, 5, 5, 4, 5, 6]^T$$

$$f_{v_{cs3}} = [10, 9, 10, 10, 9, 10, 10, 9, 10]^T$$

The minimum (min) and maximum (max) are obtained among all the feature vectors for each component as

$$(x_{nc})_{min} = \{0, 1, 2, 1, 5, 3, 2, 3, 6\}$$

$$(x_{nc})_{max} = \{10, 9, 10, 10, 9, 10, 10, 9, 10\}$$

The normalized feature vectors for three characteristic views are

$$f_{v_{cs1}}(nc) = \left[0, 0, 0, 0, \frac{3}{4}, 0, 0, 0, \frac{1}{4}\right]^T$$

$$f_{v_{cs2}}(nc) = \left[\frac{2}{5},\frac{1}{2},\frac{1}{2},\frac{5}{9},0,\frac{2}{7},\frac{1}{4},\frac{1}{3},0\right]^{T}$$

$$f_{v_{cs3}}(nc) = [1, 1, 1, 1, 1, 1, 1, 1, 1]^{T}$$

After the feature vectors are normalized, six significant rotation-invariant features will be extracted from all the feature vectors: (1) mean, (2) standard deviation, (3) entropy, (4) skewness, (5) kurtosis, and (6) histogram. These features provide good discrimination of textures and we can define the rotation-invariant features of a view which has a number of pixels (m × n) in the following [2, 7].

Feature 1: Mean

$$x_1 = \frac{1}{C}\sum_{i=1}^{C} V_i \tag{7.5}$$

Here, V_i is the value of the ith component in the feature vector with dimension C.

Feature 2: Standard Deviation

$$x_2 = \left[\frac{1}{C-1}\left(\sum_{i=1}^{C}(V_i - x_1)^2\right)\right]^{\frac{1}{2}} \tag{7.6}$$

where x_1 is the mean of feature vectors from Eq. 7.5.

Feature 3: Entropy

$$x_3 = -\sum_{i=1}^{C} p_i * lnp_i \tag{7.7}$$

where p_i is the probability of frequency of feature vector i over the total number of feature vectors.

Feature 4: Skew

$$x_4 = \frac{M_{3,3}}{\delta^3} \tag{7.8}$$

where $M_{3,3} = \frac{1}{C}\sum_{i=1}^{C}(V_i - x_1)^3$

Notations V_i and x_1 are similarly defined as in Eq. 7.5 and $M_{3,3}$ is the third-order moment of the feature vectors, and δ is the standard deviation of feature vector.

Feature 5: Kurtosis

$$x_5 = \frac{M_{4,4}}{\delta^4} \qquad (7.9)$$

where $M_{4,4} = \frac{1}{C}\sum_{i=1}^{C}(V_i - x_1)^4$

Notations V_i and x_1 are similarly defined as in Eq. 7.5 and $M_{4,4}$ is the fourth-order moment of feature vectors and δ is the standard deviation of feature vectors.

Feature 6: Histogram (a distribution of components in the feature vector)

The histogram is a graphical representation of the gray scale distribution in a digital image. It plots the number of pixels in the image (vertical axis) with a particular brightness or a particular gray-level range value (horizontal axis). In our feature vectors, it will be the number of components versus the range of values between 0 and 1 in the normalized feature vector. An increase of 0.1 is used from 0 to 1 along the horizontal axis for the histogram.

Next, we define the "correlative view". A correlative view is a view which consists of the pixel being classified as shown in Fig. 7.1 [4, 5]. It may have several correlative views (i.e., feature vectors) covering this pixel. Hence, we may call it the correlative feature vector. The probability of each correlative feature vector will be calculated to determine to which texture class that this pixel belongs.

Considering that for a pixel being classified may have many correlative views containing the current pixel as shown in Fig. 7.1, each correlative view should compete (or vote) to decide which texture class this pixel belongs to. If the view size is m by n, for each pixel there are m × n possible correlate views whose size is m × n containing the pixel. This concept is very similar to the templates used in the Tomita filter where five masks are used to determine the least variance and then calculate the mean in that mask to replace the noisy pixel being considered for

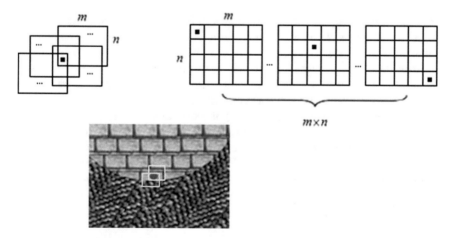

Fig. 7.1 An example of the correlative views [5] in an image

Fig. 7.2 Five masks are used in the Tomita filter; a mask of 3 × 3 in the center and four masks with a size of 3 × 3 in the four corners

10	22	3		
17	5	10	9	
11	10	5	2	12
	26	6	21	9
		17	4	10

Fig. 7.3 Eight masks are used in the Nagao filter; a square mask of 3 × 3 in the center, four masks with each covering 7 pixels in each side, and four masks with each covering 5 pixels in the four corners

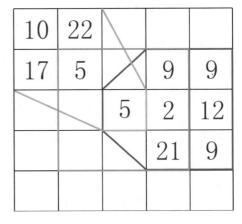

edge-preserving image smoothing as shown in Fig. 7.2 [3, 8]. The similar concept is also used in the Nagao filter which uses nine masks for image smoothing as shown in Fig. 7.3 [6].

Thus, the decision to which texture class this pixel belongs can be determined by the similarity between the correlative views and the characteristic views of a texture class. In other words, we can calculate the average similarity between all the correlative views containing the pixel being classified and all the characteristic views of each texture class. The calculation is based on their normalized feature vectors. Then, we classify this pixel to a texture class with the maximum similarity measure. The similarity of each correlative view and a characteristic view in a texture class can be calculated using the Euclidean distance and taking its inverse as shown in Eq. 7.10. We assume that there are M correlative views and V characteristic views for each of N textures.

$$S_{ij}^k = \frac{1}{|d_{ij}^k|} \tag{7.10}$$

where $i \in 1, \ldots, M, j \in 1, \ldots, V, k \in 1, \ldots, N,$ $|d_{ij}^k|$ is the absolute value of the Euclidean distance between the normalized feature vector of ith correlative view and the normalized feature vector of jth characteristic view in the kth texture class.

Then, we calculate the average similarity of all the similarities calculated in Eq. 7.10 for each texture class as shown in Eq. 7.11.

$$Avg\, S^k = \frac{1}{M \times V} \sum_{i,j} S_{ij}^k \tag{7.11}$$

where i, j, k, M and V are similarly defined as in Eq. 7.10.

The pixel will be classified to the kth texture class based on the maximum similarity obtained in Eq. 7.11.

7.2   The K-views Algorithm Using Rotation-Invariant Features (K-views-R)

We present the new K-views algorithm for texture image classification using rotation-invariant features (K-views-R) in this section [5]. These features include mean, standard deviation, entropy, skewness, kurtosis, and histogram as defined above. The proposed algorithm consists of the training process and the classification process. The training process is to pre-calculate all rotation-invariant features and then store them in a database which will be used later for the classification process.

The K-Views-R Algorithm: Training

Step 1:   Select a sample sub-image randomly for each texture class from the original image. In other words, N sample sub-images will be selected for N texture classes.

Step 2:   Extract a set of views from every sample sub-image using a suitable view size defined by the user.

Step 3:   Determine the value of K for each set of views, and select randomly K views of the view set for each sample sub-image as a set of characteristic views. Alternatively, we can select all the views in the view set as the set of characteristic views.

Step 4:   Compute the rotation-invariant features (feature 1, feature 2, feature 3, feature 4, feature 5, and feature 6) using Eqs. 7.5–7.9 for every feature vector corresponding to a view in the set of characteristic views for each texture class to obtain the normalized feature vectors.

Step 5:   Store all the normalized feature vectors in a database.

Fig. 7.4 The training
scheme for the K-views-R
algorithm

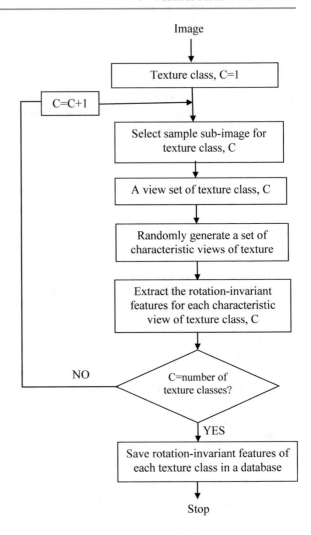

The training scheme is shown in Fig. 7.4 as the flowchart format.

The K-views-R Algorithm: Classification

Step 1:   Retrieve all the normalized feature vectors for all texture classes from the
database.

Step 2:   In the classification scheme, obtain all the correlative views for each pixel
being classified and compute the normalized feature vector of each view
in the correlative views (note that the view size should be the same as the
one used in training).

Step 3:   Use Eq. 7.10 to calculate the similarity between all the correlative views
containing the pixel being classified and all the characteristic views of
each texture class. Please note that we use the normalized feature vector
for each view (from Step 2).

Step 4:   Calculate the average similarity using Eq. 7.11 and select the maximum
similarity which will classify the pixel to the texture class it belongs.

Step 5:   Repeat Steps 2, 3, and 4 for each pixel in the original image being
classified.

The classification scheme is shown in Fig. 7.5 as the flowchart format. Some
experimental results using the K-views-R algorithm for image texture classification
are presented in the next section.

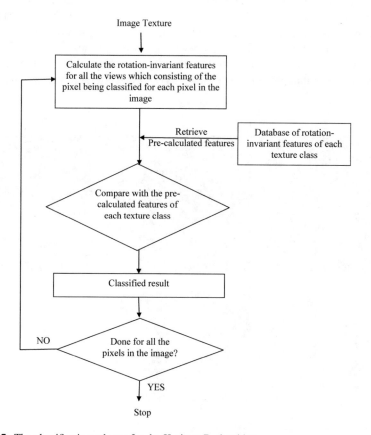

Fig. 7.5   The classification scheme for the K-views-R algorithm

7.3   Experiments on the K-views-R Algorithm

To evaluate the effectiveness of the K-views-R algorithm on the image texture classification, experiments on the Brodatz image textures were carried out and compared to the K-views-T and K-views-D algorithms. Images with different textures were tested. All the images for the testing are of 130×130 pixels, and the sample sub-images size is chosen as 40×40, K is chosen as 100, that is, a set of characteristic views contains 100 views. Different view sizes $(w = 3, 4, \ldots, 30)$ were chosen for testing. The rotation-invariant features extracted for a view are the same as those defined in Sect. 7.1. Experimental results show that the K-views-R algorithm is more robust and accurate compared with the results of the K-views-T and K-views-D algorithms.

Experimental results on some image textures [1] are shown in Figs. 7.6, 7.7, and 7.8 and the corresponding classified errors for different K-views algorithms are shown in Table 7.1. Among three textured images for the testing, the textures of the image in Fig. 7.7 are more similar both in structural and brightness compared to the other two textured images. This textured image is more challenging for the classification. Based on the experimental results, obviously, we can see that the K-views-R algorithm performs better than the K-views-T and K-views-D methods.

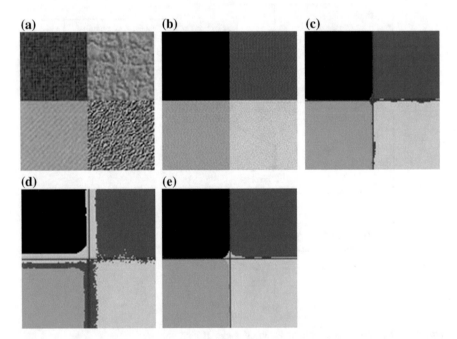

Fig. 7.6 **a** An original image, **b** an ideal classified result, **c** classified result with the K-views-D algorithm, **d** classified result with the K-views-T algorithm, and **e** classified result with the K-views-R algorithm. The red lines are drawn on the top of classified results to show the actual boundary

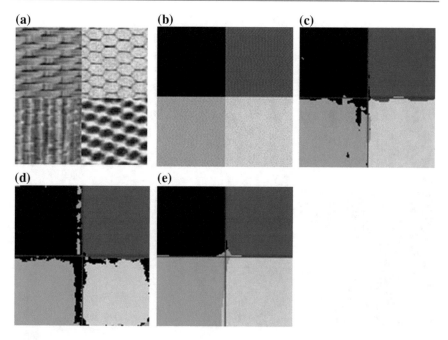

Fig. 7.7 **a** An original image, **b** an ideal classified result, **c** classified result with the K-views-D algorithm, **d** classified result with the K-views-T algorithm, and **e** classified result with the K-views-R algorithm. The red lines are drawn on the top of classified results to show the actual boundary

It also can partition well for the image texture which is difficult for the discrimination in Fig. 7.8.

Figure 7.9 shows another textured image and the classified results. This textured image was used in the comparison given in [6]. The image is composed of five textures which are quite similar, and the textural boundaries are not linear. It is more complex than the images tested in Figs. 7.6, 7.7 and 7.8. The classified result illustrated that the K-views-R algorithm performs better than the other two algorithms.

7.4 The K-views-R Algorithm on Rotated Images

In order to prove that the K-views-R algorithm is rotation-invariant, two rotated images are constructed for testing [3]. The experiment was done by following the steps listed below: Steps 1 and 2 are the same as the schemes for training and classification in the K-views-R algorithm, respectively. Step 2 is to rotate an image texture.

Step 1: Select a sample sub-image randomly for each texture class from the original image to construct normalized feature vectors (i.e., training).

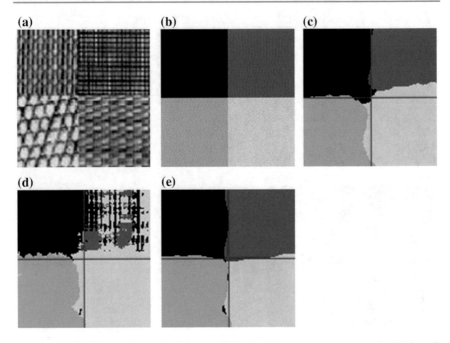

Fig. 7.8 a An original image, **b** an ideal classified result, **c** classified result with the K-views-D algorithm, **d** classified result with the K-views-T algorithm, and **e** classified result with the K-views-R algorithm. The red lines are drawn on the top of classified results to show the actual boundary

Table 7.1 Classified errors for different K-views algorithms

Algorithms			
Images	K-views-D	K-views-T	K-views-R
Image in Fig. 7.6	0.011	0.141	0.009
Image in Fig. 7.7	0.039	0.089	0.018
Image in Fig. 7.8	0.065	0.233	0.029

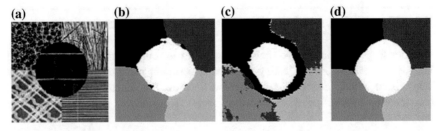

Fig. 7.9 a An original image, **b** classified result with the K-views-D algorithm, **c** classified result with the K-views-T algorithm, and **d** classified result with the K-views-R algorithm

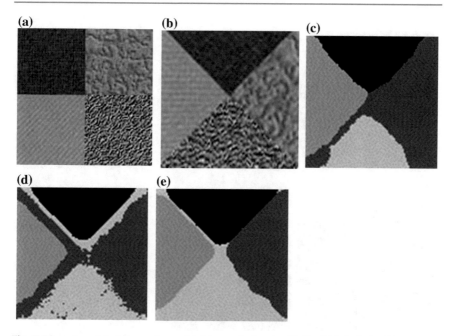

Fig. 7.10 **a** An original image, **b** a rotated image (to be classified) which is derived by rotating the original image clockwise 45 degrees, **c** classified result with the K-views-D algorithm, **d** classified result with the K-views-T algorithm, and **e** classified result with the K-views-R algorithm

Step 2:   Rotate the original image to obtain a new image (a rotated image) to be classified and construct normalized feature vectors for this rotated image.

Step 3:   Use the feature vectors for sample sub-images (obtained in Step 1) which are not rotated to classify the rotated images which are derived in Step 2 (i.e., classification).

The K-views-D method, the K-views-T method, and the K-views-R algorithm are used for the classification, and the classified results are compared. Figures 7.10 and 7.11 are two tested results. The size of both images is 130×130; sample sub-images size is chosen as 40×40, K is set to 100. The original images were rotated clockwise 45 degrees to obtain the rotated images: the size of the rotated image shown in Fig. 7.10b is 90×90 while the size of Fig. 7.11b is 96×96. The K-views-R algorithm achieves more satisfying results. The statistic features used to represent a texture class in the K-views-R algorithm are rotation-invariant, but the characteristic views extracted to represent a texture class in the K-views-D and the K-views-T are not rotation-invariant.

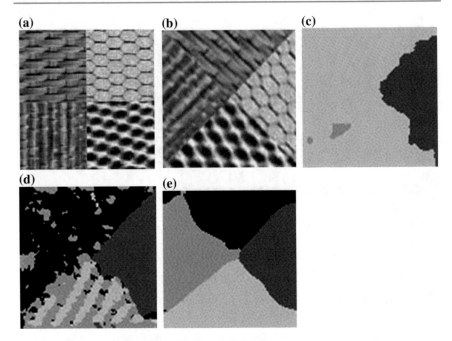

Fig. 7.11 **a** An original image, **b** a rotated image (to be classified), which is derived by rotating the original image clockwise 45 degrees, **c** classified result with the K-views-D algorithm, **d** classified result with the K-views-T algorithm, and **e** classified result with the K-views-R algorithm

7.5   The K-views-R Algorithm Using a View Selection Method to Choose a Set of Characteristic Views

We describe a method for selecting characteristic views to improve the K-views-R algorithm [4]. To be distinguished from the K-views-R algorithm, we will call this algorithm as *the K-views-R with grayness algorithm*. In the K-views-R algorithm, the set of characteristic views are selected randomly for each sample sub-image. This random selection method cannot extract a representative set of characteristic views for a texture class effectively. For example, a set of views chosen randomly are not distributed evenly by the *grayness* of a view. The grayness of a view is defined as the mean of gray levels of all pixels in that view. Some views may be centralized in the zone in which all views may have high grayness values, or in the low grayness value zone. However, one texture class may have many types of characteristic views which have different *grayness* values. Hence, this random method is not suitable for practical applications and it may not select the most representing set of characteristic views.

The selection method is based on the distribution of the grayness of a view to select a set of characteristic views for classification. The method chooses a set of characteristic views based on the interval of the minimum grayness and maximum grayness of all the views in the original (primitive) set of views and then randomly selects the same number of views in each subinterval of the grayness. Similar to the K-views-R algorithm, we select a sample sub-image randomly for each texture class and extract a set of the views from the sub-image to form a primitive view set (V_S) which contains P number of views. Then, a set of K characteristic views will be chosen using the following selection method, where K is less than or equal to P. The view selection method is listed below.

The View Selection Method:

Step 1: Select a sample sub-image randomly for each texture class from the original image and then extract a set of views (Vs).

Step 2: Compute the minimum grayness and maximum grayness for each view of the V_S represented by VSmin and VSmax, respectively.

Step 3: Calculate the zone interval (VSzone) between the VSmin and the VSmax; VSzone = VSmax − VSmin.

Step 4: Divide VSzone into m sub_zones, Length of sub_zones = VSzone/m. The ith sub_zone can be calculated as VSmin + (i − 1)* Length of sub_zones ($i \in (1, m)$).

Step 5: Select a subset of K characteristic views (i.e., K/m views) in each sub_zone from 1 to m, to form a set of characteristic views.

The K-views-R with Grayness Algorithm: Training Process

Step 1: Select a sample sub-image randomly for each texture class from the original image.

Step 2: Extract a set of views from every sample sub-image using a suitable view size.

Step 3: Determine the value of K for each view set, and select a set of K views for each sample sub-image as a set of characteristic views using the view selection method defined above.

Step 4: Compute the rotation-invariant features for each view in the set of characteristic views for each sample sub-image and obtain the normalized feature vectors of these rotation-invariant features.

Step 5: Store all the normalized feature vectors in a database.

The K-views-R with Grayness Algorithm: Classification Process

Step 1: Retrieve all the normalized feature vectors for all texture classes from the database.

Step 2: In the process of classification, derive all the correlative views for each pixel and compute the normalized feature vector of each view of all the correlative views. Note that the view size is the same as the one used in the training process.

Step 3:   Calculate the average similarity between all the correlative views containing the pixel being classified and all the characteristic views of each texture class. The calculation is based on their normalized feature vectors. Then, we classify this pixel to a texture class with the maximum similarity measure.

For example, we assume that there are four texture classes with nine correlative views containing a pixel being classified. We also assume that there are 20 characteristic views for each texture class from Step 2. The similarity of each correlative view and a characteristic view in a texture class can be calculated using the Euclidean distance and taking its inverse as shown in Eq. 7.12.

$$S_{ij}^k = \frac{1}{|d_{ij}^k|} \qquad (7.12)$$

where $i \in 1, \ldots, 9, j \in 1, \ldots, 20, k \in 1, \ldots, 4$, $|d_{ij}^k|$ is the absolute value of the Euclidean distance between the normalized feature vector of ith correlative view and the normalized feature vector of jth characteristic view in the kth texture class.

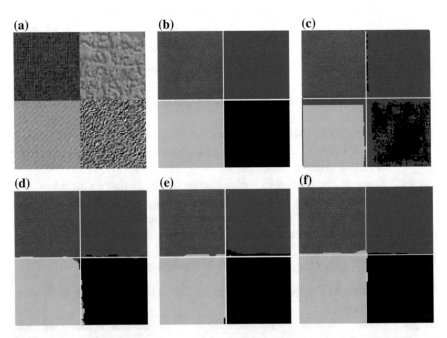

Fig. 7.12   **a** An original image, **b** an ideal classified result (ground truth), **c** classified result with the K-views-T algorithm, **d** classified result with the K-views-D algorithm, **e** classified result with the K-views-R algorithm, and **f** classified result with the K-views-R with grayness algorithm. The white lines are drawn on the top of classified results to show the actual boundary

Then, we calculate the average similarity of all the similarities calculated in Eq. 7.12 for each texture class as shown in Eq. 7.13.

$$Avg\,S^k = \frac{1}{9 \times 20} \sum_{i,j} S^k_{ij} \qquad (7.13)$$

where $i, j, and\, k$ are similarly defined as in Eq. 7.12.

The pixel will be classified to the kth texture class based on the maximum similarity obtained in Eq. 7.13.

Step 4:   Repeat Steps 2 and 3 for each pixel in the original image being classified.

To test the effectiveness of the view selection method, several images were used for the test experiment. Figures 7.12 and 7.13 show some of the experimental results on textured images. The image size is 130×130 pixels. The sample sub-images size is chosen as 40×40 and K is set to 100 in our experiments. Since the number of characteristic views used is 100, in the view selection method, the 100 views are divided into 20 intervals in the K-views-R with grayness algorithm. A rotated image is also constructed for testing. Figure 7.14 shows one of the

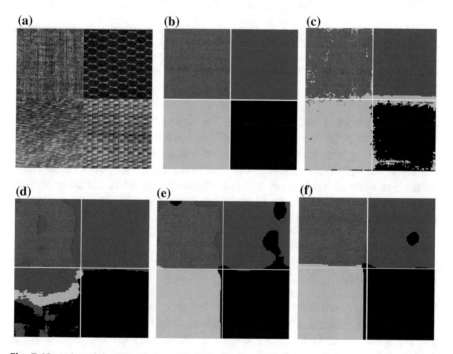

Fig. 7.13 **a** An original image, **b** an ideal classified result (ground truth), **c** classified result with the K-views-T algorithm, **d** classified result with the K-views-D algorithm, **e** classified result with the K-views-R algorithm, and **f** classified result with the K-views-R with grayness algorithm. The white lines are drawn on the top of classified results to show the actual boundary

(a)　　　　　　　　　　(b)　　　　　　　　　　(c)

(d)　　　　　　　　　　(e)　　　　　　　　　　(f)

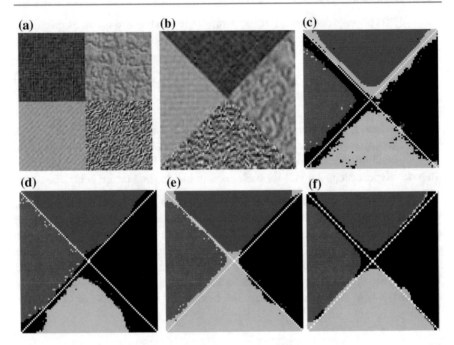

Fig. 7.14 **a** An original image, **b** a rotated image obtained by rotating the original image clockwise 45 degrees, **c** classified result with the K-views-T algorithm, **d** classified result with the K-views-D algorithm, **e** classified result with the K-views-R algorithm, and **f** classified result with the K-views-R with grayness algorithm. The white lines are drawn on the top of classified results to show the actual boundary

experimental results on the rotated image. The size is of 130×130 pixels; sample sub-images size is chosen as 40×40 with K equal to 100. The image is rotated clockwise 45 degrees to obtain the rotated image with a size of 90×90. In summary, the feature-based K-views-R algorithms are giving better classification results than those of the K-views-T and K-views-D algorithms. For some textured images such as Fig. 7.13a, the view selection method will have advantages to achieve better classification results.

7.6　Summary

This chapter presents two feature-based K-views algorithms, K-views-R and K-views-R with grayness, for image texture classification. These two algorithms use the rotation-invariant features which are statistically derived from a set of characteristic views for each texture in the image. As can be seen from the experimental results, the feature-based algorithm is superior to both the K-views-T and K-views-D algorithms. Primarily, it can obtain better results in the boundary areas between different textures.

Generally speaking, the feature-based algorithm has some significant and meaningful characteristics: the decision that a pixel belongs to a texture class is made by all the correlative "views" containing the pixel, which is based on the highest probability, and statistic features are used to represent a texture class. All the features used can be easily extracted from a view, and its computational complexity is simple. Unlike the K-views-T algorithm, the feature-based algorithm does not need to obtain a set of characteristic views through a few times of iterative computation for the K-views clustering. It just needs to directly select K-views randomly from a view set for each sample sub-image as a characteristic view set at one time. Experimental results show that both the K-views-R and K-views-R with grayness algorithm are stable.

Several improvements can be done on the K-views algorithms. For example, we can extract the image feature with affine invariants, which are scaled orthographic projection of planar objects, and projective invariants, which are the perspective projection of planar objects, and develop a method for the automatic determination of the best view size to achieve the optimum classification result.

7.7 Exercises

For a numerical image shown below, assume that there are four different textures in the image; each texture occupies one quadrant.

0	1	2	3	100	90	100	90
1	2	3	0	100	90	100	90
2	3	0	1	100	90	100	90
3	0	1	2	100	90	100	90
200	200	200	200	4	5	6	3
210	190	200	200	6	5	5	4
190	205	210	200	4	5	6	7
205	209	200	210	7	6	4	5

1. Develop a set of characteristic K-views using the K-views-T algorithm for each sub-image texture for all four textured classes.
2. Using the K-views-R algorithm to classify the image with a set of characteristic views obtained in Exercise #1.
3. Using the K-views-R with grayness algorithms to classify the image with a set of characteristic views obtained in Exercise #1.

4. Write a program to implement the K-views-R algorithm and test on some rotated image textures.
5. Write a program to implement the K-views-R with grayness algorithm and test on some rotated image textures.

References

1. Brodatz P (1966) Textures: a photographic album for artists and designers. Dover Publications, New York
2. Haralick RM, Shapiro LG (1993) Computer and robot vision, (Volume I and II). Addison Wesley, Reading
3. Hung C-C, Shin S, Jong J-Y (1996) Use of the sigma probability in Tomita's filter. In: IEEE proceedings of the IEEE southeastcon'96, Tampa, FL USA, 11–14 April 1996
4. Lan Y, Liu H, Song E, Hung CC (2010) An improved K-view algorithm for image texture classification using new characteristic views selection methods. In: Proceedings of the 25th association of computing machinery (**ACM**) symposium on applied computing (SAC 2010)—computational intelligence and image analysis (CIIA) track, Sierre, Switzerland, 21–26 March 2010. https://doi.org/10.1145/1774088.1774288
5. Liu H, Dai S, Song E, Yang C, Hung C-C (2009) A new k-view algorithm for texture image classification using rotation-invariant feature. In: Proceedings of the 24th association of computing machinery (**ACM**) symposium on applied computing (SAC 2009)—computational intelligence and image analysis (CIIA) track, Honolulu, Hawaii, 8–12 March 2009. https://doi.org/10.1145/1529282.1529481
6. Nagao M, Matsuyama T (1979) Edge preserving smoothing. Comput Graph Image Process 9:394–407
7. Palm C (2004) Color texture classification by integrative co-occurrence matrices. Pattern Recogn 37:965–976
8. Tomita F, Tsuji S (1977) Extraction of multiple—regions by smoothing in selected neighborhoods. IEEE Trans Syst Man Cybern SMC-7:107–109
9. Song EM, Jin R, Hung C-C, Lu Y, Xu X (2007) Boundary refined texture segmentation based on K-views and datagram method. In: Proceedings of the 2007 IEEE international symposium on computational intelligence in image and signal processing (CIISP 2007), Honolulu, HI, USA, 1–6 April 2007

Advanced K-views Algorithms

8

> *Kindness in words creates confidence. Kindness in thinking creates profoundness. Kindness in giving creates love.*
>
> —Lao Tzu

This chapter introduces the weighted K-views voting algorithm (K-views-V) and its fast version called the fast K-views-V algorithm. These methods are developed to improve K-views template (K-views-T) and K-views datagram (K-views-D) algorithms for image texture classification. The fast K-views-V algorithm uses a voting method for texture classification and an accelerating method based on the efficient summed square image (SSI) scheme as well as the fast Fourier transform (FFT) to enable overall faster processing while the K-views-V only uses the voting method. In classifying a pixel to a texture class in the K-views-V algorithm, it will be based on the weighted voting method among the "promising" members in the neighborhood of a pixel being classified. In other words, this neighborhood consists of all the views, and each view has this pixel in its territory. Experimental results on some textural images show that this K-views-V algorithm gives higher classification accuracy than the K-views-T and K-views-D algorithms, and improves the accurate classification of pixels near the boundary between textures. In addition, the acceleration method improves the processing speed of the K-views-V algorithm. Compared with the results from earlier K-views algorithms and those of the gray-level co-occurrence matrix (GLCM), the K-views-V algorithm is more robust, fast, and accurate. A comparison on the classified results with the selection of parameters on the view size, sub-image size, and the number of characteristic views is provided in this chapter.

8.1 The Weighted K-views Voting Algorithm (Weighted K-views-V)

The K-views-V [8] algorithm is an efficient approach to improve the K-views-T and K-views-D algorithms [4, 11] for image texture classification. The K-views-V algorithm applies a voting method for texture classification and an accelerating

© Springer Nature Switzerland AG 2019
C.-C. Hung et al., *Image Texture Analysis*,
https://doi.org/10.1007/978-3-030-13773-1_8

method based on the efficient summed square image (SSI) [10] scheme and fast Fourier transform (FFT) for fast processing. The voting method has been proven to play an important role in the group decision [3, 6]. Majority voting is the most natural voting strategy. In this strategy, each voter takes a full vote on a candidate it supports, and then the candidate with the most votes is the winner. In the application of image texture classification, one voter determines which texture class a pixel belongs to. We may consider that the texture class having the majority views in the promising neighborhood is the fittest one to the pixel as shown in Fig. 8.1. Assume that a pixel is located inside the domain of many correlated views such as views shown in Fig. 8.1a. Therefore, these views should be given an opportunity to participate in determining which texture class this pixel belongs to. If the view size is m by n, for each pixel there will be m × n possible correlative views consisting of the corresponding pixel. However, the simple majority voting strategy neglects the weighting factor of each voter. For example, V_1 and V_2 in Fig. 8.1b are two correlative views of the white pixel being classified: V_1 should be given more weight than V_2 for the relative importance of the voting since the white pixel is from texture class T_1 and V_1 is more similar to T_1 than T_2.

Similar to the rotation-invariant feature extraction method we discussed in Chap. 7, $s_{i,j}$ is the similarity measure between the ith correlative view and the jth texture class. The similarity between the corresponding feature vector of the ith correlative view and the corresponding feature vectors of the jth texture class can be defined as in Eq. 8.1:

$$S_{ij} = \frac{1}{|d_{ij}|}$$

(8.1)

where d_{ij} is the Euclidean distance between the feature vector of the ith view and all the feature vectors of the jth texture class.

The more similar a view is to a certain texture class, the more powerful the vote on that class should be. Hence, the weighting factor for the ith view to the jth texture class by W_{ij} is defined as in Eq. 8.2.

$$W_{ij} = \frac{S_{ij}}{\sum_{j=1}^{N} S_{ij}}$$

(8.2)

where N is the number of the texture classes. Therefore, the best-matched texture class (refer to T_p) would be the maximum among the weights calculated for all the correlative views, which is calculated as in Eq. 8.3:

$$T_p = \max \left(\sum_{i=1}^{V} W_{i,1}, \sum_{i=1}^{V} W_{i,2}, \ldots, \sum_{i=1}^{V} W_{i,k} \right)$$

(8.3)

(a)

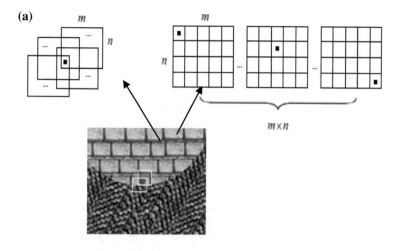

(b)

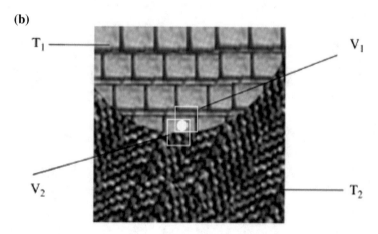

Fig. 8.1 **a** The correlative views of a pixel being classified: the dot in a small square represents the pixel being considered and **b** a voting example with two voters

where V is the number of correlative views in the neighborhood of the pixel being classified and k is the number of texture classes.

In this approach, an image texture is classified by using the weighted votes taken from all the correlative views for each pixel based on the features of characteristics views. We call this approach the weighted K-views voting algorithm (weighted K-views-V). The procedure of this algorithm is listed below:

The Weighted K-views Voting Algorithm (Weighted K-views-V) for the Classification:

Step 1: To obtain all the correlative views in the neighborhood of each pixel being classified (assume that the rotation-invariant features of each correlative views are obtained as described in Chap. 7).

Step 2: To calculate the weighting factor using Eq. 8.2.

Step 3: Determine the maximum of weighted votes using Eq. 8.3.

Step 4: Classify the pixel to the texture class, which is the maximum of the weighted votes from Step 3.

Step 5: Repeat Steps 1–4 for each pixel being classified.

Please note that the view size, the number of views, the number of characteristic views, and the size of a sample sub-image have been discussed in the previous chapters. They are selected similar to those used in the basic K-views-T algorithm. One of experimental results using the K-views-V algorithm is shown in Fig. 8.2 and compared with other K-views algorithms. Figures 8.3 and 8.4 give two more classified results using the weighted K-views-V algorithm [8].

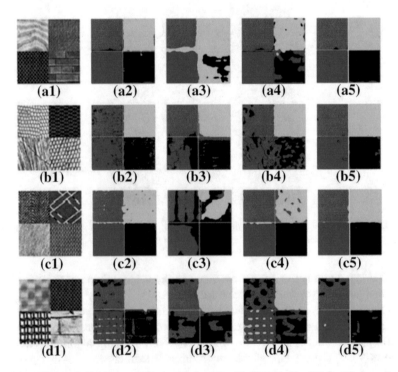

Fig. 8.2 a(1) An original image, **a(2)** classified result with K-views-T, **a(3)** classified result with K-views-D, **a(4)** classified result with GLCM, and **a(5)** classified result with the weighted K-views-V. Classified results of images in **b − d** are similarly interpreted as in **a**. White lines are drawn on the top of classified results to show the actual boundary [8]

(a) (b)

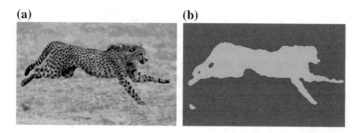

Fig. 8.3 **a** A leopard image and **b** classified result using the weighted K-views-V algorithm

(a) (b)

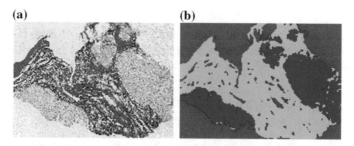

Fig. 8.4 **a** A medical image of liver organ and **b** classified result using the weighted K-views-V algorithm

In the weighted K-views-V algorithm, the Euclidean distance (i.e., similarity measure) is calculated between each view in each texture class and all correlative views for each pixel being classified. The calculation of Euclidean distance is the most time consuming in the algorithm. In order to reduce the computation time, the SSI and FFT methods are employed for the fast weighted K-views-V algorithm [9, 10]. This approach will transform the distance calculation into a simple convolution and summation operation based on the SSI and FFT methods which will be described in the next section.

8.2 Summed Square Image (SSI) and Fast Fourier Transform (FFT) Method in the Fast Weighted K-views Voting Algorithm (Fast Weighted K-views-V)

We assume that N sample sub-images are available for N texture classes. We extract a set of primitive views (S) from each sample sub-image and then derive a set of K-views of the characteristic views denoted by V_{cs} from each primitive view set using the K-means algorithm [4, 11]. Hence, the total number of calculations for obtaining the distance between a pair of two characteristic views (i.e., feature vectors) is $T = Z \times N \times K$ where Z is the number of pixels being classified. We can see that if an image is large, a number of views extracted from the image compared with the number of K-views already defined for a prototype texture are overwhelming. In other words, if we take a view, say V_1, from an image being classified, and a view, say V_2, from a set of K-views, then the number of V_1 (i.e., $Vector_1$ in Eqs. 8.6, 8.7, and 8.9) is much larger than that of V_2 (i.e., $Vector_2$ in Eqs. 8.6, 8.8, and 8.9). To reduce this tremendous amount of calculations, we introduce the summed square image (SSI) and fast Fourier transform method to expedite the computation in the following.

Without loss of generality, we take two views (i.e., V_1 and V_2) with the same view size of m × m, the Euclidean distance between two views, d, will be calculated with Eq. 8.4:

$$d = \sqrt{\|V_1 - V_2\|^2} \tag{8.4}$$

The calculation will be repeated T times to select a minimum distance between two views. This is a very time-consuming process. Equation 8.4 can be further rearranged as Eq. 8.5.

$$d = \sqrt{\|V_1 - V_2\|^2} = \sqrt{V_1^2 + V_2^2 - V_1 \times V_2} \tag{8.5}$$

We can calculate the first term (square of V_1) in Eq. 8.5 by using the summed square image (SSI) technique and calculate the third term (V_1 x V_2) by using the fast Fourier transform (FFT). The second term (square of V_2) will be calculated directly. Please note that the number of V_1 is much larger than that of V_2 as discussed above.

If we perform the calculation by using the feature vector corresponding to each view, the expansion is shown as in Eqs. 8.6−8.9.

$$d = \sqrt{\|Vector_1 - Vector_2\|^2}$$
$$= \sqrt{\sum_{l=0}^{m-1}\sum_{n=0}^{m-1}[V_1(l,n) - V_2(l,n)]^2} \tag{8.6}$$
$$= \sqrt{Vector_1^2 + Vector_2^2 - Vector_1 \times Vector_2}$$

where

$$Vector_1^2 = \sum_{l=0}^{m-1}\sum_{n=0}^{m-1}[V_1(l,n)]^2, \tag{8.7}$$

$$Vector_2^2 = \sum_{l=0}^{m-1}\sum_{n=0}^{m-1}[V_2(l,n)]^2, \text{ and} \tag{8.8}$$

$$Vector_1 \times Vector_2 = 2 \sum_{l=0}^{m-1} \sum_{n=0}^{m-1} [V_1(l,n) * V_2(l,n)] \qquad (8.9)$$

The multiplications in Eq. 8.9 is an inner product operation.

Liu et al. proposed a SSI method which is based on the integral image concept for an image de-noising algorithm [9, 10]. If a patch is in a rectangle shape (including square), its features can be computed very rapidly using an intermediate representation for an image which is called an integral image [9]. Since the view is in a rectangle shape, SSI can be used in our K-views computation. The SSI extends the concept of the integral image: the pixel value at location (x_0, y_0) contains the squared value of each pixel in the original image above and to the left of (x_0, y_0), inclusively. The SSI is then calculated as in Eq. 8.10.

$$SSI(x_0, y_0) = \sum_{x \le x_0, y \le y_0} I(x,y)^2, and \, x, y \in (l, m) \qquad (8.10)$$

where $I(x, y)$ is the pixel value in the image and l is an index for location x and m is an index for location y.

For example, if we need to calculate the sum of squares in region D as shown in Fig. 8.5, it can be obtained as follows (Eq. 8.11):

$$S_D = S_{A \cup B \cup C \cup D} + S_A - S_{A \cup C} - S_{A \cup B} \qquad (8.11)$$

where U is a notation of union.

Based on SSI shown in Fig. 8.5, we can see that

$$S_{A \cup B \cup C \cup D} = SSI(x_2, y_2); S_A = SSI(x_1, y_1);$$
$$S_{A \cup C} = SSI(x_2, y_1); S_{A \cup B} = SSI(x_1, y_2) \qquad (8.12)$$

Fig. 8.5 A summed square image (SSI) illustration

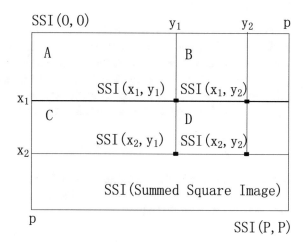

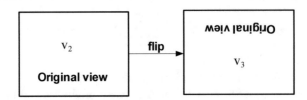

Fig. 8.6 An original view V_2 and its flipped view V_3

Therefore, we obtain the SSI for region D with Eq. 8.13.

$$S_D = SSI(x_2, y_2) + SSI(x_1, y_1) - SSI(x_2, y_1) - SSI(x_1, y_2) \qquad (8.13)$$

Each pixel in the SSI can be calculated in only one pass over the entire image. The computational complexity for computing SSI is $O(P^2)$ (P^2 is the image size). The SSI can be obtained in a linear time proportional to the image size.

The third term $V_1 \times V_2$ can be calculated quickly using the FFT transform [2]. Assuming that the view size is m $\times$ m and m is an odd number, if we flip the characteristic view, V_2, horizontally and then vertically, we will obtain a flipped view labeled as V_3 as shown in Fig. 8.6. We then compute the two-dimensional convolution of views V_1 and V_3. We can derive a $(2 \times m - 1) \times (2 \times m - 1)$ matrix denoted by MAT. According to the convolution theorem, the MAT can be calculated using Eq. 8.14.

$$V_1 \times V_2 = 2(MAT(m, m))$$

Hence,

$$MAT(m, m) = V_1 \times V_2/2 \qquad (8.14)$$

We need to compare each of correlative views (a set of characteristic views consisting of a pixel being classified) with each characteristic view of each texture class. Therefore, we can calculate the two-dimensional convolution of V_3 and the padded correlative view called PadI (PadI is that a view is padded with mirrored reflections before the first element and after the last element along each dimension in the image). The convolution is formulated as in Eq. 8.15:

$$V_3(x, y) * PadI(x, y) \Leftrightarrow IFFT(FFT(V_3(x, y))FFT(PadI(x, y))) \qquad (8.15)$$

where "*" is convolution operation, IFFT (FFT(V_3(x, y))FFT(PadI(x, y))) means that it calculates the FFT of V_3 and PadI individually, multiply them together, and then take the inverse FFT (IFFT).

In the calculation of the Euclidean distance between two views, if we calculate the Euclidean distance directly, it will take $m^2 \times P \times P \times K \times N$ subtraction operations, $(m^2-1) \times P \times P \times K \times N$ addition operations, and $m^2 \times P \times P \times K \times N$ multiplication operations (Eq. 8.4). However, by using the SSI and FFT methods, we can transform the calculations of Euclidean distance to the summation of squares and convolutions.

To compute the SSI of the image, it requires $P \times P$ multiplications and $2 \times P \times P$ addition operations; then, we can calculate the sum of each view in the SSI image. This process will need $P \times P$ additions and $2 \times P \times P$ subtractions approximately to complete the sum of square of $Vector_1$ in each characteristic view. It will take $m^2 \times K \times N$ multiplications and $(m^2-1) \times K \times N$ addition operations for $Vector_2$.

To calculate Vector1 $\times$ Vector2, the first step is to transform it into convolution operations and then calculate the FFT of V_3 and FFT of PadI. Views V_3 and PadI are extended to a size of $(P + m - 1)^2$. Thus, we will have $\frac{(p+m-1)^2}{2} \times \log(p+m-1)$ multiplications and $[(p+m-1)^2\log(p+m-1)]$ additions to calculate extended V_3 and PadI. The IFFT can be calculated similarly, and the multiplication of FFT (V_3) and FFT (PadI) will take $(p + m - 1) \times (p + m - 1)$ multiplications. Therefore, it requires a number of multiplications and additions as shown below (Eqs. 8.16 and 8.17)

$$\left[\frac{3 \times (P+m-1)^2}{2} \times \log(P+m-1) + (P+m-1)^2 \right] \times K \times N \qquad (8.16)$$

$$\left[3 \times (p+m-1)^2 \log(p+m-1) \right] \times K \times N \qquad (8.17)$$

Hence, to calculate the Euclidean distance for two views (feature vectors), we need a total of multiplications (Eq. 8.18) and additions (Eq. 8.19). In addition, there are approximately $2P^2$ subtractions.

$$P^2 + m^2 \times K \times N + \left[\frac{3 \times (P+m-1)^2}{2} \times \log(P+m-1) + (p+m-1)^2 \right] \times K \times N$$
$$(8.18)$$

$$2P^2 + (m^2 - 1) \times K \times N + \left[3(p+m-1)^2 \log(p+m-1) \right] \times K \times N \qquad (8.19)$$

Table 8.1 gives a comparison on the number of multiplications, subtractions, and additions between the direct calculation, SSI and FFT computation giving that $P = 150$, $m = 7$, $K = 30$, and $N = 4$.

Table 8.1 A comparison between the direct and SSI and FFT calculations

Calculation methods	Number of multiplications	Number of subtractions	Number of additions
(1) Direct	132,300,000	132,300,000	129,600,000
(2) SSI and FFT	34,862,249	45,000	63,900,358
Ratio of (1) versus (2)	3.795	2940	2.028

8.3 A Comparison of K-views-T, K-views-D, K-views-R, Weighted K-views-V, and K-views-G Algorithms

We developed the K-views model to characterize the gray-level primitive properties as well as the relationship among them for an image texture. In this section, we compare all the K-views related algorithms, namely, K-views Template algorithm (K-views-T), K-views datagram algorithm (K-views-D), K-views rotation-invariant feature algorithm (K-views-R) [7], and Weighted K-views voting algorithm (weighted K-views-V). In addition, we establish a new K-views algorithm using gray-level co-occurrence matrix (GLCM) , abbreviated as the K-views-G algorithm which is also compared with other K-views algorithms to demonstrate its effectiveness in image texture classification. The K-views-G algorithm in our experiments is briefly described in the following steps.

The K-views-G Algorithm:
   Please note that Steps 1–3 are the same as those in the K-views-T algorithm (in Chap. 5).

Step 1:   Select a sample sub-image randomly in the area of the texture class for each texture class from the original image. In other words, N sample sub-images will be selected for N texture classes. The size of each sub-image can be different.

Step 2:   Extract a view set from each sample sub-image.

Step 3:   Determine the value of K for each view set, and derive K-views for a set of the characteristic view from each sample sub-image using the K-means algorithm or fuzzy C-means algorithm. The number of views, K, may vary for each texture class (i.e., a sample sub-image).

Step 4:   For each characteristic view, V, of an image being classified.

(a) Compute the GLCM feature vectors (i.e., the vector is composed of contrast, correlation, energy, homogeneity and mean) values of K-views of each sub-image.

(b) Compute the GLCM feature vector values of view V. If the best-matched characteristic view belongs to characteristic view set M, classify all pixels in the view, V, from the original image to class M.

(If the view is regarded as a neighborhood of one pixel, classify that pixel only to class M). The Euclidean distance is used for the similarity match in the comparison.

Step 5:   Repeat Step 4 for each pixel in the original image being classified.

All K-views-based algorithms are tested on a set of representative texture images include coarse texture, irregular texture and regular texture which are randomly taken from the Brodatz Gallery [1]. The size of these artificial images is 150×150 pixels (the first original textured image is an exception and its size is 130×130 pixels [11]). In our experiments [5], all K-views-based algorithms were implemented with the same number of characteristic views (i.e., K) and view size. We choose K = 30, that means that there are 30 characteristic views for each texture class. The view size was set to 7×7. The features used in the GLCM include contrast, correlation, energy, homogeneity, and mean. Other parameters were set as follows: distance $\delta = 1$, $\alpha = \{0^{\circ}, 45^{\circ}, 90^{\circ}, 135^{\circ}\}$ and gray level = 16. Although the GLCM model with 0°, 45°, 90°, and 135° four directions was calculated, in our experiments, only one of the best-matched directions was selected as the final result.

By comparing the experimental results in Fig. 8.7, we can see that the weighted K-views-V performs better than K-views-T, K-views-D, K-views-R, and K-views-G. Overall, it achieves the best classification accuracy. From Fig. 8.7, we can also verify that the weighted K-views-V is more robust than the other four algorithms; the reason is that weighted K-views-V uses a decision made by the weighted voting among all the characteristic views involved. Regarding the computation time, we know that the weighted K-views-V is much faster by using the SSI and FFT methods. The K-views-D algorithm takes more computation time which is from 10 to 100 magnitudes of time used in other K-views based

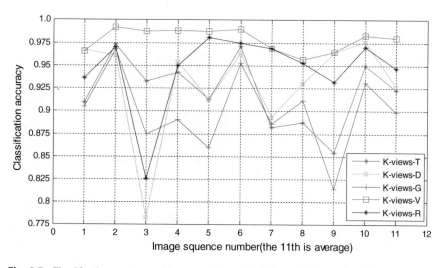

Fig. 8.7 Classification accuracy of image textures with different K-views algorithms [5]

algorithms, because of this algorithm needs to calculate the datagram (D_N) of all the characteristic views. The K-views-G algorithm needs to calculate the GLCM features of each view in the original image and characteristic views, so it is also much slower than other algorithms. Therefore, only five GLCM features were used instead of all GLCM features. In the latter case, the accuracy will be increased.

8.4   Impact of Different Parameters on Classification Accuracy and Computation Time

In those K-views based algorithms, there are three parameters which need be determined a priori: view size (VS), sub-image size (SIS), and the number of characteristic views (i.e., K). In this section, we will discuss the influence on the classification accuracy using different K-views algorithms with a variety of three parameters. Notations used to denote parameters are listed in Table 8.2. An image texture shown in Fig. 8.8 is used in our testing. Experimental results are shown in Table 8.3. We can notice that the classification accuracy can be increased at the expense of processing time by increasing the view size, sub-image size, and number

Table 8.2 Notations used to represent the parameters

Notations	Description
VS	View size
SIS	Sub-image size
K	Number of characteristic views
CA	Classification accuracy
CT	Computation time

Fig. 8.8 An original image

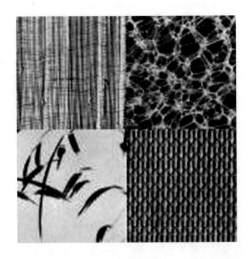

Table 8.3 Classified results of different K-views algorithms with the variety of parameters. The measurement of computation time is measured in seconds. Notations used are listed in Table 8.2

Algorithms	Parameters			Results	
	VS	SIS	K	CA	CT(seconds)
K-views-T	5	40	30	0.893	33.375
	7	40	30	0.920	35.474
	9	40	30	0.928	41.826
	15	40	30	0.919	45.240
	7	20	30	0.876	32.450
	7	30	30	0.918	34.172
	7	44	30	0.917	42.219
	7	40	20	0.912	24.906
	7	40	40	0.923	50.141
	7	40	50	0.925	59.422
K-views-D	5	40	30	0.960	871.566
	7	40	30	0.835	1178.362
	9	40	30	0.888	1642.305
	15	40	30	0.698	1983.990
	7	20	30	0.864	1171.238
	7	30	30	0.887	1172.103
	7	44	30	0.828	1164.211
	7	40	20	0.788	801.278
	7	40	40	0.806	1567.230
	7	40	50	0.842	1955.213
K-views-R	5	40	30	0.906	11.132
	7	40	30	0.948	17.954
	9	40	30	0.957	23.170
	15	40	30	0.953	53.023
	7	20	30	0.923	18.248
	7	30	30	0.943	18.005
	7	44	30	0.954	18.009
	7	40	20	0.935	16.436
	7	40	40	0.949	19.142
	7	40	50	0.951	26.093
K-views-V	5	40	30	0.970	11.563
	7	40	30	0.978	13.547
	9	40	30	0.977	16.188
	15	40	30	0.961	16.344
	7	20	30	0.959	11.188
	7	30	30	0.977	12.476
	7	44	30	0.975	14.047
	7	40	20	0.975	10.000
	7	40	40	0.978	16.375
	7	40	50	0.978	22.562

Table 8.4 Pros and cons of different K-views algorithms

Algorithms	Pros	Cons
K-views-T	Easy for implementation	(1) The behavior of K-views-T is influenced by three parameters shown in Table 8.3 and the characteristic views extracted are not rotation-invariant (2) Supervised mode
K-views-D	Easy for implementation	(1) Same as the K-views-T (2) The computation is heavy (3) Supervised mode
K-views-R	Fast, high efficiency, accurate, and rotation-invariant	(1) The characteristic views are selected randomly for each sample sub-image. This method cannot extract a representative set of characteristic views for a texture class effectively (2) Supervised mode
K-views-V	Fast, high efficiency, accurate	Same as K-views-T

of characteristic views. However, it does not mean that a larger size of those parameters yields more accurate results. For example, in the case of K-views-T, if the VS is set to 15, the classification accuracy is not the highest. Therefore, in order to achieve a higher accuracy at a less computation time, we should explore an intelligent method which can determine the reasonable view size and the number of characteristic views.

The pros and cons of different K-views-based algorithms are concluded in Table 8.4.

8.5   Summary

We give a comparison on the five K-views based algorithms, namely: K-views-T, K-views-D, K-views-R, K-views-V, and K-views-G. All of these algorithms can achieve reasonable classification accuracy in texture image classification. In particular, the K-views-V and the K-views-R algorithms perform better than K-views-T and K-views-D. In addition, we also introduced a new K-views algorithm based on the GLCM feature extractions (K-views-G). Although the feature extraction method is used in both K-views-R and K-views-G, the K-views-R performs better than K-views-G.

The decision in the K-views-D is made by a group of views composed of all "views" contained in a big patch with the current pixel (candidate for the classification) being the center, the simple majority voting strategy neglects the weighting factor of each view. This makes the algorithm less efficient than the K-views-V. Therefore, the K-views-V that utilizes a group decision made through the weighted voting among a set of correlative views is efficient and accurate in the classification. Each view in the neighborhood of the pixel being classified takes a vote weighted by the corresponding value in the voting weighted matrix for each texture class. In terms of time complexity, the K-views-D is very slow as it needs to calculate the datagram (D_N) for all the characteristic views exploited.

In order to reduce the computation time, the SSI and FFT are employed in the K-views-V algorithm which will transform the calculation of Euclidean distance into a simple convolution and summation operations. Therefore, it requires lesser computation time than other K-views based algorithms. All of these K-views based algorithms are supervised learning. With the emergence of the deep machine learning, some of these concepts may be integrated with the deep machine learning to improve the algorithms.

8.6 Exercises

Implement the following algorithms using a high-level computer language.

1. Develop a set of characteristic K-views using the K-views-T algorithm for each sub-image texture for all textured classes and test on a textured image.
2. Using the K-views-R algorithm to classify a textured image with a set of characteristic views obtained in Exercise #1.
3. Implement the K-views-R with grayness algorithms to classify a textured image with a set of characteristic views obtained in Exercise #1.
4. Use the K-views-R algorithm and test on some rotated image textures.
5. Perform the K-views-R with grayness algorithm and test on some rotated image textures.

References

1. Brodatz P (1966) Textures: a photographic album for artists and designers. Dover Publications, New York
2. Castleman KR (1996) Digital image processing. Prentice Hall, Upper Saddle River
3. Coughlin PJ (1992) Probabilistic voting theory. Cambridge University Press, Cambridge
4. Hung C-C, Yang S, Laymon C (2002) Use of characteristic views in image classification. In: Proceedings of 16th international conference on pattern recognition, pp 949–952
5. Lan Y, Liu H, Song E, Hung C-C (2011) A comparative study and analysis on k-view based algorithms for image texture classification. In: Proceedings of the 2011 ACM symposium on applied computing, Taichung, Taiwan, 21 – 25 Mar 2011. https://doi.org/10.1145/1982185.1982372
6. Li R (1999) Fuzzy method in group decision making. Comput Math Appl 38(1):91–101
7. Liu H, Dai S, Song E, Yang C, Hung C-C (2009) A new k-view algorithm for texture image classification using rotation-invariant feature. In: Proceedings of the 24th ACM symposium on applied computing (SAC 2009), pp 914 – 921. https://doi.org/10.1145/1529282.1529481

8. Liu H, Lan Y, Jin R, Song E, Wang Q, Hung C-C (2012) Fast weighted K-view-voting algorithm for image texture classification. Opt Eng 51(2) 2 Mar 2012. https://doi.org/10.1117/1.oe.51.2.027004

9. Liu YL, Wang J, Chen X, Guo YW, Peng QS (2008) A robust and fast non-local means algorithm for image denoising. J Comput Sci Technol 23(2):270–279

10. Viola P, Jones M (2001) Rapid Object Detection using a Boosted Cascade of Simple. Proceedings of the IEEE Conference on Computer Vision and Pattern Recognition 1:I511–I518

11. Yang S, Hung, C-C (2003) Image texture classification using datagrams and characteristic views. In: Proceedings of the 18th ACM symposium on applied computing (SAC), Melbourne, FL, 9 − 12 Mar 2003, pp 22 − 26. https://doi.org/10.1145/952532.952538

Part III
Deep Machine Learning Models for Image Texture Analysis

Foundation of Deep Machine Learning in Neural Networks

9

Our greatest glory is not in never falling, but in rising every time we fall.

—Confucius

This chapter introduces several basic neural network models, which are used as the foundation for the further development of deep machine learning in neural networks. The deep machine learning is a very different approach in terms of feature extraction compared with the traditional feature extraction methods. This conventional feature extraction method has been widely used in the pattern recognition approach. The deep machine learning in neural networks is to automatically "learn" the feature extractors, instead of using human knowledge to design and build feature extractors in the pattern recognition approach. We will describe some typical neural network models that have been successfully used in image and video analysis. One type of the neural networks introduced here is called supervised learning such as the feed-forward multi-layer neural networks, and the other type is called unsupervised learning such as the Kohonen model (also called self-organizing map (SOM)). Both types are widely used in visual recognition before the nurture of the deep machine learning in the convolutional neural networks (CNN). Specifically, the following models will be introduced: (1) the basic neuron model and perceptron, (2) the traditional feed-forward multi-layer neural networks using the backpropagation, (3) the Hopfield neural networks, (4) Boltzmann machines, (5) Restricted Boltzmann machines and Deep Belief Networks, (6) Self-organizing maps, and (7) the Cognitron and Neocognitron. Both Cognitron and Neocognitron are deep neural networks that can perform the self-organizing without any supervision. These models are the foundation for discussing texture classification by using deep neural networks models.

© Springer Nature Switzerland AG 2019
C.-C. Hung et al., *Image Texture Analysis*,
https://doi.org/10.1007/978-3-030-13773-1_9

9.1　Neuron and Perceptron

The traditional artificial neural networks (ANNs) have become an essential part of machine learning in artificial intelligence. The ANN is characterized by three components, namely; the architecture, transfer function (also called squashing or activation functions), and learning algorithm. Many different types of ANNs have been proposed and developed in the literature. There are two types of ANNs which are widely used for the applications; one is called the supervised ANN such as the feed-forward multi-layer neural networks (FMNN) and the other is called the unsupervised ANN such as the self-organizing map (SOM). Hence, it is very often that the SOM is used as an unsupervised classifier and the FMNN is employed as a supervised classification algorithm. In analogy, this corresponds to unsupervised and supervised learning in pattern recognition and machine learning. In general, it is time consuming for training an ANN. It acts very fast during the testing phase once an ANN is well trained [8, 10, 11, 37, 39].

Figure 9.1 illustrates an analogy between a biological neuron and an artificial neuron. The artificial neuron is a simulation of a biological neuron. The artificial neuron is called the McCulloch–Pitts model [27]. This neuron model consists of a summation function ($\sum$) and a squashing function ($f(sum)$) as shown in Eqs. 9.1 and 9.2, respectively.

$$sum = x_1w_1 + x_2w_2 + x_3w_3 + \ldots + x_nw_n = \sum_{i=1}^{n} x_iw_i \tag{9.1}$$

$$Out = f(sum) \tag{9.2}$$

where $x_1(t), x_2(t), \ldots, x_n(t)$ are the input signals and $w_0, w_1, w_2, \ldots, w_n$ are the corresponding weights.

The summation function is to calculate the total of all the multiplications for each input signal to the neuron and the corresponding weight. The squashing function will then convert the sum to fall in a controlled range. It is usually between zero and one. We can think of each neuron as a basic processing element which includes input and output functions. In addition, to accommodate the contribution of the signals traveling along the network, it depends on the strength of the synaptic connection. Figure 9.1c shows the terminology comparison between soma, synapse, dendrite, and axon in a biological neuron and neuron, weight, input, and output, respectively, in an artificial neuron.

A typical supervised ANN architecture is shown in Fig. 9.2. This architecture consists of one input layer with four neurons, one hidden layer with five neurons and one output layer with four neurons. In a network architecture, one has to determine the number of layers and the number of neurons for each layer.

Artificial neural networks (ANN) are the simulated models of the brain and nervous system of the biological neural networks in the mammals and human beings. However, the simulation is a simplified version of the biological neural networks. An ANN is a highly parallel information processing system much more

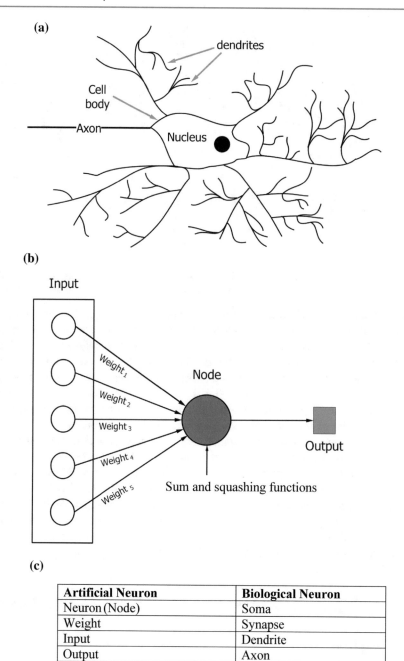

Fig. 9.1 A comparison between **a** a biological neuron and **b** an artificial neuron. The McCulloch–Pitts neuron model is used as an artificial neuron. **c** An analogy between terms used in the artificial neuron and biological neuron

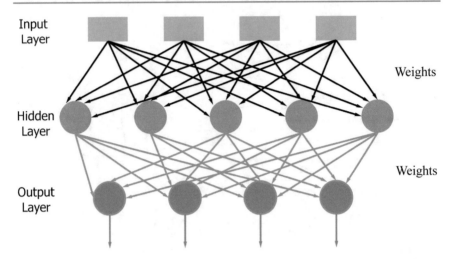

Fig. 9.2 The architecture of a traditional feed-forward multi-layer neural networks (FMNN): four neurons in the input layer, five neurons in the hidden layer, and four neurons in the output layer

like the brain. The ANN has shown its powerful capability as a complex problem solver. Watanabe et al. experimented on the discrimination of color paintings by pigeons [38]. The pigeons are able to learn and successfully recognize the paintings by Monet and Picasso. The experiments also illustrated the generalization capability of the pigeons with the unseen paintings. The experiments prove that the pigeons can extract and recognize the patterns (i.e., features) and generalize from what they have seen to make a prediction. Similar to this biological neural network (BNN), the ANN can be built to have similar functions for problem-solving.

ANN is a nonsymbolic representation as the network functions depending on how we give the weights which are small numeric values. Those weights can be trained (i.e., learned) through the learning algorithms so that an ANN can solve the problem for an application after the training. In a sense, the ANN is more like a functional approximation, which maps from the input to the output. As the transfer function is one of the characterizations in an ANN, several mathematical functions have been used as transfer functions. Figure 9.3 shows two mathematical functions which can be used for this purpose. The sigmoid function is frequently used in the FMNN network due to its simple derivative.

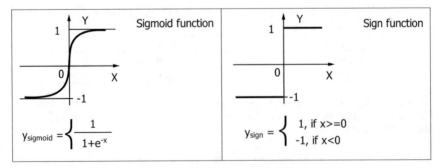

Fig. 9.3 Two mathematical functions can be used as transfer functions

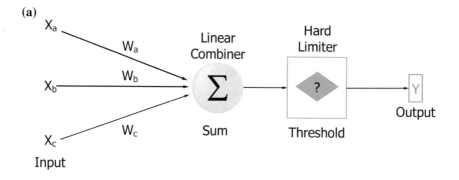

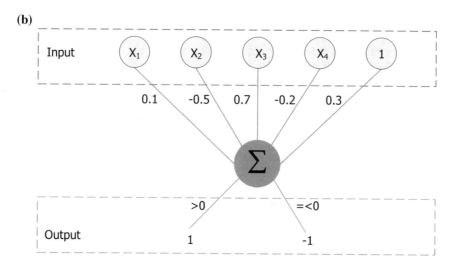

Fig. 9.4 A perceptron: **a** uses a threshold function to derive the output and **b** the threshold function is treated as a special neuron, which is a constant (numerical value one), and its corresponding weight will be learned like other weights in the network

The simplest ANN is the perceptron which consists of two layers, one for the input and the other for the output, as shown in Fig. 9.4 [28]. Similar to any ANN, each input signal for a perceptron is multiplied by the corresponding weight in the connection between the input node and the output node and all the weighted inputs will be added together. This is represented by a summation symbol $\sum$. If the sum is larger than a predetermined threshold, the output is one. Otherwise, it is zero. Instead of using a threshold function as shown in Fig. 9.4a, this threshold function can be replaced by a special neuron, which is a constant one, and its corresponding weight will be learned like other weights in the network (Fig. 9.4b).

To obtain a set of proper weights for a perceptron, the network needs to be trained using a learning algorithm. The learning algorithm usually requires many epochs to complete the proper training. An *epoch* is defined as an iteration by feeding a set of training samples to the network during the training. The following gives a general training algorithm in steps based on the architecture presented in Fig. 9.4b.

Training Algorithm for the Perceptron:

Step 1: Initialization: Set initial weights $w_0, w_1, w_2, \ldots, w_n$ to small random numbers in the range of, for example, [-0.5, 0.5].

Step 2: Activation: Activate the perceptron by applying inputs $x_1(t), x_2(t), \ldots, x_n(t)$ and desired (i.e., target) output $O_T(t)$. Calculate the actual output at iteration t, $O_A(t)$, using Eq. 9.3.

$$O_A(t) = sign\left[\sum_{i=1}^{n} x_i(t)w_i(t)\right] \tag{9.3}$$

where n is the number of the perceptron inputs, and *sign* is the sign function as shown in Fig. 9.3 used as a transfer function.

Step 3: Weight training: Update the weights of the perceptron using Eqs. 9.4 and 9.5.

$$w_i(t+1) = w_i(t) + \Delta w_i(t) \tag{9.4}$$

$$\Delta w_i(t) = \eta * (O_T(t) - O_A(t)) * x_i \tag{9.5}$$

where $\Delta w_i(t)$ is the weight correction at iteration t and η is a learning rate which is between 0.0 and 1.0. The weight correction is computed by the delta rule shown in Eq. 9.5. The learning rate is gradually decreased during the training of the network for the stabilization of the network.

Step 4: Iteration: Increase iteration t by one, go to Step 2 and repeat the process until the network converges.

Example 9.1 illustrates the steps in training a perceptron to perform a logic OR function with two input variables (x_1, x_2). In this example, there are four samples for the training as shown in Table 9.1.

Table 9.1 Illustrates a detailed training of the perceptron. The perceptron completes the training in two epochs. The threshold (θ) is set to 0.2 and learning rate (η) 0.1

Epoch (t)	Inputs (x_1, x_2)	Desired output $(O_T(t))$	Weights (w_1, w_2)	Actual output $(O_A(t))$	Error	Weight adjustment $(\Delta w_1(t), \Delta w_2(t))$	Adjusted weights (w_1, w_2)
1	(0, 0)	0	(1, 0)	0	0	(0, 0)	(1, 0)
	(0, 1)	1	(1, 0)	0	1	(0, 0.1)	(1, 0.1)
	(1, 0)	1	(1, 0.1)	1	0	(0, 0)	(1, 0.1)
	(1, 1)	1	(1, 0.1)	1	0	(0, 0)	(1, 0.1)
2	(0, 0)	0	(1, 0.1)	0	0	(0, 0)	(1, 0.1)
	(0, 1)	1	(1, 0.1)	1	0	(0, 0)	(1, 0.1)
	(1, 0)	1	(1, 0.1)	1	0	(0, 0)	(1, 0.1)
	(1, 1)	1	(1, 0.1)	1	0	(0, 0)	(1, 0.1)

Example 9.1 A perceptron which can perform the OR logic function. Please note that we ignore the biased neuron as shown in Fig. 9.4. Instead, a threshold value is used. (a) Shows an architecture for implementing the OR function and (b) Table 9.1 gives the process of the perceptron training. The threshold (θ) is set to 0.2 and learning rate (η) 0.1. The perceptron converges after two epochs of training.

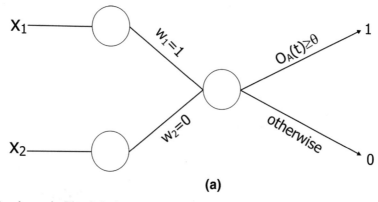

(a)

As shown in Fig. 9.4, the perceptron is nothing but a linear function which can only solve the linear type of problems. It has a very limited capability for applications [28]. However, it is fundamental for the development of more complicated nonlinear ANNs.

9.2 Traditional Feed-Forward Multi-layer Neural Networks (FMNN)

Based on the foundation of the perceptron and the invention of the *backpropagation* algorithm by Werbos [39], Parker [30], and Rumelhart et al. [32], the feed-forward multi-layer neural networks (FMNN) becomes an important model in pattern recognition and machine learning. Figure 9.5 shows a typical FMNN model which consists of three layers. In the literature, it is simply called artificial neural networks (ANN). Please note that the neurons in the input layer are used to take input signals without any functionality at all.

The backpropagation algorithm is commonly used for training a typical feed-forward multi-layer neural network (FMNN). Similar to the perception, the *forward* processing in FMNN is the same: apply an input to the network and calculate the output of each neuron in the network. This step is called *the forward pass*. If an input is represented as a vector, X, and the weights are represented as a matrix, W, then an output vector, O, can be represented as in Eq. 9.6. Here, notation f denotes the function of the FMNN.

$$O_A = f(XW) \tag{9.6}$$

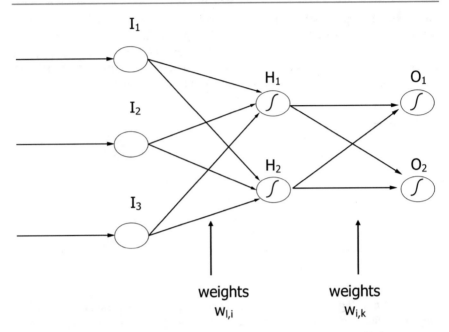

Fig. 9.5 A feed-forward multi-layer neural network with three layers: an input layer, a hidden layer, and an output layer

If the actual output, O_A, is the same as the target output, O_T, the weights remain the same without any change and this processing will be repeated for the remaining training samples. Otherwise, the weights need be adjusted using a learning algorithm such as the backpropagation algorithm.

Using the backpropagation algorithm for adjusting the weights, this algorithm is based on the gradient descent method. Hence, the activation function used for the backpropagation algorithm must be differential. The sigmoid function and its derivative as shown in Eqs. 9.7 and 9.8 are widely used for the backpropagation algorithm. Similar to other activation functions, the sigmoid function transforms the output of the summation into the range of zero and one.

$$O(I) = \frac{1}{1 + e^{-S_I}} \tag{9.7}$$

$$\frac{dO(I)}{dI} = O(I)(1 - O(I)) \tag{9.8}$$

where S_I is the sum of a neuron and $O(I)$ is the actual output of that neuron for an input I.

The adjustment of the weights connected to the neurons between the input layer and the hidden layer is different for those between the hidden layer and the output layer. This is due to the lack of target output for those neurons in the hidden layers.

Therefore, those target outputs have to be estimated for calculating the error to adjust those weights. No matter how many hidden layers are used in an FMNN, the weight adjustment for each neuron in the hidden layer is very similar. The learning rate for a network is similar to that used in the perceptron, and it is gradually decreased during the training of the network for the stabilization of the network.

Similar to the training in perceptron, the training of the FMNN is to adjust the weights by providing a set of training samples as input so that the network can function correctly for an application. A training sample is a pair of input and target output. The input is usually a vector representing a number of features. The number of features in an input vector determines the number of neurons in the input layer of the network. The target output can be in a vector format if multiple neurons are used. However, only one output will be active (means one) and others are inactive (zeros) for the categorization. The following steps give a summary for training an FMNN using the backpropagation algorithm.

Training of the FMNN Using the Backpropagation Algorithm:

Step 1: Initialize all the weights to a small random real number between zero and one. Set up a learning rate η.
Repeat Steps 2–6 for each training pair.

Step 2: Apply an input to the network and calculate the output of each neuron in the network. This step is called *the forward pass*.

Step 3: Calculate the error for a neuron k (in the output layer) between the actual output, $O_k(I)$ and the desired output, $T_k(I)$ using Eq. 9.9 for an input sample I

$$\delta_{O_k} = O_k(I)(1 - O_k(I))(T_k(I) - O_k(I)) \qquad (9.9)$$

Step 4: Adjust each weight in the connections, $w_{i,k}(t)$, between a neuron, i, in the hidden layer and a neuron, k, in the output layer by adding each $\Delta w_{i,k}$ to $w_{i,k}(t)$ using Eqs. 9.10 and 9.11.

$$w_{i,k}(t+1) = w_{i,k}(t) + \Delta w_{i,k} \qquad (9.10)$$

$$\Delta w_{i,k} = \eta \delta_{O_k} h_i(I) \qquad (9.11)$$

where η is a learning rate, t is the number of iterations, and $h_i(I)$ is the output of neuron i for an input sample, I.

Step 5: Calculate the error for a neuron i (in the hidden layer) between the input layer and the hidden layer using Eq. 9.12.

$$\delta_{H_i} = H_i(I)(1 - H_i(I)) \sum_{j \in output\ layer} \delta_{O_j} w_{ij}(t) \qquad (9.12)$$

where $H_i(I)$ is the output of neuron i for an input sample I, δ_{O_j} is the same as that calculated in Eq. 9.9 for each neuron in the output layer and $w_{ij}(t)$ is the weight between neuron i in the input layer and neuron j in the output layer. Due to the lack of a target vector for a hidden layer, the summation in Eq. 9.12 is used to estimate the error for a hidden neuron.

Step 6: Adjust each weight in the connections, $w_{l,i}(t)$, between a neuron, l, in the input layer and a neuron, i, in the hidden layer by adding each $\Delta w_{l,i}$ to $w_{l,i}(t)$ using Eqs. 9.13 and 9.14.

$$w_{l,i}(t+1) = w_{l,i}(t) + \Delta w_{l,i} \tag{9.13}$$

$$\Delta w_{l,i} = \eta \delta_{H_i} I_l \tag{9.14}$$

where I_l is the input to the neuron l in the input layer for an input sample I.

Step 7: Stop the training if the network converges.

Example 9.2 A feed-forward multilayer neural network which is trained to perform the OR logic function; (a) the FMNN architecture and (b) Table 9.2 shows the forward pass and backward propagation. To simplify the operation, an input of $(x_1, x_2) = (1, 1)$ is used for the illustration. We assume that the target output is $(O_1, O_2) = (1, 0)$. In other words, O_1 represents the true output and O_2 the false output. The learning rate is set to 0.1. Initial weights are given as shown in the architecture.

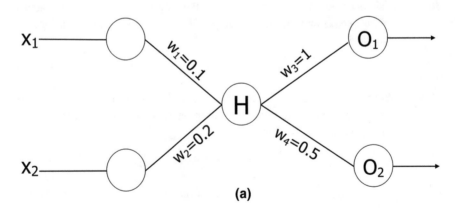

(a)

There are several issues related to the backpropagation training algorithm: network training paralysis, local minima, and long training time. The local minima problem is due to the gradient descent technique used in the backpropagation algorithm and can be solved using an additional term, called *momentum*, in the weight adjustment [8, 10, 11, 37, 39]. In many applications, a biased neuron is added to each neuron in an FMNN. This is very similar to a special neuron used in the perceptron shown in Fig. 9.4. In other words, the input for this biased neuron is always a constant one, and the corresponding weight will be learned precisely the

Table 9.2 Illustrates a detailed training of the neural network only for the input of $(x_1, x_2) = (1.\ 1)$. The first table shows the calculated results for the forward pass. The second and third tables give the weight adjustment between the neurons during the backward propagation. The learning rate (η) is set to 0.1

Forward pass:

Inputs (x_1, x_2)	Hidden neurons (H)		Output neurons		Target output
	Weighted sum		Weighted sum		
	Input	Output	Input	output	
$x_1 = 1$	0.3	0.29	$O_1 = 0.29$	0.29	$T_1 = 1$
$x_2 = 1$	0.3	0.29	$O_2 = 0.14$	0.28	$T_2 = 0$

Backward propagation: adjust weights between the input and hidden layer.

Inputs (x_1, x_2)	Hidden neurons (H)	η	δ_H	$\Delta = \eta\delta_H x_i$	Old weight	New weight
$x_1 = 1$	H	0.1	0.024289	0.002429	$w_1 = 0.1$	$w_1 = 0.102429$
$x_2 = 1$	H	0.1	0.024289	0.002429	$w_2 = 0.2$	$w_2 = 0.202429$

Backward propagation: adjust weights between hidden and output layers.

Hidden neurons (H)	Output Neuron s	η	δ_O	$\Delta = \eta\delta_O H$	Old weight	New weight
H = 0.29	O_1	0.1	0.146189	0.004239	$w_3 = 1$	$w_3 = 1.004239$
H = 0.29	O_2	0.1	−0.056448	−0.001637	$w_4 = 0.5$	$w_4 = 0.498363$

same as other weights. It works similar to adjust the threshold used in the perception and bring about the faster convergence of the training. Several advanced training algorithms such as genetic algorithms have also been proposed in the literature as alternatives for the backpropagation algorithm.

9.3 The Hopfield Neural Network

The Hopfield neural network (HNN) is a recurrent artificial neural network (ANN). It is a very simple, but, useful ANN which can store the patterns [8, 10, 17]. The HNN is different from the FMNN and in that, there is no feedback (i.e., recurrent) from any of the network outputs to their inputs. The HNN is an auto-associative network which will output an entire pattern if the network recognizes an input which may be incomplete or noise-corrupted pattern. Figure 9.6 shows an HNN with three neurons in a single layer. Each neuron is connected to every other neuron in the network. Each neuron is an input, but also an output. The weights in the connection between each pair of neurons are symmetric: in other words, $w_{12} = w_{21}, w_{13} = w_{31},$ *and* $w_{23} = w_{32}$. There are three important properties associated with the HNN: (1) each neuron is a nonlinear unit, (2) synaptic connections (weights) are symmetric, (3) recurrent feedback to each neuron, and (4) the weight is zero for self-feedback of each neuron (it is not shown in Fig. 9.6).

Fig. 9.6 An HNN with three neurons: neurons are denoted as N_1, N_2, and N_3. The weights in the connection between each pair of neurons are symmetric

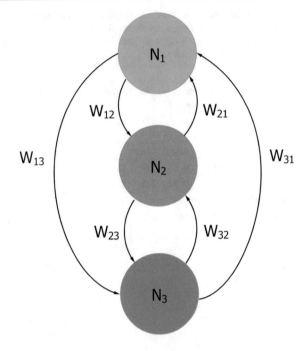

Each neuron in an HNN is always in one of two-state (+1 and −1) at any time. Equation 9.15 is used to calculate the state (S_i) of a neuron i. This equation indicates that the state of a neuron, i, depends on the states of other neurons, j.

$$S_i = +1, \quad if \sum_{j=1}^{N} w_{ij}S_j > \theta_i \tag{9.15}$$

$$else \ S_i = -1$$

where w_{ij} is the weight in the connection between neurons i and j, N is the number of neurons and θ_i is a threshold associated with the neuron i. Please note that we usually use zero for threshold θ_i in Eq. 9.15. An update of a neuron in HNN can be randomly selected in the asynchronous mode. A simultaneous update for all neurons in the synchronous mode is also used.

The energy concept in a system, similar to the Ising model [2], is used in the HNN. Hence, to obtain a solution of the HNN, the network will have to converge to a stable state which indicates the system has reached a minimum energy in the network. The energy function (or called Liapunov function) used in the HNN is defined as in Eq. 9.16 [39].

$$E = -\frac{1}{2}\left(\sum_i \sum_j w_{ij}S_iS_j - \sum_j I_jS_j + \sum_j \theta_jS_j\right) \qquad (9.16)$$

where notations are similarly defined as in Eq. 9.15, the mutual interactions between neurons i and j are characterized by the first term, I_j is an external input to neuron j, and θ_j is the threshold of a neuron j. Since there are only two states (+1 and −1) for each neuron, the state of HNN can be represented by using a binary vector with each component either +1 or −1. Therefore, the state of HNN can be shown as an n-dimensional hypercube for n neurons with 2^n states. Example 9.3 shows a three-dimensional hypercube for the HNN in Fig. 9.6.

Example 9.3 All $2^3 = 8$ states of the HNN with three neurons as shown in Fig. 9.6.

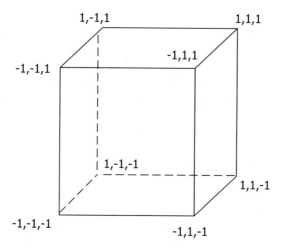

Since the HNN is an auto-associative network, we should be able to store the patterns and then retrieve them later. Hence, there are two modes in the operation of the HNN; the storage mode and the retrieval mode. Similar to a traditional ANN, the storage mode of the HNN is the training of the network. The stochastic dynamics of the network allows the learning of HNN for a set of binary state vectors that represent good solutions. Once the training is completed, the pattern retrieval can be achieved using the retrieval mode (i.e., testing). Some researchers call the training and the testing as encoding and decoding of the patterns, respectively. The HNN can be trained with either Hebbian or Storkey learning [17, 35]. The following algorithm presents steps used for the HNN training using Hebbian learning.

Training of the Hopfield Neural Network (HNN):

Step 1:   Present a set of training patterns $X = \{x_1, x_2, \ldots, x_p\}$ one at a time to all the neurons. We assume that each pattern vector is of p-dimensional and p neurons in the HNN. In other words, the dimensionality of a pattern vector is the same as the number of neurons.

Step 2:   Using the Hebbian learning to train the weight with Eq. 9.17.

$$w_{ij} = \frac{1}{p} \sum_{C=1}^{p} S_i^c S_j^c \; if \; i \neq j$$

$$w_{ij} = 0, \; if \; i = j \tag{9.17}$$

where p is similarly defined as in Step 1, S_i and S_j are the states of neurons i and j, and C is the index of a component in a pattern vector.

The above training can be compactly represented in the matrix format as described in [8]. Once the training is completed, we can think of the HNN is an auto-associative memory. To retrieve a pattern from the HNN, an input vector is presented to the network for the *probe*. The state of the network will be dynamically changed until it stabilizes. The stabilized state will be the retrieved output pattern. The pattern retrieval in the HNN is presented in the following procedure.

Pattern Retrieval in the HNN:

Step 1:   Present an input vector for the probe to the HNN. We assume that the dimensionality of an input vector is the same as the number of neurons in the network. A neuron is randomly selected for the update.

Step 2:   The energy function in Eq. 9.16 is used for testing the stability of the network. If the energy function decreases, the network will change the state. The network will change to a stable state which is the minimum of the energy function. The update of the energy function due to a change in neuron j is done using Eq. 9.18. The change in Eq. 9.18 will then be added to Eq. 9.16 to obtain an updated energy function.

$$\delta E = -\left(\sum_{i \neq j} w_{ij} S_i + I_j - \theta_j \right) \delta S_j \tag{9.18}$$

where notations are similarly defined as in other equations and δS_j is the change in neuron j. Please note that threshold θ_j is zero. It has been illustrated that the network energy must either decrease or remain constant [39].

Example 9.4 Assume that the following training set was used to train a Hopfield network with three neurons as shown in Fig. 9.6.

$$(\ \ 1 \ \ \ 1 \ -1 \ )^T$$
$$(-1 \ -1 \ -1 \ )^T$$
$$(\ \ 1 \ -1 \ -1 \ )^T$$

If this HNN is well trained, a new pattern $new = (1 - 1 \ \ 1)^T$ is presented to this HNN, the state of HNN should return the following pattern: $output = (1 - 1 - 1)^T$.

The HNN discussed so far is a deterministic machine which can be trapped to a local optimal solution. A so-called statistical Hopfield machine has been established by using the Boltzmann distribution to make a probabilistic transition among the state change in the HNN [39]. The Boltzmann distribution function was discussed in the simulated annealing in Chap. 3. A general learning procedure of the statistical Hopfield machine is described below:

Learning of the Statistical Hopfield Machine:

Step 1: For each neuron i, to set its state to one or zero using Eq. 9.19.

> If $P_i = e^{-\delta E_i/(T+1)} > \theta_i$, set the state to 1,
> Otherwise, set the state to -1.
> where
> $\qquad\qquad\qquad\qquad\qquad\qquad\qquad\qquad\qquad\qquad\qquad$ (9.19)

δE_i = the change in the energy function between the next state and the current state of a neuron i,
T = the current temperature, and
θ_i = a random number between 0 and 1.

when the temperature T is high, the probability is close to 1. This means that the probability of setting the state to one is very high. If the temperature is low, the probability is close to 0.

Step 2: Reducing the temperature T and repeat Step 1 until the stable state of the network is reached or the temperature has been reduced to zero.

9.4 Boltzmann Machines (BM)

Similar to many clustering algorithms, the Hopfield neural network also tends to stabilize on a local optimal state in the energy space. Hinton, Ackley, and Sejnowski [1, 13, 14] introduced the Boltzmann machine (BM) which can be considered as an extension of the Hopfield network by using simulated annealing. Besides Hebbian learning, the Boltzmann distribution is used in the BM. The BM is a type of neural networks in which the neurons change the state using the Boltzmann distribution function. Hence, there is a similarity between the simulated annealing (SA) introduced in Chap. 3 and the BM as both use the Boltzmann

Fig. 9.7 An example of the
Boltzmann machine with four
neurons in the visible layer
and three neurons in the
hidden layer

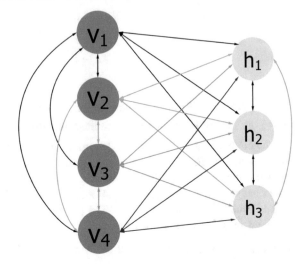

distribution function. The optimization method used in the SA is employed in the
BM to avoid the local optimal problem. The architecture of BM consists of the
visible layer and hidden layer. Hence, the neurons in the visible layer are called
visible neurons. Those neurons in the hidden layer are labeled as *hidden* neurons.
Figure 9.7 shows an example of the BM with visible and hidden layers. The BM is
a fully connected neural network.

The stochastic dynamics of a Boltzmann machine allows this machine to sample
binary state vectors that represent good solutions to the optimization problem. The
Boltzmann machine has two modes: training (i.e., learning) and testing (i.e.,
searching or recall). Due to the hidden neurons used in the Boltzmann machine, its
training is more complicated than that of the HNN. The testing, or recall, is
straightforward. The training procedure has been given by Hinton and Sejnowski
[14] and other researchers [8, 10, 33, 39]. A general training procedure is summarized in five steps in the following: the training will reduce the difference
between what the network settles to in the positive phase and what it settles to in the
negative phase.

Step 1:   Select an example randomly from a training set.
Step 2(a): Train the network in a *positive phase* with a selected example: let the
          network settle using the simulated annealing.
Step 2(b): Calculate the statistics on a pair of neurons which are both on.
Step 3(a): Train the network in a *negative phase* without a training example: let
          the network settle using the simulated annealing.
Step 3(b): Calculate the statistics on a pair of neurons which are both on.
Step 4:   Update the weights based on statistics from Steps 2(b) and 3(b).
Step 5:   Go to Step 1 and repeat.

Similar to [33], a procedure with details is given below:

Training of the Boltzmann Machine:

Step 1:   Calculate the clamped probabilities:

Step 1(a):   Clamp each of a set of training patterns $X = \{x_1, x_2, \ldots, x_p\}$ one at a time to input and output neurons. We assume that each pattern vector is of p-dimensional and p neurons in the input and output layers of the BM. In other words, the dimensionality of a pattern vector is the same as the number of neurons in the input and output layers.

Step 1(b):   Allow the network to settle into equilibrium and record the output values of all neurons.

Step 1(c):   Repeat Steps 1(a) and 1(b) for all training patterns.

Step 1(d):   Calculate the probability (P_{ij}^+) for all training patterns that neurons i and j are both ones using Eq. 9.20

$$P_{ij} = e^{-\delta E_{ij}/(T+1)} \tag{9.20}$$

where δE_{ij} = the change in the energy function between neurons i and j, and T = the current temperature.

Step 2:   Calculate the unclamped probabilities:

Step 2(a):   Start from a random state with the "free run" of the network. "free run" means that no pattern is clamped to the input and output neurons.

Step 2(b):   Repeat step 2(a) (it should be long enough) and record the output values of all neurons.

Step 2(c):   Calculate the probability (P_{ij}^-) for all training patterns such that neurons i and j are both one using Eq. 9.20.

Step 3:   Adjust the weights, w_{ij}, of the network with the amount, δW_{ij}, using Eq. 9.21.

$$\delta W_{ij} = \eta \left(P_{ij}^+ - P_{ij}^- \right) \tag{9.21}$$

where η is the learning rate of the network and probabilities, P_{ij}^+ and P_{ij}^- are from Steps 1 and 2.

Recall in the Boltzmann Machine:

Step 1: The output of a neuron i in the hidden layer is obtained by using Eq. 9.22.

$$H_i = f\left(\sum_{I=1}^{n} S_I W_{Ii} \right) \tag{9.22}$$

where f is a step function, S_I is the state of each neuron in the input layer, and W_{Ii} is the weight in the connection from each neuron in the input layer to neuron i in the hidden layer.

The visible neurons in some Boltzmann machine are divided into the input layer and the output layer [8]. In such a situation, the formula for the output of a hidden neuron can be revised for the output of a visible neuron in the output layer.

9.5 Deep Belief Networks (DBN) and Restricted Boltzmann Machines (RBM)

The traditional multi-layer ANN which uses the gradient descent algorithm such as the backpropagation can be trapped into a local minima solution. Deep belief networks (DBN) are proposed to solve this local optimal problem [12, 15, 25, 36]. The DBN is trained by using a mixture of unsupervised and supervised training. The basic module (a layer) of the DBN is the restricted Boltzmann machine (RBM) and each RBM is trained using a so-called unsupervised pretraining without labeled data [12, 15]. Once each module is well trained, the backpropagation algorithm is then used for the fine-tuning with a set of labeled training data to reduce the overall error for the DBN. Since the RBM is the foundation of the DBN, the RBM is discussed first in the following.

The restricted Boltzmann machine (RBM) is a "restricted" version of the Boltzmann machine (BM). Similar to other ANNs, the neurons in the RBM are massively connected between layers. The restriction means that there are no connections among neurons at the same layer. In other words, there are no intra-layer connections. The architecture is very similar to a symmetrical bipartite and bidirectional graph in graph theory [36]. Figure 9.8 illustrates a 4-3 architecture of RBM. The neurons in the input layer are called visible neurons (denoted by v) while the neurons in the hidden layer are called hidden neurons (denoted by h). The weights between the visible neurons and the hidden neurons are symmetrically connected [12, 15, 34]. The visible neurons will take an input and pass it through the weighted connections to the neurons in the hidden layer. Therefore, hidden neurons are usually called feature detectors. Hinton and Salakhutdinov [15] presented an unsupervised pretraining for the RBM.

An energy function E(v, h), similar to the function used in the HNN, of the visible and hidden neurons is defined in Eq. 9.23.

$$E(v, h) = - \sum_{i \in pixels} b_i v_i - \sum_{j \in features} b_j h_j - \sum_{i,j} v_i h_j w_{ij} \qquad (9.23)$$

where v_i and h_j represent the states of visible neuron i and hidden neuron j, respectively, b_i is a bias in neuron i, and w_{ij} denotes the weight between these two neurons.

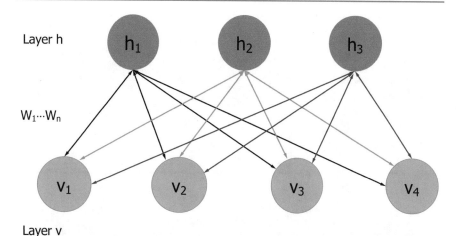

Fig. 9.8 The Restricted Boltzmann Machine (RBM) with 4-3 architecture. Neurons in the visible layer is denoted by v_i with i = 1, 2, 3, and 4, whereas neurons in the hidden layer are labeled as h_j with j = 1, 2, and 3. RBM is a symmetrical, bipartite, and bidirectional graph with shared weights

The network assigns a probability to every input via this energy function [12, 15]. The probability of an input is adjusted by changing the weights and biases for each neuron. The pretraining of the RBM based on those presented in [15] is given below.

The Pretraining of Restricted Boltzmann Machines (RBM):

Step 1:   Given an input, the binary state h_j of each neuron j is set to 1 with probability $P(h_j)$,

$$P(h_j) = \frac{1}{1 + \exp(-(b_j + \sum_i v_i w_{ij}))} \tag{9.24}$$

where b_j is the bias of neuron j, v_i is the state of neuron i, and w_{ij} is the weight between neurons i and j. Once binary states have been chosen for the hidden units h_j, neuron v_i is then set to 1 with probability $P(v_i)$,

$$P(v_i) = \frac{1}{1 + \exp(-(b_i + \sum_j h_j w_{ij}))} \tag{9.25}$$

where symbols are similarly defined as in Eq. 9.24.

Step 2:   The states of the hidden units are then updated so that they represent features of the confabulation (repeat Step 1). The change in a weight is given by Eq. 9.26.

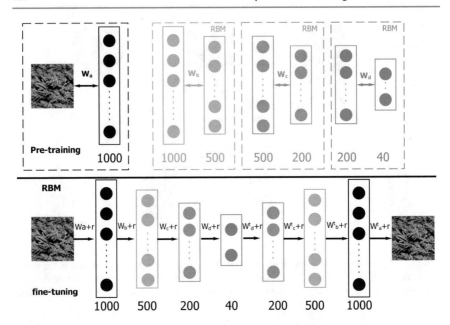

Fig. 9.9 A DBN consists of three RBMs are stacked together (top) and each RBM can be trained separately. A fine-tuning will be done using the backpropagation (bottom) [15]

$$\Delta W_{ij} = \eta \left(v_i h_j^{(Data)} - v_i h_j^{(Recon)} \right) \tag{9.26}$$

where η is a learning rate, the first term $v_i h_j^{(Data)}$ is the fraction of times that neurons i and j are on together when neurons j are being driven by neurons i, and the second term $v_i h_j^{(Recon)}$ is the corresponding fraction for confabulations [12, 15].

As demonstrated by Hinton and Salakhutdinov [15], a stack of RBMs, called DBN, is used for the application as shown in Fig. 9.9. Each RBM will be pretrained separately, and then the backpropagation algorithm will be used to fine-tune the entire stack of RBMs. For this fine-tuning, a labeled dataset must be used for learning the entire network.

Hence, the training of the DBN can be established with the following steps:

The Training of Deep Belief Networks (DBN):

Step 1: To train each module of RBM using the unsupervised pretraining of RBMs above. Please note that an output from a module becomes an input to the next module.

Step 2: To train the entire DBN using the backpropagation algorithm.

9.6 The Self-Organizing Map (SOM)

Researchers in the area of artificial neural networks have proposed and developed many interesting self-organizing neural networks to mimic the functions of human brains. These networks are capable of detecting various features presented in input signals. They have been widely used in applications such as graph bipartitioning, vector quantization, etc. [11]. Among the self-organizing networks developed, the Kohonen's self-organizing feature map (SOM) is perhaps one of the most popular model used in remote sensing image analysis.

The artificial neural network has been an important platform for many years in many different application areas such as speech recognition and pattern recognition [24]. In general, these models are composed of many nonlinear computational elements (neural nodes) operating in parallel and arranged in patterns reminiscent of biological neural nets [11, 21, 24]. One type of these networks, which possess the self-organizing property, is called a competitive learning network [11, 21, 24]. The simple competitive learning network (SCL) has been used as unsupervised training methods in the hybrid image classification system [21].

An artificial neural network model is characterized by the topology, activation function, and learning rules. The topology of SOM is represented as a two-dimensional one-layered output neural net as shown in Fig. 9.10. Each input node is connected to each output node. The dimension of the training patterns determines the number of input nodes. Therefore, for a color image, the number of input neurons is three. During the process of training the network, the input vectors representing signals are fed into the network sequentially one vector at a time. The classes trained by the network are represented by the output nodes with the centroids of each class are stored in the connection as weights between input and output nodes.

The algorithm for SOM that forms feature maps (i.e., the output layer) requires a neighborhood to be defined around each winning node. The size of this neighborhood is gradually decreased [26]. The following algorithm outlines the operation of the SOM algorithm as applied to unsupervised learning [21]; let L denote the dimension of the input vectors, which for us is the number of spectral bands (or spectral features). We assume that a 2-D (N x N) output layer is defined for the algorithm, where N is chosen so that the expected number of classes is less than or equal to N^2

The Competitive Learning in SOM:

Step 1: Initialize weights W_{ij} (t) (i = 1, ..., L and j = 1, ..., N x N) to small random values and iteration count (t) to 1. Choose a maximum number of iterations (Max-It). Determine a learning rate η (t).

Step 2: Present an input pixel $X(t) = (x_1, x_2, x_3, ..., x_i, ..., x_L)$ at time t.

Step 3: Compute the distance d_j between the X(t) and each output node using Eq.9.27

Fig. 9.10 The $X_1, X_2, X_3, \ldots, X_L$ are inputs, one for each component of the feature vectors (i.e., in the three-dimensional case, L is 3). Each node in the SOM (shown as a connected network in two-dimensional space) corresponds to one output. Each output defines a spectral class where its center values are stored in the connections between inputs and the output nodes

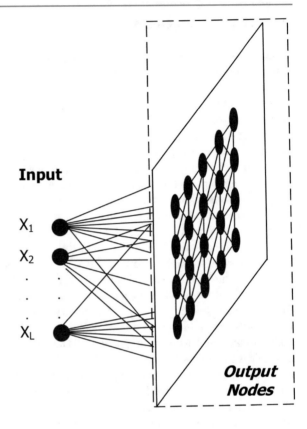

Input

X_1

X_2

X_L

Output Nodes

$$d_j = \sum_{i=1}^{L} \left(x_i - w_{ij}(t)\right)^2 \tag{9.27}$$

where i, j, L, x_i, and w_{ij} are similarly defined as in Steps 1 and 2.

Step 4: Select an output node j^* which has the minimum distance as the winner and update its weights using Eq. 9.28

$$w_{ij^*}(t+1) = w_{ij^*}(t) + \eta(t)\left(x_i - w_{ij^*}(t)\right) \tag{9.28}$$

where i, j, L, x_i and w_{ij} are similarly defined and $1 \leq j^* \leq N \times N$, where $\eta(t)$ is a monotonically slowly decreasing function of t and its value is between 0 and 1.

Step 5: Update the weights of the nodes in the neighborhood of the winning node j^* using the similar formula as Eq. 9.28. The size of the neighborhood is defined as M x M (M $\leq$ N) and M is decreasing as the learning progresses [26].

Step 6: Increase the iteration count (t) by 1 and check if it meets Max-It. If not, repeat steps 2 to 5.

Step 7: Select a subset of these N^2 output nodes as spectral classes; the classification will be the assignment of each pixel in the image to one of N^2 classes based on the minimum distance between each pixel and the N^2 classes.

9.7 Simple Competitive Learning Algorithm Using Genetic Algorithms (SCL-GA)

Competitive learning provides a way to discover the salient general features that can be used to classify a set of patterns [34]. However, there exist some potential problems with the application of competitive learning neural networks: 1) the underutilization of some neurons [11, 21], 2) the learning algorithm is very sensitive to the learning rate, $\eta(t)$, and 3) the number of output nodes in the network must be greater than the number of classes in the training set [21]. Ideally, the number of output nodes should be dynamically determined in the training (learning) environment instead of being specified a priori.

Genetic algorithms (GA) have been used to prevent fixation to the local minima. GA is a randomized heuristic search strategy [16, 29]. It is an evolutionary algorithm, which is a simulation of natural selection in which the population is composed of candidate solutions. The diverse candidates can emerge via the mating process (mainly the mutation and crossover operations) through the evolution of the population. The purpose of crossover and mutation operators is to move a population around on the landscape defined by the fitness function [16, 29]. Evolution begins with a population of randomly selected chromosomes (candidate solutions). Chromosomes will compete with one another for reproduction in each generation. This is based on the Darwinian principle of survival of the fittest. After a number of generations during the evolutionary process, the chromosomes that survived in the population are the optimal solutions. A simple genetic algorithm consists of four basic elements namely, (1) generation of populations of chromosomes, (2) reproduction, (3) crossover, and (4) mutation.

The simple competitive learning algorithm using genetic algorithms (SCL-GA) consists of the following steps [22]; we assume that the string with the lowest mean square error (MSE*) is the optimal solution. The algorithm will search such a string for the solution. The cluster centers will be encoded into the string. The crossover is to combine two subsequences on two strings. The chromosomes in the SCL-GA are a population of a number of strings (say P), which are generated randomly at the beginning. Each string represents a set of K class centers. In the reproduction, the MSE for each string of the population is calculated using Eq. 9.29. The inverse, of the MSE is used as the fitness function. The half of strings will survive and the other half will be regenerated randomly. The MSE is defined as in the following:

String #1	$C_{11}...C_{1L}$	$C_{21}...C_{2L}$	...	$C_{k-1,1}...C_{k-1,L}$	$C_{k1}...C_{kL}$
String #2	$C_{11}...C_{1L}$	$C_{21}...C_{2L}$	...	$C_{k-1,1}...C_{k-1,L}$	$C_{k1}...C_{kL}$
String #3	$C_{11}...C_{1L}$	$C_{21}...C_{2L}$	...	$C_{k-1,1}...C_{k-1,L}$	$C_{k1}...C_{kL}$
$\vdots$	$\vdots$	$\vdots$	...	$\vdots$	$\vdots$
String #P	$C_{11}...C_{1L}$	$C_{21}...C_{2L}$	...	$C_{k-1,1}...C_{k-1,L}$	$C_{k1}...C_{kL}$

Fig. 9.11 A population of P strings with the length of each string, L x K (K is the same as N^2) where L is the dimension of each cluster center and K is the number of clusters

$$\sigma^2 = \frac{1}{m} \sum_{i=1}^{k} \sum_{x \in \theta_i} (x - v_i)^2 \tag{9.29}$$

where m represents the number of pixels in the training set, K is the number of classes, x is the pixel which is an N-dimensional vector in the training set, v_i is the mean of class i, and θ_i is the collection of data points belonging to class i.

Strings using decimal numbers are implemented as arrays in the simulation. Assume that a 2-D (N x N) output layer is defined for the algorithm, where N is chosen so that the expected number of classes is less than or equal to N^2. Hence, the number of classes (clusters), K, is less than or equal to N^2. For the convenience, K is equal to N^2 and L denotes the number of feature vector dimensions used in training. The topology of competitive learning networks is similar to that shown in Fig. 9.10. A population of P strings is shown in Fig. 9.11. The SCL-GA algorithm can be described in the following steps. Please note that we assume that the training dataset has been normalized to the range between 0.0 and 1.0.

The SCL-GA algorithm:

Step 1: Define a number of neural networks, say *P*, and each neural network is similar to that shown in Fig. 9.10. Initialize the center weights $w_{ij}(t)$ at time t = 1 (i = 1, ..., L and j = 1, ..., N x N) to small random values for each neural network. These *P* set of neural networks are identical except their weights are different.

Step 2: Apply the simple competitive learning (SCL) algorithm to each neural network defined in Step 1. Note that only the weight of the winning neuron and its neighboring neurons (for example, in the neighborhood of 3×3 or 5×5) will be updated in each neural network.

Step 3: Generate *P* strings of cluster centers. That is, $S_1 = \{C_1, C_2, ..., C_{N^2}\}$, $S_2 = \{C_1, C_2, ...,C_{N^2}\}$, $S_3 = \{C_1, C_2, ..., C_{N^2}\}$, ..., $S_p = \{C_1, C_2, ..., C_{N^2}\}$, where C_i is the mean of class i in each set (i.e., weights in the connections between the input and the output neurons as shown in Fig. 9.10) and i is from 1 to N^2. The length of each string is L x N^2.

Step 4:   Distribute the pixels in the training set among N^2 clusters by the minimum distance criterion using the Euclidean Distance measure for each string separately and calculate the centroid of each cluster. This step is repeated P times for each string.

Step 5:   (**Crossover**) For each string, a one-point crossover is applied with probability p_c. A partner string is randomly chosen for the mating. Both strings are cut into two portions at a randomly selected position between j and j + 1, and the portions are mutually interchanged where j = 1 to N^2.

Step 6:   (**Mutation**) Mutation with probability p_m is applied to an element for each string. Either −1 or +1 is selected randomly by comparing with probability 0.5 (if the random probability is less than 0.5, −1 is selected. Otherwise, +1 is selected) and added to the chosen element. The mutation operation is used to prevent fixation to the local minimum in the search space.

Step 7:   (**Reproduction**) The inverse of the mean squared error (MSE) is used as the fitness function for each string. All strings are evaluated with the fitness function and pairwise compared. In each comparison, the string with the lowest MSE will be retained and the other one will be discarded and replaced by a new string generated randomly. In other words, only half of the strings in a population are survived and the other half are regenerated by new random strings representing new class means.

Step 8:   Replace all the connection weights of each neural network with each new set of strings obtained in Step 7 for all P neural networks.

Step 9:   Repeat Steps 2–8 for several generations defined by the user.

Step 10: Select a subset of these N^2 output nodes as spectral classes by the user.

Step 11: (**Clustering**) Classify each of all the pixels to one of the clusters based on the minimum distance between the pixel and the clusters (based on the selected output nodes solution obtained in Step 10).

As the training of the SCL-GA involves many iterations of the training samples, it may be time consuming. A systematic sampling from the whole data set (or an image) can be used as a training sample set. Figure 9.12 shows an original thematic mapper (TM) multispectral image and the classified results. The number of iterations used for all algorithms was 10. The crossover probability and mutation probability used was 0.9 and 0.3, respectively, and the population was set to 10 for SCL-GA. For SCL and SCL-GA, the learning rate was generated randomly between 0.0 and 1.0 and divided by the number of iterations. Since three bands were used in the experiments, the dimension of the input vector for SCL and SCL-GA was three. From these experiments, SCL-GA yields better classification results. The SCL is a stable algorithm and the GA makes a significant contribution to the SCL for enhancing the performance.

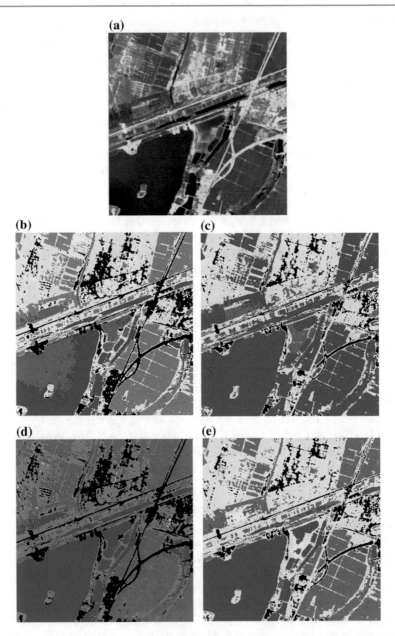

Fig. 9.12 **a** An original image, **b** classified result using the K-means algorithm, **c** classified result using the K-means-GA algorithm (described in Chap. 3), **d** classified result using the SCL algorithm, and **e** classified result using the SCL-GA algorithm. The number of clusters used in the classification was 6

9.8 The Self-Organizing Neocognitron

Neocognitron is a deep neural network model for the visual recognition [4–6]. This might be one of the pioneering works in the research of deep neural network models although some models existed earlier than the neocognitron [3, 7, 23, 31]. The neocognitron is an improved model of cognitron proposed by Fukushima based on the hypothesis that *"the synapse from neuron* x *to neuron* y *is reinforced when* x *fires provided that no neuron in the vicinity of* y *is firing stronger than* y" [3]. This type of neural networks is termed hierarchical neural networks in which sparse and localized synapses are used in the connections between layers [10, 39]. Cognitron is a self-organized model in which the receptive fields of the cells (i.e., neurons) become relatively larger in a deeper layer [3]. In the deeper layer, a neuron can integrate low-level features from previous layers to form high-level features in the hierarchy of cognitron.

Neocognition is more like the biological visual system model proposed by Hubel and Wiesel [18–20]. Hubel and Wiesel proposed a neural model called *cortical plasticity*, also known as *neuroplasticity*. This term refers to the changing of the structure, function, and organization of neurons in response to the new environmental experiences. The network works similar to the traditional ANNs: it takes stimulus input signals and processes them in the successive layers. Similar to cognitron, the neocognitron is also a self-organized model which can extract higher level of features (information) if the network is stimulated with the pattern repeatedly [4–6]. The receptive fields of the cells (neurons) are important mechanisms in the biological visual cortex [18–20]. Unlike the most traditional neural networks which take a feature vector as an input, the input of neocognitron is usually an image since the network was developed for visual recognition.

The neocognitron possesses the characteristics of recognizing patterns from an image based on the geometrical similarity (Gestalt) of the shapes of the objects. Unlike the cognitron, the recognition in this model is not affected by their different position nor by small distortion of their shapes [4–6]. Figure 9.13 shows the architecture of neocognitron. The architecture has an input layer along with several module structures. Each module structure consists of a pair of S-layer and C-layer. The S-layer represents simple neurons and C-layer means complex neurons. In addition, the synaptic weight connections between the S-layer and C-layer is fixed and other synaptic weight connections are trainable, i.e., the synaptic weight connections from the previous C-layer in module n-1 to the current S-layer in the module n.

The input layer consists of a two-dimensional array of cells (neurons), which correspond to photoreceptors of the retina in the biological visual cortex. There is a mapping of visual input from the retina to neurons in the S-layer. This is so-called *retinal mapping* which are the synaptic weight connections between the cells of the input layer and S-layer. Each cell in the S-layer receives signals through the connections that lead from the cells in a neighborhood, i.e., the receptive field, on the preceding layer. Each module consisting of a pair of the S-layer and C-layer can be duplicated many times to form a deep neural network.

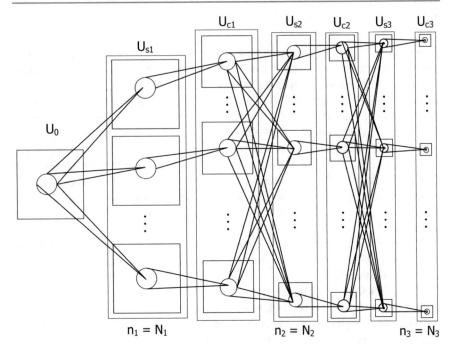

Fig. 9.13 A schematic diagram showing the interconnections between a pair of S-layer and C-layer in a module [4]

Similar to the functions in the visual cortex, neurons in the beginning level respond to low-level features such as lines and edges in a specific orientation. The neurons in the higher level of the neocognitron respond to more complex and abstract objects such as parts. This is due to the deeper the layer is, the receptive field of each neuron becomes larger in the layer [4]. Each neuron in the final layer integrates the information from the previous layers and selectively responds to a specific stimulus pattern (i.e., a feature). Figure 9.14 shows the receptive fields in a layer.

Recall that one of the hypotheses used in neocognitron is that all the S-cells in the same S-plane have input synapses of the same spatial distribution and only the positions of the presynaptic cells shift in the parallel according to the shift in the position of the individual receptive field of S-cells [4]. Figure 9.15 shows an example of how the neurons in the different layers of neocognitron respond to patterns through the synaptic weight connections between cells (neurons) [4]. In the early stage, the neurons identify the low-level features such as partial patterns of an object. Gradually, the neurons in the latter stage of the network can recognize the higher level features such as the complete patterns of an object. In other words, this higher level features are composed of low-level features learned from the early stage in the front layers. For example, in the task of automatic target recognition such as camouflaged enemy tanks detection, the low-level features such as corners and partial edges and lines may be detected in the early stage. The higher level features such as

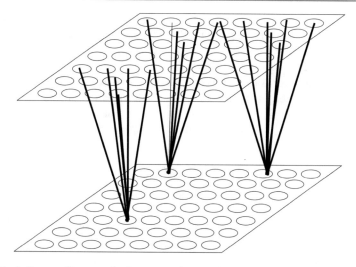

Fig. 9.14 A diagram illustrates the interconnections to the neurons in the receptive fields [4]

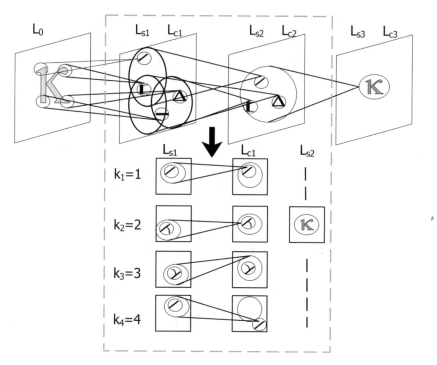

Fig. 9.15 An example shows how the neocognitron works in recognizing partial and complete patterns through the different layers in the process of self-organization [4]

wheels of the tank may be gleaned in the latter stage. As we continue to go more in–depth of the layers in the neocognitron, some complex high-level features such as the shape of the tank may appear in recognition of the final layer. This process is completely a self-organized procedure for performing pattern recognition.

To make the neocognitron to be a self-organized network, the trainable synapses are reinforced (learned) using the winner-take-all method which is very similar to that used in the SOM [10, 39]. The detail to select the winner (i.e., the representative cell) is given in [4]. The procedure for self-organizing learning is summarized below:

The Self-organizing Learning of Neocognitron :

Step 1: A set of images is applied to the neocognitron one at a time and the synaptic weights are adjusted layer by layer from the input layer until the last layer. Please note that only the synaptic weights from the C-layer in the module n − 1 to the S-layer in the module n will participate in the training.

Step 2: A synaptic weight will be increased if (a) the complex neuron is responding or (b) the simple neuron is responding more strongly than any of its immediate neighboring neurons within the competition area.

The neocognitron, when its self-organizing learning is completed, will obtain a neural structure similar to the model of the visual nervous system proposed by Hubel and Wiesel [18–20].

9.9 Summary

This chapter introduces the basics of artificial neural networks for the foundation of deep neural networks. Perceptron is a simple neural network which can only solve the linear type of problems. Traditional neural networks such as feed-forward multi-layer neural networks (FMNN) are the foundation for many advanced neural networks in the deep machine learning. This traditional multi-layer neural network requires a representative dataset for supervised training. Kohonen's self-organizing map (SOM) is an unsupervised clustering method which is useful in the mapping from an high-dimensional space into a two-dimensional map. To improve the performance of the SOM, the population of the SOM is diversified through the evolutionary scheme using the genetic algorithm. An algorithm of SOM-GA is briefly described, and it is tested on the image classification. Both FMNN and SOM are widely used for categorization. Hopfield neural network is an associative-memory network for storing patterns and retrieving them. This pioneering work has led to the development of the Boltzmann Machine (BM) and restricted Boltzmann machine (RBM). A stack of RBMs is formed for multiple layers to become a generative model for deep machine learning. This generative model is called Deep Belief Networks which is popular for many applications. A self-organizing deep neural network, Neocognitron, is briefly described for its superior characteristic of arranging cells (neurons) which is much like the human visual cortex. We may be able to find some roots of popular deep machine learning such as convolutional neural networks (CNN) from the concept used in Neocognitron and others.

9.10 Exercises

Implement the following algorithms using a high-level computer language.

1. Develop a perceptron which can perform as a logic OR function.
2. Perform a feed-forward three-layer neural network which can classify the Iris pattern dataset into three classes (https://archive.ics.uci.edu/ml/datasets/iris).
3. Develop a Kohonen's self-organizing map (SOM) and classify a color image into a two-dimensional class map.
4. Implement the SCL–GA using a computer language. Classify a color image using the SCL-GA and compare with the result obtained from SOM.

References

1. Ackley DH, Hinton GE, Sejnowski TJ (1985) A Learning Algorithm for Boltzman Machines. Cognit Sci 9:147–169
2. Binder K (1994) Ising model. in Hazewinkel, Michiel, Encyclopedia of mathematics. Springer Science + Business Media B.V./Kluwer Academic Publishers, Berlin. ISBN 978-1-55608-010-4
3. Fukushima K (1975) Cognitron: a self-organizing multilayered neural network. Biol Cybern 20:121–136
4. Fukushima K (1980) Neocognitron: a self-organizing neural network model for a mechanism of pattern recognition unaffected by shift in position. Biol Cybern 36:193–202
5. Fukushima K, Miyake S (1982) Neocognitron: A new algorithm for pattern recognition tolerant of deformation and shifts in position. Pattern Recogn 15(6):455–469
6. Fukushima K, Miyake S, Takayuki I (1983) Neocognitron: a neural network model for a mechanism of visual pattern recognition. IEEE Trans Syst Man Cybern SMC-13(5):826–834
7. Giebel H (1971) Feature extraction and recognition of handwritten characters by homogeneous layers. In: Griisser O-J, Klinke R (eds) Pattern recognition in biological and technical systems. Springer, Berlin, pp. 16–169
8. Haykin S (1994) Neural networks: a comprehensive foundation. IEEE Press
9. Heaton J (2015) Artificial Intelligence for Humans (Volume 3): Deep Learning and Neural Networks, Heaton Research Inc. 2015
10. Hecht-Nielsen R (1990) Neurocomputing. Addison-Wesley, Boston. (Good in Hopfield and Boltzmann machines)
11. Hertz J, Krogh A, Palmer RG (1991) Introduction to the theory of neural computation. Addision-Wesley, Boston
12. Hinton GE (2002) Training Products of Experts by Minimizing Contrastive Divergence. Neural Comput 14:1771–1800
13. Hinton GE, Sejnowski TJ (1983) Optimal perceptual inference. In: Proceedings of the IEEE conference on computer vision and pattern recognition, Washington, pp 448–453
14. Hinton GE, Sejnowski TJ (1986) Learning and relearning in Boltzmann machines. In: Rumelhart M et al (ed) Parallel distributed processing, vol 1

15. Hinton GE, Salakhutdinov RR (2006) Reducing the dimensionality of data with neural networks, science, vol 313, 28 JULY 2006
16. Holland JH (1975) Adaptation in natural and artificial systems.The MIT Press, Cambridge
17. Hopfield JJ (1982) Neural networks and physical systems with emergent collective computational abilities. In: Proceedings of the national academy of sciences of the USA, vol 79, pp 2554–2558
18. Hubel DH, Wiesel TN (1959) Receptive fields of single neurones in the cat's visual cortex. J Physiol 148:574–591
19. Hubel DH, Wiesel TN (1962) Receptive fields, binocular interaction and functional architecture in the cat's visual cortex. J Physiol 160:106–154
20. Hubel DH, Wiesel TN (1965) Receptive fields and functional architecture in two nonstriate visual areas (18 and 19) of the cat. J Neurophysiol 28:229–289
21. Hung C-C (1993) Competitive learning networks for unsupervised training. Int J Remote Sens 14(12):2411–2415
22. Hung C-C, Fahsi A, Coleman T (1999) Image classification. In: Encyclopedia of electrical and electronics engineering. Wiley, pp 506–521
23. Kabrisky M (1967) A proposed model for visual information processing in the human brain. Psyccritiques 12(1):34−36
24. Kohonen T (1989) Self-organization and associative memory. Springer, New York
25. Lee H (2010) Unsupervised feature learning via sparse hierarchical representations, Ph.D. dissertation, Stanford University
26. Lippmann RP (1987) Introduction to computing with neural nets. IEEE ASSP Mag
27. McCulloch WW, Pitts W (1943) A logical calculus of the ideas imminent in nervous activity. Bull Math Biophys 5:115–133
28. Minsky ML, Papert S (1969) Perceptrons. MIT Press, Cambridge
29. Mitchell, M., An Introduction to Genetic Algorithms, The MIT Press, 1999
30. Parker DB (1982) "Learning Logic", Invention Report S81–64, File 1. Stanford University, Stanford, CA, Office of Technology Licensing
31. Rosenblatt F (1962) Principles of neurodynamics, perceptrons and the theory of brain mechanisms. Spartan Books, Washington
32. Rumelhart DE, Hinton GE, Williams RJ (1986) Learning internal representations by error propagation. In: Parallel distributed processing, Vol. 1, pp 318–362. MIT Press, Cambridge
33. Simpson PK (1990) Artificial neural systems: foundations, paradigms, applications, and implementation. Pergamon Press, Oxford
34. Smolensky P (1986) In: Rumelhart DE, McClelland JL (eds) Parallel distributed processing: volume 1: foundations. MIT Press, Cambridge, pp 194–281
35. Storkey AJ (1999) Efficient covariance matrix methods for Bayesian Gaussian processes and hopfield neural networks. Ph.D. thesis, University of London
36. Trudeau RJ (2013) Introduction to graph theory, Courier Corporation, 15 Apr 2013
37. Wasserman PD (1989) Neural computing: theory and practice. Van Nostrand Reinhold, New York
38. Watanabe S, Sakamoto J, Wakita M (1995) Pigeons' discrimination of paintings by Monet and Picasso. J Exp Anal Behav 63(2):165–174. https://doi.org/10.1901/jeab.1995.63-165
39. Werbos PJ (1974) Beyond regression: New tools for prediction and analysis in the behavioral sciences. Master Thesis, Harvard University

Convolutional Neural Networks and Texture Classification

10

I have just three things to teach: simplicity, patience, compassion. These three are your greatest treasures.

— Lao Tzu

Convolutional neural networks (CNN) model is an instrumental computational model not only in computer vision but also in many image and video applications. Similar to Cognitron and Neocognitron, CNN can automatically learn the features of data with the multiple layers of neurons in the network. There are several different versions of the CNN which have been reported in the literature. If an original image texture is fed into the CNN, it will be called an image-based CNN. A major problem with the image-based CNNs is that the number of training images is very demanding for the good generalization of the network due to the rotation and scaling change in images. An alternative method is to divide an image into many small patches for the CNN training. This is very similar to the patches used in the K-views model. In this chapter, we will briefly explain the image-based CNN and patch-based CNN for image texture classification. The LeNet-5 neural network architecture will be used as a basic CNN model. CNN is useful not only in the image recognition but also in the textural feature representation. Texture features, which are automatically learned and extracted from a massive amount of images using the CNN, become the focus of developing feature extraction methods.

10.1 Convolutional Neural Networks (CNN)

Deep machine learning is a trend in recent years for the general pattern recognition and machine vision. Most deep machine learning is based on the neural networks approach which uses many layers of neurons; it is more than the number of layers used in the traditional artificial neural networks. Hence, it is called "deep" neural networks. Due to the advance of high-speed computing devices, several high-performance deep neural network models based on the foundation of the

© Springer Nature Switzerland AG 2019
C.-C. Hung et al., *Image Texture Analysis*,
https://doi.org/10.1007/978-3-030-13773-1_10

traditional neural networks have been proposed and widely used in the broad domain of artificial intelligence. One of the deep neural networks, which is called the convolutional neural networks (CNN), might be the most popular in applications [3, 6, 7, 16, 24]. Unlike most traditional pattern recognition systems which require engineer-designed feature extractors, the CNN can automatically learn the feature maps through the deep layers of the networks. This characteristic feature makes CNN suitable for the big data analysis in machine learning. Even more, some advanced CNN has been developed for understanding convolutional networks and generating image descriptions [12, 31].

Convolutional neural networks (CNN) has become a de facto neural network used in visual recognition recently. The architecture of CNN is more or less similar to that of Neocognitron which is one of the earliest deep neural network models although several features used in CNN are quite new [4]. If we consider the traditional multi-layer neural networks (MLNN) as a general architecture, the CNN is a special kind of the MLNN. However, the CNN architecture is still somewhat different although both models use the backpropagation training algorithm for the network parameters learning for their adaptive weights in the connections between the layers. A general architecture of CNN is shown in Fig. 10.1 [16]. The architecture consists of a convolutional layer followed by the pooling layer (we may call this pair of layers as a component). This pair of convolution and pooling layers can be duplicated many times and cascaded to form a "deep" neural network. Then, the fully connected layers will be added in the final stage in the network to serve as the classification for the output of the CNN. The fully connected layers take the high-level feature vectors as the input extracted from the preceding components.

Although the backpropagation algorithm can be used in the training of both ANN and CNN neural networks, some parameters of the networks in CNN are shared by the filters which are called the receptive fields. This sharing will significantly reduce the number of parameters used in the CNN. The pooling layer is the same as the spatial subsampling technique which is used to reduce the dimension of *activation maps* generated from each convolution layer. Hence, it will make the recognition and

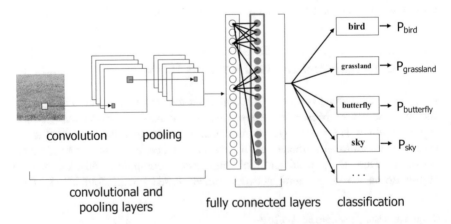

Fig. 10.1 A general architecture of CNN [16]

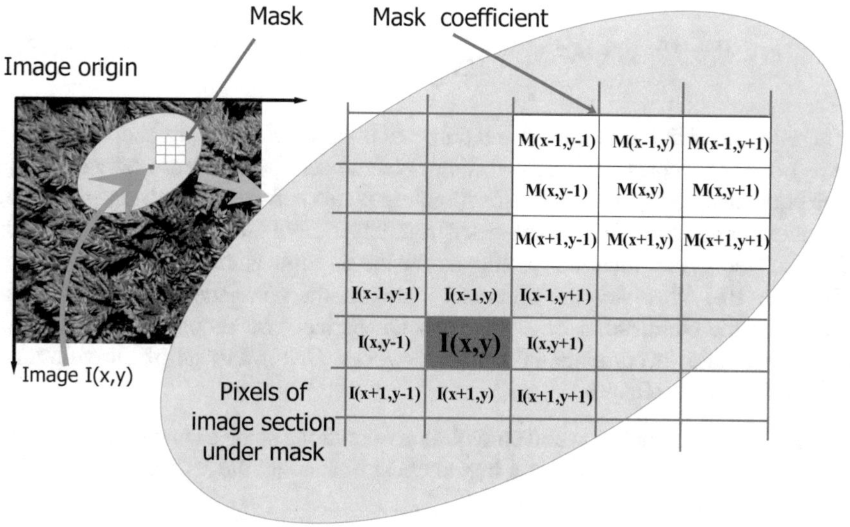

Fig. 10.2 A spatial filter used in the digital image smoothing

detection robust to a limited distortion of objects. The convolutional layer is very similar to the spatial filter design in digital image processing [5, 21]. As shown in Fig. 10.2, a spatial filter (commonly used in digital image smoothing) which is very similar to the filter used in CNN. The filter convolves with an image patch defined by a neighborhood function that is called the *receptive field* in the CNN. Each filter will produce an activation map. In general, *a kernel operator* is used to denote the operation of a spatial filter [5, 21]. The filter scans the entire image in the defined neighborhood from left to right, and then top to bottom of the image. The difference between filters used in CNN and digital image smoothing is that the former can be learned with the backpropagation algorithm, but the latter is engineer-designed and fixed. That is the reason that the filter used in CNN is called the *learnable filter*. The similarity is that both filters are used to detect low-level features from the image. Due to the multiple (i.e., deep) convolution layers used in the CNN network, the learnable filter can gradually derive high-level features in the deep layers. Feature extraction is an essential component of learning in CNN [18].

Please note that there are two important operations called *convolution* and *correlation* [5, 21]. Snyder and Qi pointed out the difference between these two operations in which the correlation refers to a kernel operator [21]. The mathematical expressions for the correlation and convolution are listed in Eqs. 10.1 and 10.2, respectively.

$$g(x,y) = f(x,y)oh(x,y) = \frac{1}{MN}\sum_{m=0}^{M-1}\sum_{n=0}^{N-1}f(m,n)h(x+m,y+n) \qquad (10.1)$$

$$g(x, y) = f(x, y) * h(x, y) = \frac{1}{MN} \sum_{m=0}^{M-1} \sum_{n=0}^{N-1} f(m, n)h(x - m, y - n) \qquad (10.2)$$

where M and N denote the rows and columns of an input image, respectively, and h (x, y) function represents a spatial filter. We can see the difference between these two equations; in Eq. 10.1, the corresponding pixels between the sub-image and the spatial filter are multiplied in the order from left to right and top to bottom while in Eq. 10.2 the spatial filter will be flipped for the multiplications with the sub-image. Example 10.1 illustrates the difference between the correlation and convolution. Based on the clarification of Snyder and Qi, perhaps we should call this type of neural networks as correlational neural networks (CNN), instead of Convolutional Neural Networks (CNN).

Example 10.1 Correlation and convolution operations using a spatial filter: the first two-dimensional (2-D) array is a hypothetical image and the second 2-D array is a spatial filter..

A hypothetical image

1	2	3	5	4
4	5	6	7	8
7	8	9	2	3
3	2	1	4	5
6	7	8	7	9

A spatial filter

1	2	3
4	5	6
7	8	9

For the correlation, we simply multiply the corresponding elements in the sub-image and the spatial filter and sum them together. The result is $1 \times 1 + 2 \times 2 + 3 \times 3 + 4 \times 4 + 5 \times 5 + 6 \times 6 + 7 \times 7 + 8 \times 8 + 9 \times 9 = 285$.

For the convolution, we need to flip the spatial filtering mask based on Eq. 10.2 and then perform the multiplications and summation same as the correlation. The flipped spatial filter is illustrated below:

5	4	6
2	1	3
8	7	9

The result for the convolution is $1 \times 5 + 2 \times 4 + 3 \times 6 + 4 \times 2 + 5 \times 1 + 6 \times 3 + 7 \times 8 + 8 \times 7 + 9 \times 9 = 255$.

However, if multiple pairs of convolutional and pooling layers are used, the learnable spatial filters in the latter stage of the CNN will be able to recognize the higher level features instead of just low-level features. This higher level features are composed of low-level features learned from the early stage in the pair of convolutional and pooling layers. This property is very similar to that demonstrated in the Neocognitron [4]. For example, in the alphabet character recognition [4], the low-level features may be partial lines or curves of characters, and the higher level features are the partial or entire alphabet character. The output of each component in the CNN is called the *activation map or feature map*. As we continue to go more in–depth of the multiple layers in the CNN, some complex high-level features such as the entire alphabet character may appear in the activation map.

In a sense, the CNN uses the concept of a spatial filtering method from digital image processing for its multiple convolution layers along the networks. With this interpretation, the idea on *the number of spatial filters, filter size, stride,* and *padding* used in the CNN is similar to those used in the digital image processing. The number of layers in a CNN, the number of convolutional layers, the number of spatial filters, filter size, stride, and padding are called hyperparameters of a CNN. This means that we need to specify the hyperparameters for training a CNN for a task to be solved. There are some constraints on the stride (S) in terms of relationship among filter width (W_F), the width (i.e., column) of an image (W_I), and padding (P) [9]. The relationship is made easy for the CNN network design. It is expressed in Eq. 10.3.

$$S = \frac{W_I - W_F + 2P}{S + 1} \tag{10.3}$$

The stride must be an integer. Otherwise, the spatial filter cannot be moved around on the input image. We can adjust the padding that adds the extra rows and columns to an image making the result of Eq. 10.3 as an integer. Please note that the stride here is for moving the filter from left to right in an image, i.e., horizontally. It is implicitly assumed that the move from top to bottom (i.e., vertically) is one row at a time. If we need to move the filter vertically similar to the horizontal, we may use Eq. 10.3 to calculate the stride for the vertical movement.

The CNN has shown its robustness to a certain degree of pattern distortions and simple geometric transformations in image recognition. The popular LeNet-5, one of the foundational CNN models, introduced by LeCun et al. is mainly for handwritten and machine-printed character recognition that possesses the property of feature invariance [16]. In other words, LeNet-5 is robust in the image recognition regardless of shift, scale and distortion variance to a certain degree. This is due to the use of the pooling layer. LeNet-5 and its variations are widely used for image classification and recognition. The LeNet-5 architecture consists of *local receptive fields, shared weights, subsampling (i.e., pooling),* and *fully connected layers connected to the output layer.* The local receptive field is very similar to the spatial

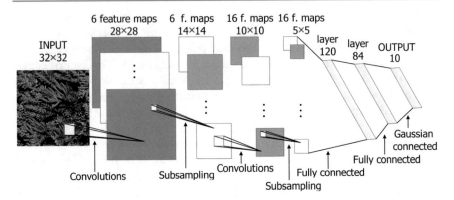

Fig. 10.3 LeNet-5 architecture. The subsampling is also called pooling [16]

filter such as a size of 3×3 or 5×5 neighborhood window in digital image smoothing. Each neuron is connected to only a local subregion of the input image or activation map generated from a layer. The shared weights capture the translational invariances and other invariances in the input image and activation maps.

Similar to the CNN architecture as shown in Fig. 10.1, LeNet-5 shown in Fig. 10.3 which consists of the convolutional layer, pooling layer, fully connected layer, and output layer. In addition, the transfer function called ReLU is used for squashing the output of the convolutional layer. Similar to the traditional neural network training, the weights are randomly generated at the beginning with the proper variance. The activation function ReLU uses a small positive bias before the mapping [16].

The convolutional layer in the CNN is somewhat similar to the Neocognitron as shown in Fig. 10.4. A neuron of a spatial filter in Layer L is connected to a small neighborhood in the previous Layer L-1. These receptive fields form a set of trainable filters which will generate activation (i.e., feature) maps. This is very similar to the spatial filter used in digital image processing to obtaining the most appropriate response from an input image. However, the weights for each filter are trainable and shared across the neurons by adjusting the associated weights by learning the features and patterns from the image or feature map.

The spatial kernel operator of the trainable filters is similar to Eq. 10.1, however, now we are working on the neurons that are trainable and adaptive. Since the CNN is supervised learning, we need to provide a set of labeled images for optimizing the weights of filters. The initial weights are randomly given just the same as most traditional neural networks. A mathematical formula for each spatial filter in the convolutional layer is given in Eq. 10.4.

$$f_{rc}^{l} = \varphi \left(\sum_{i=1}^{S_r} \sum_{j=1}^{S_c} f_{(r+i-1)(c+j-1)}^{l-1} w_{ij}^{l} + b^{l} \right) \qquad (10.4)$$

Fig. 10.4 A diagram illustrates the relations of an input layer (Layer L-1) and an output layer (Layer L) for the receptive fields

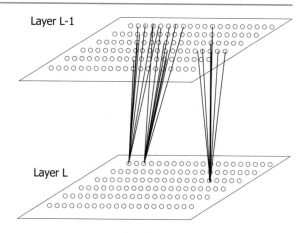

Fig. 10.5 A rectified linear function (ReLU)

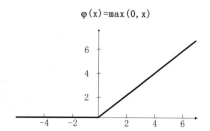

where f_{rc}^l denotes an output neuron in the location (r,c) of layer l, S_r and S_c the number of rows and columns of a spatial filter, w_{ij}^l is the weight of connections between the neuron in the receptive field of layer l and each pixel in the location (i, j) of layer l-1, and b^l is a corresponding bias for the filter. Notation φ is the rectified linear function (ReLU) to model the output of a neuron. The ReLU is defined in Eq. 10.5 and plotted in Fig. 10.5.

$$\varphi(x) = \max(0, x) \qquad (10.5)$$

To visualize the operations of a convolutional layer, a simple diagram is given in Fig. 10.6.

A pooling layer performs a downsampling function which is used to reduce the dimension of a feature map. This function is also used to make the feature extraction robust for the invariance due to some minor deviations. It has been demonstrated that the pooling function can improve classification accuracy [15]. For example, the maximum pooling function is to select the maximum value in a neighborhood with a *stride* 2 as shown in Fig. 10.7. Here, *stride* refers to how many columns and rows we are moving the sampling window from left to right and top to bottom in a feature map. Among the spatial filters used in CNNs, a 1 × 1 filter is often used for computation reduction and increased nonlinearity of feature

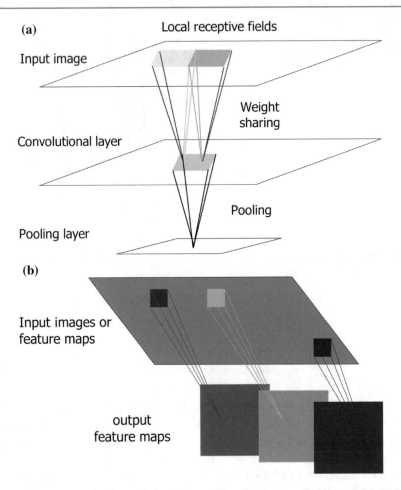

Fig. 10.6 **a** An example of convolutional layer and pooling layer and **b** the operation of three receptive fields (i.e., spatial filters) will generate three activation (feature) maps

Fig. 10.7 An example of the maximum pooling layer in LeNet-5 [16]

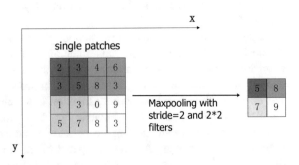

representation [25]. This filter with a size of 1×1 will reduce multiple feature maps by pooling the features across the various feature maps and constructing a single feature map. Unlike the spatial filter such as a size of 3×3, the 1×1 filter does not consider the correlation of features in a single feature map.

The fully connected layers used in the LeNet-5 are exactly same as those traditional multi-layer feed-forward neural networks as we discussed in Chap. 9. Similar to the traditional neural networks, CNNs can be an over-fitted network. Several methods have been proposed to avoid the overfitting problem such as the dropout technique [23].

10.2   Architectures of Some Large Convolutional Neural Networks (CNNs)

Similar to the topology of a traditional neural network, researchers in the area of deep machine learning have proposed several different architectures of convolutional neural networks (CNN) for solving problems of challenging visual recognition. Based on the general architecture of the CNN in Fig. 10.1, almost all of CNNs proposed has its basic structure similar to the layout shown in Fig. 10.8. We will introduce three popular CNNs namely, AlexNet, ZFNet, and VGG Net [13, 22, 31].

AlexNet is an extraordinary CNN network which is the winner of ImageNet Large-Scale Visual Recognition Challenge (ILSVRC) 2012 for a large dataset called ImageNet [13]. AlexNet has a relatively simple layout consisting of five convolutional layers, max-pooling layers, dropout layers, and three fully connected layers. ImageNet which is a challenging benchmark case for a machine learning algorithm has more than 15 million of labeled high-resolution images with 22000 categories. The ILSVRC only uses a subset of ImageNet with approximately 1000 images per category and 1000 categories. The AlexNet architecture is shown in Fig. 10.9. This architecture has about 650,000 neurons and 60 million of trainable parameters. Due to such a large number of parameters, the AlexNet uses the data augmentation and dropout techniques to reduce overfitting. Experimental results show that the AlexNet is capable of achieving record-breaking results in the competition of ILSVRC. The performance of AlexNet will degrade if a single convolutional layer is removed.

Zeiler and Fergus developed a CNN, called ZFNet, in which its architecture is very similar to AlexNet [31]. The ZF Net was the winner of 2013 ILSVRC competition. The objective of ZFNet was to explore two important issues: why a large

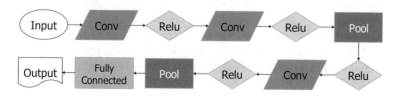

Fig. 10.8 A basic topology of a CNN

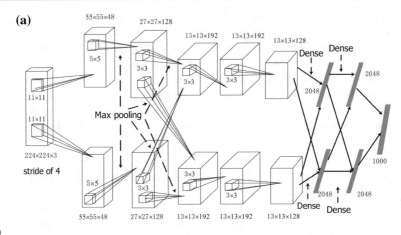

(b)

Layer	C1	S1	C2	S2	C3	C4	C5	S5	F6	F7	Output
Depth	96	96	256	256	384	384	256	256	4096	4096	1000
Dimension	55x55	27x27	27x27	13x13	13x13	13x13	13x13	6x6	6x6	1	1
Filter Size	11x11	3x3	5x5	3x3	3x3	3x3	3x3	3x3	1x1	1	1
Stride	4	2	1	2	1	1	1	2	1	1	1

C: Convolutional layer
S: Sampling layer
F: Fully Connected layer

Fig. 10.9 a An illustration of AlexNet architecture which contains five convolutional layers, three maximum pooling layers, and three fully connected layers; **b** Numeric values specify hyperparameters used in AlexNet [13]

CNN performs so well on the ImageNet benchmark and how they might be improved [31]? Hence, ZFNet was re-architectured based on the modification of AlexNet. The DeconvNet was introduced as a visualization technique that provides an insight about the function of intermediate activation layers and illustrates how the improvement of a CNN can be made. With the DeconvNet, the authors were able to find CNN model architectures that outperform AlexNet on the ImageNet benchmark. As a matter of fact, ZFNet also works very well for Caltch-101 and Caltech-256 datasets. Figure 10.10 shows the first eight-layer of ZFNet. It can be seen that a smaller spatial filter size is used in the first layer of ZFNet compared with 11×11 filter size used in AlexNet. The effect of the filter size is already discussed in many digital image processing books.

As most CNNs are constructed using the trial-and-error method, the DeconvNet gives us a valuable tool for analyzing the excitation of the input stimuli on the activation maps at any layer and observing the evolution of features during the training. The latter provides a tool for diagnosing potential problems in the CNN model. Figure 10.11 shows how a DeconvNet layer is attached to a convolutional layer. This DeconvNet can be a reverse process of any convolutional layer for an activation map that will be "mapped" back to the input image. In other words, it

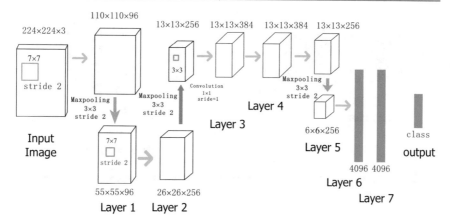

Fig. 10.10   The ZFNet architecture [31]

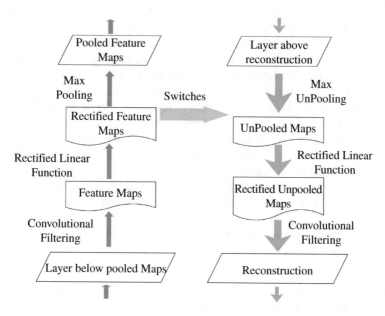

Fig. 10.11   The DeconvNet used in ZFNet architecture [31]: the right column shows a DeconvNet is attached to a convolutional layer on the left column

traces back from the features to the input pixels. A DeconvNet uses the same filters as the original ZFNet. The reverse process will start from the current layer and go through a series of unpooling, rectify, and filtering operations for each preceding layer until the input layer is reached [31]. The diagnosis of DeconvNet will discover the pros and cons of a CNN.

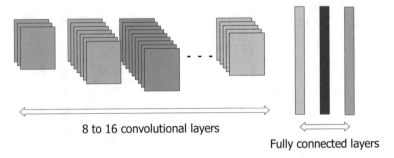

Fig. 10.12 An example of VGGNet architecture shows that 8 to 16 convolutional layers and three fully connected layers [22]

Simonyan and Zisserman developed a CNN, called VGGNet, which won the first place and second place in the localization and classification tracks, respectively, in the competition of 2014 ILSVRC [22]. The goal of VGGNet was to investigate the effect of depth of CNN on the accuracy of a large-scale image recognition task. Experimental results show that the VGGNet will have a significant improvement over the current state-of-the-art CNNs with a depth of 16–19 layers and small 3×3 spatial filters. An example of VGGNet is shown in Fig. 10.12. It can be observed that there is not much difference in terms of architecture between AlexNet and VGGNet except for the depth of layers and size of spatial filters used. In addition, 1×1 filter is used to increase the degree of nonlinearity without affecting the receptive field. An important contribution made in VGGNet is that the deeper layers work better for the recognition in a CNN network. It also indicates that multiple small spatial filters can detect features better than a large spatial filter.

There exist several software tools for constructing CNNs for training and testing. These tools include Convnet for MATLAB [33], Theano for CPU and GPU [34], Pylearn2 for python [35], TensorFlow developed by Google [36], Caffe [37], Wavenet (generate human speech by Deepmind) [26], and Project Catapult (Microsoft using special hardware) [38].

10.3   Transfer Learning in CNNs

We can think of CNN as a heterogeneous parallel computing paradigm in which the features are extracted and distributed from a low level to a higher level in the multiple layers of the entire network. To extract representative features in such a deep network, CNN training requires a significant amount of sample images to achieve higher accuracy for a task in the application. Therefore, a tremendous amount of time is required for training. The graphical processing units (GPU) and special hardware are commonly used for expediting the computation. It is also quite common to normalize the dataset in which each sample subtracted the mean of the dataset and divided by the standard deviation that is similar to what has been used in the traditional artificial neural networks.

Since it is required of a large dataset to train the CNN for an application, we will not be able to have full utilization of the CNN for solving the problem if a sufficient amount of data is not available for an application. To solve this problem, transfer learning is widely used for overcoming the shortage of dataset for CNN training [7, 10, 19, 20, 24, 30]. It will be useful that CNN learns the knowledge from a sufficient amount of the dataset and store the knowledge in the distributed weights (synaptic connections) over the entire network. This is usually called the source domain. We can then copy those weights to another similar CNN architecture for fine-tuning and solving different problems. This is called the target domain. In other words, we do not have to train a CNN from scratch in the target domain, as we may not have enough amount of data. However, we still need to retrain the CNN with "cloned" weights and a limited amount of data in the target domain.

There are several successful applications by using the transfer learning in the CNN [10, 19]. Oquab et al. designed a scheme in which the knowledge learned with CNNs in the source domain dataset was transferred to the CNNs in the target domain which has a limited amount of training data. They trained a CNN using the ImageNet dataset, which is a large-scale annotated dataset, as a generic feature extractor and then reused this generic feature extractor in the target domain [19]. In the target domain, all pre-trained parameters from layer C1 to layer FC7 are transferred to this new CNN as depicted in Fig. 10.13. A new adaptation layer (fully connected between FC_a and FC_b) is then created and trained with a limited number of the labeled dataset, which is the PASCAL VOC dataset, for the target domain. With this transfer learning, they were able to achieve the state-of-the-art

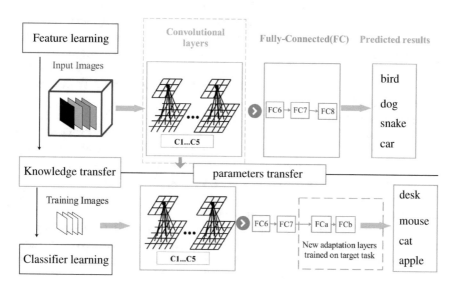

Fig. 10.13 A transfer learning scheme from the source domain to the target domain [19]

visual recognition results on the PASCAL VOC dataset. However, Yosinski et al. studied the transfer learning used in CNNs and discovered that some issues based on their experiments affect the transferability [30].

10.4 Image Texture Classification Using Convolutional Neural Networks (CNN)

Convolutional neural networks (CNN) almost becomes a de facto neural network in the area of visual and pattern recognition nowadays. Image texture classification is an application of visual and pattern recognition. Therefore, the way it works for the image texture classification is similar to those tasks in the visual and pattern recognition applying the CNN. Some excellent work has been reported in the literature for the image texture classification by using the convolutional neural networks (CNN) [7, 11, 13, 24]. As stated earlier, CNNs will extract the hierarchical features automatically from an input when the learning moves from a layer to the next layer in a deep neural network. The CNNs used for image texture classification are either image-based or patch-based networks [24]. It requires many training samples for both methods. However, in the patch-based method, we can have a sufficient amount of different patches from an input image and apply the data augmentation technique to generating enough number of samples for training. The data augmentation technique is mainly used to generate new image samples in which the variations such as rotation, different illumination, and scale changes that are different from the original samples [29].

The motivation that we can apply the patch-based CNN is due to the periodical property of the image texture [24]. Figure 10.14 shows an example by taking some textural images, randomly selecting some patches, and swapping them. Although the patch is quite small compared with the original image, it still provides adequate information for different texture discrimination. Hence, the patch-based CNN can recognize a randomly selected patch as good as an entire image. Even some patches are swapped, the image texture re-constructed still appear very similar to the original image [24].

There are some advantages associated with patch-based CNNs [24]. It is well known that natural images including the textural images are usually captured under different imaging conditions such as illumination, rotated angles, partially occluded, and scales due to varying distances between the sensor and the target. In such a state, a robust classifier must be able to accommodate all of these variations. In other words, a classifier should be provided all of these variations as inputs for the model learning. The data augmentation method is a good fit for the patch-based CNN by adding to the set of training samples with many of such new patches obtained through the transformation of the original patches. Two types of transformation are widely used: the Gaussian pyramid method to create a set of multi-scale patches in the scale space, and the rotation transformation using different angles [24].

(a)   (b)

(c)   (d)

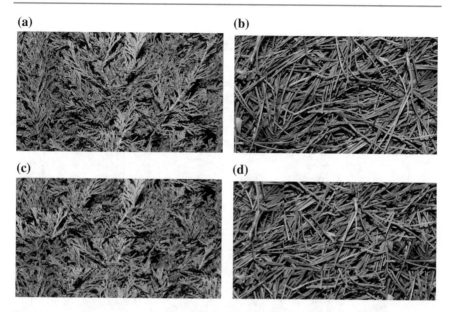

Fig. 10.14 **a** and **b** show two image textures: leaves and pine straw needles, and **c** and **d** illustrate if some patches are randomly selected for swapping, the image texture reconstructed still appear very similar to the original image [24]

Sun designed two different CNN architectures for image texture classification and compared their performance [24]: the image-based CNN and the patch-based CNN. The former is similar to the regular CNN. The patch-based CNN, abbreviated as p-CNN, is shown in Fig. 10.15. It consists of one p-CNN for training and the other p-CNN for the classification. The first four layers of both p-CNNs for training and classification are identical. The difference between these two p-CNNs is that there is an extra layer for the bag-of-patches pooling to obtain the confidence scores for the classification of a patch to a texture class in the p-CNN for classification.

To show the effectiveness of the CNN on the image texture classification, Sun conducted experiments on four-benchmark image texture dataset including Brodatz, CUReT, KTH-TIPS, and UIUC [1, 2, 8, 14]. The image-based CNN and p-CNN are also compared with four image texture classification methods [17, 27, 28, 32] namely, (1) SRP that is an extension of the patch-based method, (2) VZ_Joint that is a patch-based method, (3) VZ_MR8 that is a filter-bank-based method, and (4) Zhang's method that is a bag-of-keypoints method. These four methods differ in the algorithmic aspect of how the features are extracted from image textures. Their experimental results on the four-benchmark datasets show that the p-CNN has much higher classification accuracies than the image-based CNN on three datasets and slightly lower on the CUReT dataset. However, among the comparison with four image texture classification methods, the p-CNN achieves either the competitive or the better results.

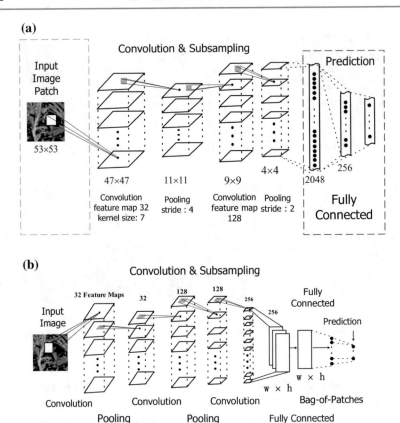

Fig. 10.15 An architecture of the patch-based CNN: **a** a patch-based CNN consisting of two convolutional layers (include pooling layers) and two fully connected layers for training and **b** a patch-based CNN for the classification that has an extra layer for the bag-of-patches pooling [24]

It is ideal to use the p-CNN for image texture classification. Similar to the selection of a size for a K-views template discussed earlier, it is a challenge to choose an appropriate size of the patch for the p-CNN to achieve the high classification accuracy. Sun used the patch size of 53 × 53 in his experiments of image texture classification and concluded that the p-CNN is suitable for any type of datasets including patches generated using the data augmentation technique while the image-based CNN is more appropriate for image textures with the homogeneity and fewer variations in the image [24].

10.5 Summary

Deep machine learning techniques have emerged as the state-of-the-art methods for computer vision and pattern recognition. Convolutional neural networks (CNN), which is one of deep machine learning techniques, have been widely used for image texture recognition. The features generated by the CNN provide a new set of textural characteristics for the image texture classification. This is a different approach from the traditionally handcrafted features in the traditional pattern recognition. The CNN can learn and transform the input image texture into a set of feature descriptors.

LeNet-5 is one of the CNN models that is frequently used for image recognition and classification. There are many advantages associated with the CNN model such as its robustness to a certain degree of variation on the shift, scaling, and rotation. This spatial invariance is achieved through the convolutional and pooling layers in the CNN. However, the CNN model requires a tremendous amount of representative data for learning. We may not be able to obtain a sufficient amount of data for a task being solved by the CNN. Transfer learning is thus used to supplement the lack of training data. In other words, we borrow the knowledge from another dataset which has been trained in a CNN in a so-called source domain and used the well-trained weights for the current CNN for fine-tuning in the target domain. In a sense, we pre-train the current CNN on a large dataset, for example, ImageNet. Then, we will fine-tune the parameters of the current CNN with the dataset in the current task domain. Several extremely large CNNs have been proposed for image classification and achieved a significant breakthrough in the development of CNNs. These include AlexNet, ZFNet, and VGGNet.

The patch-based CNN model has shown its promising in the image texture classification. As new convolutional neural networks are evolved rapidly, we may expect that the accuracy of image texture classification will be improved significantly in the near future.

10.6 Exercises

1. Perform experiments on the different size of patches for image texture classification using the patch-based CNN.
2. Apply the data augmentation technique to the patches extracted in Exercise #1.
3. Compare the accuracy of image texture classification using the image-based and patch-based CNN models.
4. Compare the accuracy of image texture classification on the CNN models with the transfer learning and without the transfer learning.

References

1. Brodatz P (1999) Textures: a photographic album for artists and designers. Dover Publications. ISBN 0486406997
2. Dana KJ, van Ginneken B, Nayar SK, Koenderink JJ (1999) Reflectance and texture of real-world surfaces. ACM Trans Graph 18(1):1–34
3. Davies ER (2018) Computer vision: principles, algorithms, applications, and learning, 5th edn. Academic, New York
4. Fukushima K, Miyake S, Takayuki I (1983) Neocognitron: a neural network model for a mechanism of visual pattern recognition. IEEE Trans Syst Man Cybern SMC-13(5):826–834
5. Gonzalez RC, Woods RE (2002) Digital image processing, 2nd edn. Prentice Hall, Englewood Cliffs
6. Goodfellow I, Bengio Y, Courville A (2016) Deep learning. The MIT Press, Cambridge
7. Hafemann LG (2014) An analysis of deep neural networks for texture classification. M.S. thesis, Universidade Federal do Parana,
8. Hayman E, Caputo B, Fritz M, Eklundh J (2004) On the significance of real-world conditions for material classification. In: European conference on computer vision, vol 4. pp 253–266
9. Heaton J (2015) Artificial intelligence for humans: deep learning and neural networks, vol 3. Heaton Research, Inc.,
10. Huang Z, Pan Z, Lei B (2017) Transfer learning with deep convolutional neural network for SAR target classification with limited labeled data. Remote Sens 9:907. https://doi.org/10.3390/rs9090907
11. Jarrett K, Kavukcuoglu K, Ranzato M, LeCun Y (2009) What is the best multi-stage architecture for object recognition? In: IEEE 12th international conference on computer vision, Kyoto, Japan, 29 Sept–2 Oct 2009, pp 2146–2153
12. Karpathy A, Li F-F (2015) Deep visual-semantic alignments for generating image descriptions, CVPR
13. Krizhevsky A, Sutskever I, Hinton GE (2017) Imagenet classification with deep convolutional neural networks. Commun ACM 60(6):84–90
14. Lazebnik S, Schmid C, Ponce J (2005) A sparse texture representation using local affine regions. IEEE Trans Pattern Anal Mach Intell 27(8):1265–1278
15. Lecun Y, Boser B, Denker JS, Henderson D, Howard RE, Hubband W, Jackel LD (1989) Backpropagation applied to handwritten zip code recognition. Neural Comput 1(4):541–551
16. Lecun Y, Bottou L, Bengio Y, Haffner P (1998) Gradient-based learning applied to document recognition. In: Proceedings of the IEEE, pp 2278–2324
17. Liu L, Fieguth P, Clausi D, Kuang G (2012) Sorted random projections for robust rotation-invariant texture classification. Pattern Recogn 45(6):2405–2418
18. Liu L, Chen J, Fieguth P, Zhao G, Chellappa R, Pietikainen M (2018) BoW meets CNN: two decades of texture representation. Int J Comput Vis 1–26. https://doi.org/10.1007/s11263-018-1125-z
19. Oquab M, Bottou L, Laptev I, Sivic J (2013) Learning and transferring mid-level image representations using convolutional neural networks, INRIA, Technical report, HAL-00911179
20. Pan SJ, Yang Q (2010) A survey on transfer learning. IEEE Trans Knowl Data Eng 22 (10):1345–1359
21. Snyder WE, Qi H (2004) Machine vision. Cambridge University Press, Cambridge
22. Simonyan K, Zisserman A (2015) Very deep convolutional networks for large-scale image recognition, ICLR
23. Srivastava N, Hinton G, Krizhevsky A, Sutskever I, Salakhutdinov R (2014) Dropout: a simple way to prevent neural networks from overfitting. J Mach Learn Res 15:1929–1958
24. Sun X (2014) Robust texture classification based on machine learning, Ph.D. thesis, Deakin University

25. Szegedy C, Liu W, Jia Y, Sermanet P, Reed S, Anguelov D, Erhan D, Vanhoucke V, Rabinovich A (2015) Going deeper with convolutions. In: 2015 IEEE conference on computer vision and pattern recognition (CVPR), Boston, MA, USA, 7–12 June 2015

26. Van Den Oord A, Dieleman S, Zen H, Simonyan K, Vinyals O, Graves A, Kavukcuoglu K (2016) WaveNet: a generative model for raw audio. In: SSW, 125 pp

27. Varma M, Zisserman A (2005) A statistical approach to texture classification from single images. Int J Comput Vis 62(1):61–81

28. Varma M, Zisserman A (2009) A statistical approach to material classification using image patch exemplars. IEEE Trans Pattern Anal Mach Intell 31(11):2032–2047

29. Wong SC, Gatt A, Stamatescu V, McDonnell MD (2016) Understanding data augmentation for classification: when to warp?" In: International conference on digital image computing techniques and applications (DICTA), Gold Coast, QLD, Australia, 30 Nov–2 Dec 2016

30. Yosinski J, Clune J, Bengio Y, Lipson H (2014) How transferable are features in deep neural networks? In: Advances in neural information processing systems (NIPS 2014), vol 27

31. Zeiler MD, Fergus R (2014) Visualizing and understanding convolutional networks. In: Fleet D et al (eds) ECCV 2014, Part I, LNCS, vol 8689. Springer International Publishing, Switzerland, pp 818–833

32. Zhang J, Marszalek M, Lazebnik S, Schmid C (2007) Local features and kernels for classification of texture and object categories: a comprehensive study. Int J Comput Vis 73 (2):213–238

33. https://www.mathworks.com/products/deep-learning.html

34. http://deeplearning.net/software/theano/

35. http://deeplearning.net/software/pylearn2/

36. https://www.tensorflow.org/

37. http://caffe.berkeleyvision.org/

38. https://www.microsoft.com/en-us/research/project/project-catapult/

Index

© Springer Nature Switzerland AG 2019
C.-C. Hung et al., *Image Texture Analysis*,
https://doi.org/10.1007/978-3-030-13773-1

Printed in the United States
By Bookmasters